Fifth Workshop on NLP for Indigenous Languages of the Americas (AmericasNLP 2025)

Albuquerque, New Mexico, USA
4 May 2025

ISBN: 979-8-3313-1911-3

Printed from e-media with permission by:

Curran Associates, Inc.
57 Morehouse Lane
Red Hook, NY 12571

Some format issues inherent in the e-media version may also appear in this print version.

Association for Computational Linguistics
209 N. Eighth Street
Stroudsburg, Pennsylvania 18360

Phone: 1-570-476-8006
Fax: 1-570-476-0860

acl@aclweb.org

Additional copies of this publication are available from:

Curran Associates, Inc.
57 Morehouse Lane
Red Hook, NY 12571 USA
Phone: 845-758-0400
Fax: 845-758-2633
Email: curran@proceedings.com
Web: www.proceedings.com

NAACL 2025

The Fifth Workshop on NLP for Indigenous Languages of the Americas

Proceedings of the Workshop

May 4, 2025

The NAACL organizers gratefully acknowledge the support from the following sponsors.

Sponsor

Google

Order copies of this and other ACL proceedings from:

Association for Computational Linguistics (ACL)
317 Sidney Baker St. S
Suite 400 - 134
Kerrville, TX 78028
USA
Tel: +1-855-225-1962
acl@aclweb.org

Introduction

We would like to welcome you to AmericasNLP 2025, the Fifth Workshop on Natural Language Processing for Indigenous Languages of the Americas!

The main goals of the workshop are to:

- encourage research on NLP, computational linguistics, corpus linguistics, and speech around the globe to work on Indigenous American languages.
- promote research on both neural and non-neural machine learning approaches suitable for low-resource languages.
- connect researchers and professionals from underrepresented communities and native speakers of endangered languages with the machine learning and NLP communities.

In 2025, AmericasNLP will be held in Albuquerque, USA, on May 4th. Prior to the workshop three shared tasks were hosted: (1) the Shared Task on Machine Translation into Indigenous Languages, (2) the Shared Task on the Creation of Educational Materials for Indigenous Languages, and new for 2025 (3) the Shared Task on Machine Translation Metrics for Indigenous Languages. During the workshop, there will be two invited talks, a panel, poster session, as well as multiple paper and shared task submission presentations.

We received a total of 22 submissions: 12 research papers, 1 extended abstract, and 8 shared task system description papers (across all shared tasks). 8 archival papers were accepted (acceptance rate: 66%) – in addition to the previously published and system description papers.

We would like to acknowledge all the time and effort put into the reviewing process, and thank for program committee members for helping us create a high-quality program in a short amount of time. AmericasNLP would not have been possible without the help our sponsor for 2025: Google. Finally, we would also thank all the authors who submitted their work to the workshop, the participants of the shared tasks, and everyone who will be at the workshop, both in-person and remote, to exchange and discuss their ideas for improving natural language technologies for Indigenous languages of the Americas!

Manuel Mager, Abteen Ebrahimi, Shruti Rijhwani, Robert Pugh, Arturo Oncevay, Luis Chiruzzo, Rolando Coto-Solano, and Katharina von der Wense

AmericasNLP 2025 Organizing Committee

Program Committee

Program Committee

Eduardo Blanco, University of Arizona
Ruixiang Cui, University of Copenhagen
Cristina España-Bonet, DFKI GmbH
Silvia Fernandez Sabido, CentroGeo
Luke Gessler, Indiana University Bloomington
Santiago Góngora, Universidad de la República
Éric Le Ferrand, Boston College
Zoey Liu, Department of Linguistics, University of Florida
Daniela Moctezuma, Centrogeo
Sarah Moeller, University of Florida
Alejandro Molina-Villegas, SECIHTI
Remo Nitschke, University of Arizona
John E. Ortega, Northeastern University
Tanmay Parekh, University of California Los Angeles
Nathaniel Robinson, Johns Hopkins University
Atnafu Lambebo Tonja, Instituto Politécnico Nacional (IPN), Centro de Investigación en Computación (CIC)
Daan Van Esch, Google Research
Si Wu, Northeastern University

Keynote Talk

Alexis Palmer
University of Colorado Boulder

Bio: Dr. Palmer is an expert in computational discourse and semantics; computational linguistics for low-resource languages and language documentation; discourse structure and coherence, and modes of discourse and social analytics, including automated detection of offensive language in social media. She received her PhD from UT Austin in 2009, has held a number of prestigious post docs and research positions in Germany (including positions at the Institute for Computational Linguistics in Heidelberg and the Institut für Deutsche Sprache in Mannheim). Until her move to CU in 2021, she was an assistant professor at the University of North Texas, Denton. Dr. Palmer brings a prestigious National Science Foundation CAREER grant with her to CU. In this project, she is working on cross-linguistic methods for better development of language processing tools for low-resource languages. The project is called FOLTA (From One Language to Another). She has also recently become interested in the question of how we can make the outcomes of linguistic documentation more useable and accessible, particularly to support development of pedagogical materials for a language.

Table of Contents

Text-to-speech system for low-resource languages: A case study in Shipibo-Konibo (a Panoan language from Peru)

Daniel Menéndez
Postgraduate School
Pontificia Universidad Católica del Perú
dmenendez@pucp.edu.pe

Héctor Erasmo Gómez
Chana Research Group
Postgraduate School
Pontificia Universidad Católica del Perú
hector.gomez@pucp.edu.pe

Abstract

This paper presents the design and development of the first Text-to-Speech (TTS) model and speech dataset for Shipibo-Konibo, a low-resource indigenous language spoken mainly in the Peruvian Amazon. Despite the challenge posed by data scarcity, data was gathered and structured for the dataset, thus the TTS model was trained with over 4 hours of recordings and 3,025 written sentences. The test results demonstrated an intelligibility rate (IR) of 88.56% and a mean opinion score (MOS) of 4.01, confirming the quality of the generated audio using Tacotron 2 and HiFi-GAN. This study highlights the potential for extending this approach to other indigenous languages in Peru, contributing to their documentation and revitalization.

1 Introduction

With over 7,000 languages worldwide (SIL, Accessed March 14 2024), many of them face extinction, threatening linguistic diversity and indigenous knowledge (Evans and Levinson, 2009; Spiegelhalter et al., 2002; Campbell and Rehg, 2018). In the particular case of Peru, official statistics recognize 48 indigenous languages, while Glottolog lists 90 (Hammarström et al., 2021). Among these, Shipibo-Konibo, part of the Pano family, is spoken by approximately 40,000 people[1]; however, NLP efforts for the language face challenges such as at least two orthographic traditions and limited digital resources. For more details about the Shipibo-Konibo communities and its current writing and speech systems, see Appendix A.

Thus, to continue previous efforts made in projects like Huqariq (Zevallos et al., 2022), where a combined speech corpus of Quechua, Aymara, and Shipibo-Konibo was collected, this paper presents the development of the first Shipibo-Konibo TTS model. The study includes dataset creation, model selection, training, and evaluation. The goal is to facilitate future NLP applications for Shipibo-Konibo and other indigenous languages. Furthermore, we aim to support language revitalization by offering audio resources that facilitate pronunciation practice beyond the classroom. Additionally, integrating synthesized speech into educational tools such as dictionaries and verb conjugators enhances language accessibility as it was done in other countries (Pine et al., 2022).

[1]The 2017 Peruvian census estimates the total Shipibo-Konibo population at 34,000, but the actual figure is expected to be higher (INEI, 2018)

2 Speech synthesis for low-resource languages

Developing a TTS model for low-resource languages presents challenges, primarily the lack of structured data. This limitation impacts training strategies, requiring transfer learning and specialized neural architectures as Transformer-TTS (Li et al., 2019) or Glow-TTS (Kim et al., 2020). Additional challenges include the estimation of computational resources, as renting the necessary capacity was the only viable option, leading to additional expenses within our limited budget.Another challenge arose in selecting the most suitable metrics for this low-resource scenario. While MOS is the most commonly used in such cases, the evaluations were also designed to extract computable data on intelligibility (Xu et al., 2020).

3 Data Collection

No existing Shipibo-Konibo speech dataset was available, so creating one from scratch was necessary. Texts published after 2015 alphabet normalization were prioritized for relevance, and corresponding audio recordings were collected.

Proceedings of the Fifth Workshop on NLP for Indigenous Languages of the Americas (AmericasNLP), pages 1–7
May 4, 2025 ©2025 Association for Computational Linguistics

3.1 Text Compilation

Key sources included the Shipibo-Konibo translation of The Little Prince (*Jatibi Ibo Bake*) and some bilingual educational materials from the Peruvian Ministry of Education, resulting in a corpus of 3,025 sentences.

3.2 Audio Compilation

Audio recordings were done following the LJ Speech (Ito and Johnson, 2017) dataset requirements:

- Sampling rate of 22,050Hz or higher.
- Single speaker.
- The sentences must contain diverse phonemes.
- Audio duration must be between 1-10 seconds.
- Audio segments must not have long silence at the beginning or at the end.
- Audio segments must not contain long pauses.

The recording sessions featured a native Shipibo-Konibo speaker with prior experience in voice documentation, which were conducted over three months in intervals of up to two hours to ensure vocal consistency.

By the end of all the sessions, the final dataset exhibited the characteristics shown in Table 1.

Characteristics	**Value**
Number of sentences	3025
Total duration	$4h37m14s$
Minimum sentence duration	$1.08s$
Maximum sentence duration	$12.1s$
Average sentence duration	$5.1s$

Table 1: Details of the audio clips collected from the Shipibo-Konibo language.

Finally, all the sentences were trimmed and re-sampled to 22.05KHz. Long silences were removed, volume, speed, and text were normalized as required by the Tacotron 2 model (Shen et al., 2018).

4 The proposed TTS model

A previous evaluation of many TTS models led to the selection of Tacotron 2 as a result of its success in low-resource environments, showing promising results using datasets of less than 3 hours (Debnath et al., 2020; Dasare et al., 2022; Gopalakrishnan et al., 2022) and the vibrant state of development also. Previous models like Voice Loop 2 (Taigman et al., 2017), FastSpeech2 (Ren et al., 2020) and Transformer-TTS (Li et al., 2019) were discarded due to factors such as their fall into disuse or their inferior performance.

4.1 Tacotron 2

Tacotron 2 (Shen et al., 2018) was chosen for its encoder-attention-decoder architecture, which improves speech quality. Our model was implemented in PyTorch and trained using transfer learning techniques.

4.2 The HiFi-GAN vocoder

Unlike the original Tacotron 2 approach using WaveGlow (Prenger et al., 2019), this study employed HiFi-GAN (Kong et al., 2020) due to its recent superior performance. HiFi-GAN, a GAN-based vocoder, generates waveforms from Tacotron 2 spectrograms.

A summary of the entire proposed model is shown in Figure 1.

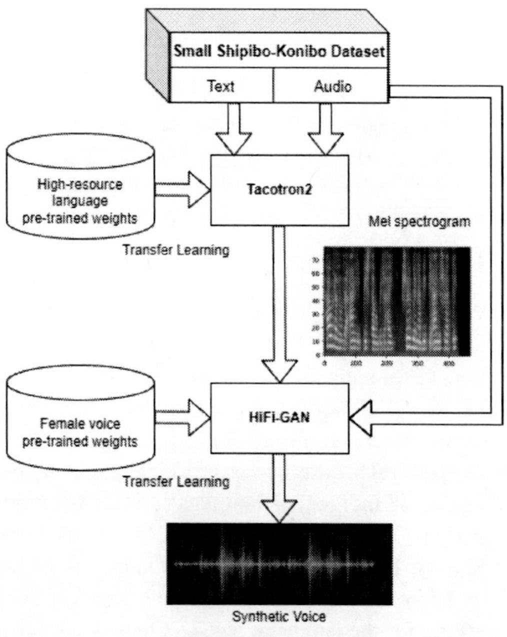

Figure 1: Architecture of the proposed TTS model.

5 Experimentation and Results

Tacotron 2 and HiFi-GAN were trained separately, as the vocoder relied on the spectrogram predictions generated by the fully trained Tacotron 2 model. Hyperparameter tuning was optimized using insights from similar projects (Debnath et al., 2020; Dasare et al., 2022).

5.1 Training the Tacotron 2 Model

We used Google Colab with an Nvidia A100 GPU for the training process, and we fine-tuned a pre-trained Latin American Spanish model from Hugging Face (Cedillo, 2023), where the best hyper-parameters achieved are displayed on tables 2 and 3, showing promising encoder-decoder alignment from the first epoch.

Hyperparameters	Value
Epochs	225
Batch size	16
Gate threshold	0.5
Decoder dropout	0.1
Attention	0.1

Table 2: Final Tacotron2 Hyperparameters.

Optimizer Parameters	Value
Learning rate	3.10^{-4}
β_1	0.9
β_2	0.999
Weight decay	1.10^{-5}

Table 3: Parameters used for the Adam optimizer.

The training process took about 225 epochs until it stalled at a validation loss of 0.1434 (Figure 2) and encoder-decoder alignment as shown in Figure 3.

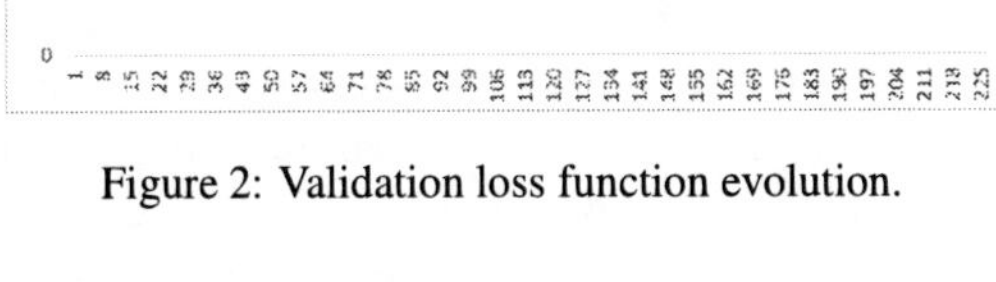

Figure 2: Validation loss function evolution.

5.2 Training the HiFi-GAN vocoder

The vocoder was trained after Tacotron 2 using a transfer learning strategy with a pre-trained universal female voice model to achieve faster convergence with the native speaker's voice. After 34 epochs, loss stabilization indicated convergence.

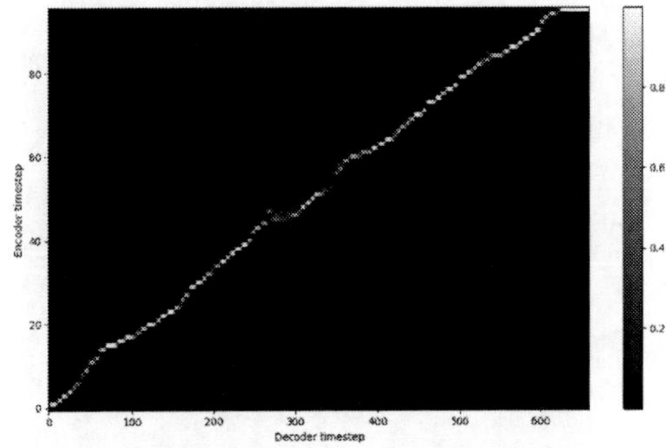

Figure 3: Epoch 225 final encoder-decoder alignment.

5.3 Evaluation and Results

For model evaluation, we extracted 400 additional sentences from the book Koshi Shinanya Ainbo (The Testimony of a Shipibo Woman) (Valenzuela and Rojas, 2005), a pre-2015 Shipibo-Konibo book with an alphabet easily adaptable to the modern one. It narrates the life and traditions of Mrs. Ranin Ama and her community.

As an initial inference test, Figure 4 presents a five-word phrase from the book, lasting three seconds: Nokon titan ea axeani jawékibo ("The things my mother taught me").

Objective metrics like PESQ (Rix, 2003) and POLQA (Beerends et al., 2013) require extensive high-quality reference data, which is unavailable for Shipibo-Konibo. Instead, we followed subjective evaluations by several native speakers, despite being more time-consuming. The Mean Opinion Score (MOS) is the most commonly used metric in low-resource scenarios, while the Intelligibility Rate (IR) can also provide valuable insights.

The Intelligibility Rate (IR) measures how accurately listeners transcribe synthesized speech, calculated as the percentage of correctly identified words. The Mean Opinion Score (MOS) evaluates speech quality based on clarity, naturalness, and fluency, rated on a scale from 1 to 5 (see Table 4). The average score given by the evaluators is used to determine the final mean opinion score.

Value	Descripción
1	Unacceptable or very poor quality
2	Poor quality
3	Acceptable or adequate quality
4	Good quality
5	Excellent quality

Table 4: MOS metric scale.

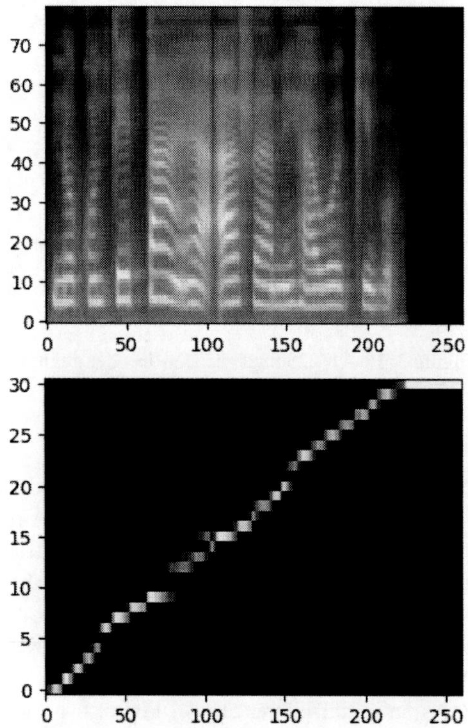

Figure 4: Spectrogram and encoder-decoder alignment graph of a 3-second synthetic phrase.

A total of 26 native Shipibo-Konibo speakers (11 men, 15 women), all under 30 and university-educated, participated as evaluators. All of them familiar with the use of PC and office software tools to make evaluations easier. To compare natural and synthetic speech, 25% of the evaluated phrases were natural samples, randomly included in a set of 20 audios per evaluator. Table 5 presents the intelligibility rate (IR) results for both speech types.

Type of voice	IR
Natural	83.45%
Synthetic	88.56%

Table 5: Intelligibility rate results.

Meanwhile, the results obtained from the same evaluators for the mean opinion score (MOS) are shown in Table 6.

Type of voice	MOS
Natural	3.75 ± 1.2
Synthetic	4.01 ± 1.09

Table 6: Mean opinion score results.

Furthermore, Figure 5 illustrates the comparison between the MOS distributions for natural and synthetic voices.

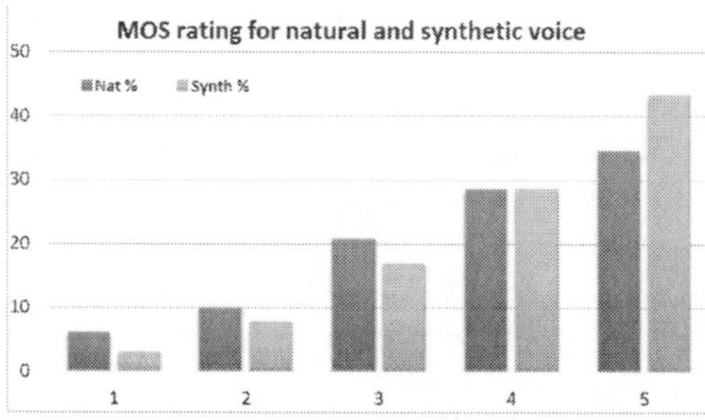

Figure 5: MOS percentage distribution for natural and synthetic voice.

5.4 Discussion

The results were highly positive, with an IR of 88.56% and MOS of 4.01, meeting expectations. Surprisingly, the synthetic voice outperformed the natural voice in both metrics.

However, a parallel qualitative analysis revealed issues such as ambiguous intonation, improper punctuation handling, and pronunciation inconsistencies. The encoder-decoder alignment analysis during sentence synthesis identified some recurring synthesis faults, particularly in the suffixes *titai*, *tiai*, *tian* and *wai*, due to insufficient training data. Additionally, significant pronunciation variations were observed across recordings for the sounds *iki*, *nai*, *non*, *ani*, *ja*, *ea*, *baon*, *kon*, *xe*, and *noa*.

6 Conclusions and future work

We successfully designed, developed, and evaluated the first TTS model for the Shipibo-Konibo language. For this task, we compiled speech corpus of over 4 hours and 3,025 labeled sentences.

The Tacotron 2 spectrogram predictor and HiFi-GAN vocoder were effectively trained, achieving an IR of 88.56% and an MOS of 4.01, which indicates that the synthetic speech samples surpassed the natural ones in some tests. These results show the potential of the model for other Panoan and Amazonian languages with similarly limited speech data.

Future work will focus on improving corpus quality, refining audio recording conditions, and incorporating more diverse sentence structures. This model serves as a foundation for adapting TTS systems to other indigenous languages within the Pano family and beyond.

Limitations

Despite promising results, this study has some limitations:

- The corpus consists of only 4 hours and 3,025 sentences, which may not fully capture the phonetic and prosodic variability of Shipibo-Konibo. A larger dataset could improve generalization.
- Our was trained on a young female single speaker, limiting voice diversity. Multi-speaker training for broader applicability should be included.
- Although our collaborator is a native Shipibo-Konibo speaker, she has been living in the capital, Lima, for several years. The distance from her community and the reduced daily use of her language have led to variations in her pronunciation, which are reflected during evaluations in the intelligibility rate (IR) and mean opinion score (MOS) metrics for natural voice.
- Due to the absence of high-quality reference data, PESQ and POLQA were not used. Subjective evaluations (IR and MOS) were employed, but they are more time-consuming and dependent on evaluator bias.
- While the model provides a framework for low-resource TTS development, its adaptation to other Panoan or Amazonian languages requires additional data and fine-tuning.
- Shipibo-Konibo has at least two writing conventions. The dataset prioritizes the 2015 standard, but variations may affect the model's usability in different communities.

Ethics statement

This study was conducted with ethical considerations in mind, ensuring respect for the Shipibo-Konibo community and its linguistic heritage. The native speaker who contributed to the dataset participated voluntarily, providing informed consent before any recording sessions. Additionally, she was fairly compensated for her time and contributions.

We acknowledge the importance of responsible data collection and ensure that all linguistic resources were gathered and processed with the utmost respect for cultural sensitivity. The project aligns with ethical guidelines for language documentation and preservation, aiming to empower indigenous communities by providing AI tools that support language revitalization.

Any future use of the dataset and TTS model will be governed by principles of transparency and community engagement, ensuring that the benefits of this research extend directly to the Shipibo-Konibo people.

Acknowledgments

We would like to express our gratitude to the *Chana Project* of the *Pontificia Universidad Católica del Perú (PUCP)* and prof. Roberto Zariquiey for their support and for providing us with literature in the Shipibo-Konibo language, which was essential for conducting the evaluations.

Additionally, we extend our appreciation to the *Universidad Intercultural de la Amazonía (UNIA)* for their support in providing facilities and student participation during the evaluation process.

Finally, we would like to sincerely thank Ms. Seleni Rojas, an activist dedicated to the preservation of Shipibo-Konibo culture, whose invaluable contribution made the creation of both the dataset and the TTS model possible.

References

John G Beerends, Christian Schmidmer, Jens Berger, Matthias Obermann, Raphael Ullmann, Joachim Pomy, and Michael Keyhl. 2013. Perceptual objective listening quality assessment (polqa), the third generation itu-t standard for end-to-end speech quality measurement part i—temporal alignment. *journal of the audio engineering society*, 61(6):366–384.

Lyle Campbell and Kenneth Rehg. 2018. Introduction. In Lyle Campbell and Kenneth Rehg, editors, *The Oxford Handbook of Endangered Languages*, pages 1–18. Oxford: Oxford University Press.

Rene Cedillo. 2023. taco2-checkpoints. `https://huggingface.co/datasets/rmcpantoja/taco2-checkpoints/tree/main/es`,[Accesed: (2024-02-09)].

Ashwini Dasare, KT Deepak, Mahadeva Prasanna, and K Samudra Vijaya. 2022. Text to speech system for lambani-a zero resource, tribal language of india. In *2022 25th Conference of the Oriental COCOSDA International Committee for the Co-ordination and Standardisation of Speech Databases and Assessment Techniques (O-COCOSDA)*, pages 1–6. IEEE.

Ankur Debnath, Shridevi S Patil, Gangotri Nadiger, and Ramakrishnan Angarai Ganesan. 2020. Low-resource end-to-end sanskrit tts using tacotron2, waveglow and transfer learning. In *2020 IEEE 17th*

India Council International Conference (INDICON), pages 1–5. IEEE.

Nicholas Evans and Stephen Levinson. 2009. The myth of language universals: Language diversity and its importance for cognitive science. *Behavioral and Brain Sciences*, 32(5):429–492.

Thirumoorthy Gopalakrishnan, Syed Ayaz Imam, and Archit Aggarwal. 2022. Fine tuning and comparing tacotron 2, deep voice 3, and fastspeech 2 tts models in a low resource environment. In *2022 IEEE International Conference on Data Science and Information System (ICDSIS)*, pages 1–6. IEEE.

Harald Hammarström, Robert Forkel, Martin Haspelmath, and Sebastian Bank. 2021. Glottolog 4.4. Leipzig: Max Planck Institute for Evolutionary Anthropology. Available at `http://glottolog.org`. Accessed on 2021-05-20.

INEI. 2018. *Perú: Resultados definitivos de los Censos Nacionales 2017*. Instituto Nacional de Estadística e Informática, Lima, Perú.

Keith Ito and Linda Johnson. 2017. The lj speech dataset. `https://keithito.com/LJ-Speech-Dataset/`.

Jaehyeon Kim, Sungwon Kim, Jungil Kong, and Sungroh Yoon. 2020. Glow-tts: A generative flow for text-to-speech via monotonic alignment search. *Advances in Neural Information Processing Systems*, 33:8067–8077.

Jungil Kong, Jaehyeon Kim, and Jaekyoung Bae. 2020. Hifi-gan: Generative adversarial networks for efficient and high fidelity speech synthesis. *Advances in neural information processing systems*, 33:17022–17033.

Naihan Li, Shujie Liu, Yanqing Liu, Sheng Zhao, and Ming Liu. 2019. Neural speech synthesis with transformer network. In *Proceedings of the AAAI conference on artificial intelligence*, volume 33, pages 6706–6713.

Aidan Pine, Dan Wells, Nathan Brinklow, Patrick Littell, and Korin Richmond. 2022. Requirements and motivations of low-resource speech synthesis for language revitalization. In *Proceedings of the 60th Annual Meeting of the Association for Computational Linguistics (Volume 1: Long Papers)*, pages 7346–7359.

Ryan Prenger, Rafael Valle, and Bryan Catanzaro. 2019. Waveglow: A flow-based generative network for speech synthesis. In *ICASSP 2019-2019 IEEE International Conference on Acoustics, Speech and Signal Processing (ICASSP)*, pages 3617–3621. IEEE.

Yi Ren, Chenxu Hu, Xu Tan, Tao Qin, Sheng Zhao, Zhou Zhao, and Tie-Yan Liu. 2020. Fastspeech 2: Fast and high-quality end-to-end text to speech. *arXiv preprint arXiv:2006.04558*.

Antony W Rix. 2003. Comparison between subjective listening quality and p. 862 pesq score. *Proc. Measurement of Speech and Audio Quality in Networks (MESAQIN'03), Prague, Czech Republic*.

Jonathan Shen, Ruoming Pang, Ron J Weiss, Mike Schuster, Navdeep Jaitly, Zongheng Yang, Zhifeng Chen, Yu Zhang, Yuxuan Wang, Rj Skerrv-Ryan, et al. 2018. Natural tts synthesis by conditioning wavenet on mel spectrogram predictions. In *2018 IEEE international conference on acoustics, speech and signal processing (ICASSP)*, pages 4779–4783. IEEE.

SIL. Accessed March 14 2024. *Ethnologue: Languages of the World*. SIL International, https://www.ethnologue.com/.

David J. Spiegelhalter, Nicola G. Best, Bradley P. Carlin, and Angelika van der Linde. 2002. Bayesian measures of model complexity and fit. *J. R. Statist. Soc. B*, 64(4):583–639.

Yaniv Taigman, Lior Wolf, Adam Polyak, and Eliya Nachmani. 2017. Voiceloop: Voice fitting and synthesis via a phonological loop. *arXiv preprint arXiv:1707.06588*.

Pilar Valenzuela and Agustina Valera Rojas. 2005. *Koshi shinanya ainbo*. Fondo Editorial de la Facultad de Ciencias Sociales UNMSM.

Jin Xu, Xu Tan, Yi Ren, Tao Qin, Jian Li, Sheng Zhao, and Tie-Yan Liu. 2020. Lrspeech: Extremely low-resource speech synthesis and recognition. In *Proceedings of the 26th ACM SIGKDD International Conference on Knowledge Discovery & Data Mining*, pages 2802–2812.

Rodolfo Zevallos, Luis Camacho, and Nelsi Melgarejo. 2022. Huqariq: A multilingual speech corpus of native languages of peru for speech recognition. *arXiv preprint arXiv:2207.05498*.

A About de Shipibo-Konibo community

The Shipibo-Konibo community is an indigenous Amazonian group located primarily in the Ucayali region of Peru, with additional populations in Loreto, Huánuco, Madre de Dios and urban areas such as Lima and Pucallpa. They are known for their rich cultural heritage, textile art, and deep spiritual connection to nature.

In 2015, the Peruvian Ministry of Education formalized an official alphabet as shown in Figure 7, though older orthographies still exist as can be seen on the Figure 8.

Figure 6: Map of Peru showing the areas where various Shipibo-Konibo communities are located.

Vowels

a	e	i	o
[ɐ/ã]	[e]	[i̞/ĩ]	[ö̞/õ]

Consonants

b	ch	j	k	m	n	p	r
[β/β̞/b/bβ]]	[tʃ]	[h]	[k]	[m]	[n]	[p]	[ɹ̝/z̞/d͡z/dɹ/ɾ]
s	sh	t	ts	x	w	y	
[s]	[ʂ~ʃ]	[t̪]	[ts]	[ʃ]	[w/w̃/ŋʷ]	[j/j̃/ɲ]	

Figure 7: Current Shipibo-Konibo normalized graphemes and phonemes

Vowels

a	e	i	o	u
[ɐ/ã]	[e]	[i̞/ĩ]	[ö̞/õ]	[ɯ/ɨ/ɯ̃]

Consonants

b	c	ch	j	k	l	m	n
[β/β̞/b/bβ]]	[ts]	[tʃ]	[h]	[k]	[l]	[m]	[n]
p	qu	r	s	sh	t	w	y
[p]	[k]	[ɹ̝/z̞/d͡z/dɹ/ɾ]	[s]	[ʂ~ʃ]	[t̪]	[w/w̃/ŋʷ]	[j/j̃/ɲ]

Figure 8: One of the old Shipibo-Konibo graphemes and phonemes

Does a code-switching dialogue system help users learn conversational fluency in Choctaw?

Jacqueline Brixey
USC Institute for Creative Technologies
brixey@usc

David Traum
USC Institute for Creative Technologies
traum@ict.usc.edu

Abstract

We investigate the learning outcomes and user response to a chatbot for practicing conversational Choctaw, an endangered American Indigenous language. Conversational fluency is a goal for many language learners, however, for learners of endangered languages in North America, access to fluent speakers may be limited. Chatbots are potentially ideal dialogue partners as this kind of dialogue system fulfills a non-authoritative role by focusing on carrying on a conversation as an equal conversational partner. The goal of the chatbot investigated in this work is to serve as a conversational partner in the absence of a fluent Choctaw-speaking human interlocutor. We investigate the impact of code-switching in the interaction, comparing a bilingual chatbot against a monolingual Choctaw version. We evaluate the systems for user engagement and enjoyment, as well as gains in conversational fluency from interacting with the system.

1 Introduction and Motivation

Conversational fluency is a goal for many language learners. However, for learners of endangered languages like Choctaw, access to fluent speakers may be limited. This lack of access may be due to geographical features, such as not living on or near tribal lands, or because there are few remaining fluent speakers of the language. It is unclear how many Indigenous languages are still spoken today in the United States; one source (Moseley, 2010) estimated there were 256 in 2010, while the 2010 US census estimated 165[1]. At the time of writing, no similar summary could be found for the results of the 2020 census. However, it is anticipated that the number of speakers has declined over time (Simons and Fennig, 2018), particularly after the devastating effects of the COVID-19 pandemic (Healy and Blue; Rogers), thus support for learning these languages is time critical.

The goal of the chatbot investigated in this work is to serve as a conversational partner in the absence of a fluent Choctaw-speaking human interlocutor. The goal of the interaction is for the user to gain conversational fluency in Choctaw, such as through increased vocabulary or greater sense of ease, by interacting with the system. We compare a monolingual version of the chatbot against a code-switching one.

This work builds on our previous work on Masheli, a simplified Choctaw-English code-switching chatbot (Brixey and Traum, 2021). However, we address several new questions, such as: Will code-switching lead to a better user experience? Will users show a higher preference for the code-switching chatbot? Will code-switching improve the learning outcomes? Will Indigenous language learners want to use this technology? Our results indicate that interactions with the code-switching chatbot suggest a slight improvement in user experience but did not find significant learning benefits compared to the monolingual chatbot.

2 Relevant Literature

Technology developed for learning purposes, especially language learning, is a well-established area of research. Technology, particularly dialogue systems, has been implemented in this sphere for several reasons. While traditional classroom settings may attempt to create conversational opportunities, many student factors, such as shyness or fear of making errors, can prevent learners from engaging fully in conversation with a human partner (Shawar and Atwell, 2007). Chatbots are well suited for language learning environments since they can serve as an equal conversational partner without expectations of explicit correction on errors (Chou et al., 2003), and learners have reported

[1] https://www2.census.gov/library/publications/2011/acs/acsbr10-10.pdf

Proceedings of the Fifth Workshop on NLP for Indigenous Languages of the Americas (AmericasNLP), pages 8–17
May 4, 2025

feeling more comfortable chatting with a dialogue system than with a human interlocutor (Fryer and Carpenter, 2006).

2.1 Second language acquisition literature

Second language acquisition is learning a second language other than the first after the first language has been acquired (Ortega, 2014). Theories, frameworks, and descriptions for second language acquisition abound (For a more detailed overview, see Ortega (2014); Mitchell et al. (2013); Lightbown and Spada (2013)). This section is thus related to Indigenous language learning and systems and emerging bilingual conversational behaviors and pedagogy that supports these behaviors.

2.1.1 Indigenous language pedagogy and language learning systems

Learning an Indigenous language differs from other second languages due to factors like a limited number of fluent speakers, often dispersed geographically, and the dominance of English in many Indigenous communities (2015). Language suppression and forced cultural assimilation have contributed to these challenges, along with a lack of published literature and media in the language. Moreover, the scarcity of learning opportunities and spaces to practice the language, even on reservations, further complicates revitalization efforts (White, 2006). Additionally, Indigenous language teachers may not always have formal training in pedagogy, and there may not be enough instructors to meet the growing demand for learners of all ages (Lukaniec and Palakurthy, 2022).

Technology has become a significant tool for overcoming some of these challenges, providing new opportunities for language learning and connecting speakers across geographical distances (Cassels and Farr, 2019). While technology alone cannot revitalize a language, it can supplement the efforts of motivated learners and serve as one of many tools for language revitalization (Cassels and Farr, 2019). The Choctaw Nation of Oklahoma has long utilized technology for language teaching, from early telecourses to more recent Zoom classes, which became especially popular during the pandemic and continue to thrive today [2]. As Mark Turin, former chair of the First Nations and Endangered Languages Program at the University of British Columbia, states, "tools and technology don't save language — speakers do" (Karstens-Smith).

2.1.2 Emerging Bilingual Conversational Behaviors and Translanguaging

Emerging bilinguals often code-switch, combining elements from different languages to communicate, even in non-grammatical ways, but they still co-construct meaning with interlocutors (Cenoz and Gortegaorter, 2017; Canagarajah, 2011). This is common in casual conversations where interlocutors share multiple languages and the language choice is not fixed (Auer, 1995). While learning a language is ultimately an individual endeavor, supportive pedagogy can enhance the process. Traditional immersion pedagogy required learners to interact only in the target language, but translanguaging—intentionally using multiple languages in a learning environment—has become more widely accepted in second-language pedagogy, especially for teaching endangered languages (Cenoz and Gortegaorter, 2017).

The literature differentiates code-switching from translanguaging. Code-switching involves shifting between languages in any conversational setting, while translanguaging encourages emerging bilinguals to use all their languages purposefully in a learning setting, with the instructor gradually reducing support as learners progress (Cenoz and Gortegaorter, 2017; Makalela, 2015). Originating in bilingual English-Welsh education, translanguaging emphasizes interaction and participation, even if not entirely in the target language, allowing learners to use other languages to fill gaps in their knowledge (Makalela, 2015; García, 2009). This contrasts with immersion-style teaching, which often discourages or ignores the use of the non-target language.

In monolingual settings, emerging bilinguals often avoid addressing their language confusion, hoping that future encounters or additional context in the same conversation will provide clarification (Canagarajah, 2011). This is known as the "let it pass" principle (Firth, 1996), the act of not addressing misunderstandings, which can hinder comprehension if additional examples do not occur. However, classrooms using translanguaging have seen better outcomes for second-language learners, as fewer "let it pass" instances happen (Champlin, 2016). While translanguaging is frequently considered a verbal act (Canagarajah, 2011), the literature supports translanguaging in text form. For example,

[2] `https://www.choctawnation.com/about/language/classes/`

Māori literacy improved when students used English to process Māori texts (Lowman et al., 2007). Translanguaging has also been shown to be psychologically beneficial for emerging bilinguals. It is suggested to legitimize a student's relationship with both languages and foster self-identification as a speaker of both languages (Makalela, 2015), while encouraging the use of all linguistic resources, rather than suppressing specific repertoires, can enhance students' self-confidence.

There are strategies to use translanguaging in a learning environment effectively. The most common approaches emphasize linking translanguaging to content in lessons, such as important vocabulary, and that the instructor should utilize translanguaging and encourage its use by individual students and within groups (Cenoz and Gortegaorter, 2017; Dougherty, 2021; Seals and Olsen-Reeder, 2020).

2.2 Hypotheses

To summarize the prior research, translanguaging and using an already known language can enhance a learner's learning gains and sense of comfort in a classroom setting with human-human interactions (Butzkamm and Caldwell, 2009). The literature also shows that code-switching can lessen the feeling of distance between conversational human interlocutors. Based on the literature, the hypotheses for this experiment are as follows.

1. H1: Code-switching bilingual chatbots that use translanguaging techniques and code-switching frameworks lead to a better learning experience, possibly through learning gains or a greater sense of rapport, comfort, or enjoyment for language learning users.
2. Users will demonstrate the highest learning gains with a code-switching system.
3. Users will have a lower user experience with the monolingual system than with the code-switching bilingual system.

3 System Design

For this work, we implemented two chatbots: a monolingual Choctaw version, and an English-Choctaw code-switching one. The backend of the chatbots is NPCEditor, a response classifier and dialogue management system (Leuski and Traum, 2011). NPCEditor uses a statistical classifier that is trained on linked questions and responses. The classifier is trained on a question-answer (QA) corpus.

Figure 1: Example conversation with the chatbot.

For each user input, the classifier ranks all the available responses. NPCEditor also contains a dialogue manager, which selects an appropriate response from the ranked responses. Previous applications of NPCEditor have been used for interactive characters in multiple domains, such as interviews with Holocaust survivors (Traum et al., 2015). This was also the backend for an earlier version of Masheli (Brixey and Traum, 2021).

An example dialogue with the code-switching chatbot is in Figure 1, demonstrating some greetings (the first two complete turns) and then telling a story about a fox in Choctaw.

We elected to use NPCEditor and handcrafted utterances over LLMs or other approaches for two primary reasons. First, we wanted to implement a consistent strategy for code-switching, which we found LLMs struggled to produce reliably. Second, through experimentation, we discovered that LLMs often failed to generate syntactically correct Choctaw utterances. Since one of the chatbot's main goals is to help learners improve their language fluency, providing incorrect Choctaw would contradict that objective.

3.1 QA Corpus

Each question in the QA corpus is matched to at least one appropriate answer that serves as a response for the chatbot. There is no explicit module for recognizing the language in which the user is communicating. The knowledge base of the chatbot is sharing stories about animals. We made this selection because pedagogy literature, especially for American Indigenous languages (Cantoni, 1999), indicates that story-based instruction is beneficial in language learning environments (Kickham, 2015; Andrews et al., 2009).

3.1.1 Questions

We implemented a Python script to generate questions for the question portion of the QA corpus. The script included several sentences with predominantly English syntax, such as "Can I have a story about ..." or "Tell me about ..." and the list of animals from the stories in Choctaw to be added at the end of the sentence. The result produced a sentence like "Can I have a story about shawi?" (Can I have a story about raccoons?)

The monolingual chatbot version was intended to mimic an immersion-style pedagogy, so we only added a handful of English and code-switched sentences. Most of these were mapped to an off-topic response encouraging the user to speak in Choctaw. This type of response aligns with the immersion-style curriculum, which will ignore or discourage statements made in the non-target language.

3.1.2 Answers

To form the chatbot's domain knowledge, ten animal stories were selected from ChoCo (Brixey et al., 2018), a Choctaw language corpus. All stories are originally in Choctaw and have English translations. We created handcrafted responses for the two chatbots. To incorporate translanguaging strategies in the code-switching chatbot, we repeated key vocabulary to understand the story in English in parentheses. Repetition was one non-spontaneous strategy for effective translanguaging (Seals and Olsen-Reeder, 2020). The examples in Table 1 show how code-switching and translanguaging were incorporated into a given line in a story.

Code-switching was generated in two options, insertional and switching at clauses, which follows the linguistic literature on code-switching and the model described in Ahn et al. (2020). There were two options for the matrix language, either Choctaw or English. Not every sentence in a story includes code-switching. Instead, we aimed for roughly 75% of a given Choctaw story to have code-switching.

3.2 Dialogue manager

The dialogue manager can choose a lower-ranked response to avoid repetition. If the score of the top-ranked response is below the threshold that was selected during training, the dialogue manager will instead select a response that indicates non-understanding or that aims to end a conversation topic. For example, the expression "Mihacha?" ("It really is, isn't it?") might be selected as a response when no other response scores above the threshold.

3.3 Orthographic considerations

One challenge to support Choctaw is that the language does not have a fully standardized written form. Each training example in the question portion of the QA corpus was written in multiple formats to support many different possible orthographic presentations. For example, the sentence "Do you know a story about a woodpecker?" could be written with different formats of nasalized characters a̱ and i̱:

1. Biskinik am anumpa nan anoli ish i̱shi?
2. Biskinik a anumpa nan anoli ish i̱shi?
3. Biskinik an anumpa nan anoli ish i̱shi?
4. Biskinik a̱ anumpa nan anoli ish i̱shi?
5. Biskinik a̱ anumpa nan anoli ish inshi?

4 Methods

This section discusses consultations with the Choctaw Nation of Oklahoma, the IRB review process, and how we ensured tribal data rights. We also describe methods to assess the user experience: a language test to evaluate the user's learning and a survey to gauge their sense of rapport, comfort, and enjoyment.

4.1 Tribal review

Several steps are required to conduct research on the Oklahoma Choctaw language or with Choctaw tribal members. First, a sponsor must review and support the work. A sponsor must be someone who works for the tribal nation. The sponsors for this work evaluated the proposal for sensitivity to the community, adequate protection of tribal members, and alignment with tribal initiatives. Following a sponsor's approval and support, we then applied to

English	One day a man riding in a boat came to the end of the water.
Monolingual Choctaw	Mak atoko̱ nittak himona ka̱ hattak mvt oka peni fokka osh ont aivhli ma̱ ona tok.
Insertional-Cho matrix	Mak atoko̱ nittak himona ka̱ hattak mvt **a boat** fokka osh ont aivhli ma̱ ona tok.
Clausal-Cho matrix	**One day**, hattak mvt oka peni fokka osh ont aivhli ma̱ ona tok.
Insertional-Eng matrix	**One day a man riding in** oka peni **came to the end of the water**.
Clausal-Eng matrix	Mak atoko̱ nittak himona ka̱ **a man riding in a boat came to the end of the water**.
Repetition	**One day a man riding in** oka peni **(a boat) came to the end of the water**.

Table 1: Framework-based utterances examples. English portions are bolded in code-switched utterances.

Choctaw Nation's IRB. Our university's IRB then reviewed and approved the protocol.

4.2 Language Test

We created a 15-question language test to be administered before and after the interaction. The test determines whether learners gained any new vocabulary ("What is the word for deer in Choctaw?", 12 questions) or any new syntax ("How would you say, 'Do you know a story about deer?' in Choctaw?", three questions).

The language test also served to inform all participants about the chatbot's domain knowledge of animal stories, a fact given in the instructions read to each participant, so that participants would have more consistent experiences and not have to spend time discovering which stories the chatbot knows.

4.3 Survey design

The survey was designed to evaluate the user's sense of rapport, the naturalness of the code-switching, and the feeling of connection because of language identity.

The survey consisted of twelve 5-point Likert scale questions, and the answers were scored from 1 strongly disagree to 5 strongly agree. Many questions came from previous research on rapport (Novick and Gris, 2014; Gratch et al., 2007). Questions 7 and 10 are novel and tailored to this experiment. All survey questions were optional, and participants could choose to skip any questions.

1. The system understood me.
2. The system seemed unengaged.
3. The system was friendly.
4. The system and I worked towards a common goal.
5. The system and I did not seem to connect.
6. I didn't understand the system.
7. The system knows the Choctaw language.
8. The interaction was interesting.
9. The interaction felt natural.
10. I felt the system and I were in the same social group.
11. I would be willing to continue the conversation with the system for longer.
12. I would recommend interacting with this system to a friend.
13. Was there anything else that you wanted to talk to the system about? (open-ended)
14. Do you have any other comments to share about your experience? (open-ended)

Questions were selected to determine levels of rapport (1, 2, 4, 5, 6, 9) and engagement and connection (3, 8, 10, 11, 12). We hypothesized that the code-switching cohort would score the chatbot higher on these questions. The survey also measured people's perception of the chatbot's knowledge of the Choctaw language (7) to gauge how users perceived the fluency of the chatbot's code-switching.

4.3.1 Experiment session

Participants began by reading and signing a consent form, followed by an oral explanation. The experiment started with the language test, after which participants interacted with the chatbot for 15 minutes. They then completed the language test again and finished with a post-interaction survey to rate their experience and provide comments. Participants were encouraged to have a dictionary on hand; if not, they were given links to two online dictionaries, a 1915 publication (Byington, 1915) and a 2016 publication (The Choctaw Nation of Oklahoma Dictionary Committee, 2016).

4.3.2 Inclusion and exclusion criteria

Inclusion and exclusion criteria, in this case, specify which individuals from the participant population are eligible or ineligible to be included in the research study. The inclusion criteria required participants to follow instructions, engage meaningfully with tasks, and provide on-topic interactions with the chatbot. They were instructed to communicate with the session leader only for questions or technical issues. Participants were expected to complete all tasks, including language proficiency tests, surveys, and structured interactions with the chatbot, ensuring data integrity. While participants were not required to spend the full 15 minutes interacting with the chatbot and would not be excluded for finishing early, they were encouraged to take time referencing the dictionary. No specific number of chatbot interactions was required, but at least one turn was necessary to demonstrate participation. Exclusion criteria included multiple off-topic utterances, inappropriate comments, or off-topic survey responses. Non-engagement was identified as discussing unrelated topics with the session leader, except for technical issues or clarifications.

5 Results

In total, 23 participants completed the experiment. Twelve participants interacted with the monolingual Choctaw chatbot, while eleven participants interacted with the framework-based code-switching chatbot. One participant from the monolingual chatbot met the exclusion criteria, so their survey and language test responses were omitted.

Two participants requested to finish the chat portion early. Their data was retained as they followed all protocols and engaged with the chatbot, albeit for less time. One participant using the monolingual chatbot ended the session after 6 minutes due to frustration, while another using the code-switching chatbot ended it after 13 minutes, citing frustration and disinterest. Many participants asked the chatbot for definitions and translations despite having a dictionary, suggesting future work could include providing these directly.

5.1 Language Test

All language tests (pre- and post-test) were scored for two factors. The first factor was how many questions were attempted, regardless of correctness. The second factor was correctness. A correct answer was one point; thus, a perfect score on the quiz would be 15.

For the first 12 questions on the language test, we applied a rubric for grading the questions. Since Choctaw is not standardized and can require a keyboard with the unique characters, we made allowances for differences in spelling. Half a point was deducted if an extra syllable was added, a vowel was sufficiently incorrect to impact the pronunciation, or a consonant was substantially incorrect. Likewise, half of a point was deducted for the syntax questions if the words were correct, but the ordering was off, or the pronoun was incorrect.

Next, we evaluated the average change for attempted and correct responses. The average change in the number of vocabulary questions attempted was 1.18 for the monolingual group and 1.36 for the code-switching group. This indicates that the code-switching group was slightly more inclined to try more questions after interacting with the chatbot. The average change in correct answers for vocabulary questions for the monolingual group was 1.5, while the code-switching group was 1.36. This indicates that all groups benefited from the interaction, with the monolingual group improving slightly more. No participants had decreased test scores. Several participants in both groups showed no improvement via the language test. The participant with the greatest improvement was in the code-switching group, with a gain of 4.5 points between pre- and post-interaction tests, and this participant also showed the greatest change in the number of questions attempted. For the grammar questions of the language test, the monolingual group showed an average increase of 0.1 in the number of grammar questions attempted. In contrast, the code-switching group had an average increase between pre- and post-grammar questions attempted of 0.09. The monolingual group improved in correct responses on average by 0.2 points, while the code-switching group improved by 0.18.

An overall positive finding is that learning occurred with both chatbots. Additionally, we did not observe a significantly higher level of learning with the monolingual chatbot, the "immersion" style of learning, over the translanguaging, code-switching chatbot.

5.2 Responses to survey

The results of comparing the two groups' survey responses using a one-tailed T-test are shown in Table 2. The table also shows the average score for each group, with the standard deviation given in parentheses next to the mean value.

We observed two $p<0.10$ values: (1) The code-switching group scored their chatbot as friendlier than the monolingual group, and (2) the code-switching group reported that they would be more likely to recommend the system to others.

	Question	T-test result	Mean Mono (std dev)	Mean CSW (std dev)
1	The system understood me.	0.25	3(1)	3.54(1.03)
2	The system seemed unengaged.	0.73	2.54(1.50)	2.36(1.36)
3	The system was friendly.	*0.07	3.18 (1.47)	4.36 (0.80)
4	The system and I worked towards a common goal.	0.65	3.36 (1.36)	3.54 (0.82)
5	The system and I did not seem to connect.	0.34	2.90 (1.51)	2.45 (1.12)
6	I didn't understand the system.	1	2.54 (1.29)	2.54 (1.29)
7	The system knows the Choctaw language.	0.64	3.9 (0.87)	4 (0.89)
8	The interaction was interesting.	0.16	3.63 (1.36)	4.36 (0.92)
9	The interaction felt natural.	0.19	2.81 (1.32)	3.45 (0.82)
10	The system and I were in the same social group.	0.16	2.45 (1.21)	3.18 (1.16)
11	I would be willing to continue the conversation with the system for longer.	0.13	3.63 (1.74)	4.45 (0.52)
12	I would recommend interacting with this system to a friend.	*0.06	3.63 (1.62)	4.54 (0.52)

Table 2: The results of comparing survey responses between the monolingual and code-switching interactions. p<0.10 results are marked with one asterisk. Standard deviations are given in parentheses next to the average in the final two columns.

We then analyzed the survey responses by clustering the questions by rapport (1, 2, 4, 5, 6, 9) and engagement and connection (3, 8, 10, 11, 12). We then summed the scores for each participant in the given cluster. We reversed the polarity for negatively phrased questions (2, 5, 6). The p-value for the clustered questions on rapport was 0.24. The p-value for engagement and connection was 0.04, a significant value.

6 Discussion

First, we will review the findings for the main research questions.

- *Will code-switching lead to a better user experience? Will users show a higher preference for the code-switching chatbot?*
  The survey results indicate that users had a better, more satisfying experience with the code-switching, translanguaging chatbot.
- *Will code-switching lead to an increase in learning?*
  The language tests indicate that participants learned new vocabulary while interacting with the code-switching chatbot. However, they did not learn significantly more than the monolingual group, indicating that interacting with any chatbot will lead to a learning experience.
- *Will Indigenous language learners want to use this technology?*
  Some participants expressed interest in interacting with the chatbot again, we invited them to chat with it again during one weekend over the month that experiments were held. The conversations that day were recorded via a log, but no information was noted about who spoke to the chatbot at any given time.

Now, we will review the findings in relation to the hypotheses.

H1: Code-switching bilingual chatbots that use translanguaging techniques and code-switching frameworks lead to a better learning experience, possibly through learning gains or a greater sense of rapport, comfort, or enjoyment for language learning users.

The code-switching chatbot followed translanguaging principles in its code-switching but also followed linguistic frameworks that produced insertional and clause switches. The survey results suggest that modeling code-switching aspects using linguistic frameworks leads to higher levels of reported rapport and enjoyment. The final question of the survey indicates that the code-switching cohort would be more likely to interact with the chatbot again; thus, it is possible that learning gains could be achieved over multiple interactions.

Survey results also show that participants found the code-switching chatbot more enjoyable and better suited as a language partner for Choctaw learners, with many describing it as friendlier. This aligns with the literature on face, suggesting that participants felt their face was threatened when the chatbot didn't understand their Choctaw attempts. Face is the image one has of oneself and emerges during interactions (Haugh, 2009). Face is important in any conversation as humans want to be liked and respected by others, but face is a key factor in learning scenarios (Wang et al., 2008) and particularly in second language conversations (Piirainen-Marsh, 1995; Ahvenainen, 2021).

H2: Users will demonstrate the highest learning gains with a code-switching system.

The language test results show no significant learning gains with immersion (interacting with the monolingual chatbot), either in the number of correct answers or the number of attempted questions. Participants interacting with the code-switching chatbot had slightly lower correct answers but were more likely to attempt vocabulary questions, possibly due to increased confidence. These results suggest that both chatbots lead to positive learning gains.

H3: Users will have a lower user experience with the monolingual system than with the code-switching bilingual chatbot.

Based on the $p<0.10$ results for questions 3 and 12 on the user survey, a preference was observed for the code-switching system.

Literature on face and face-work explains why participants preferred the bilingual chatbot. As face is tied to emotional reactions, it can be threatened in language learning, leading to frustration, shame, or anger (Spencer-Oatey, 2007; Holtgraves, 2009; Ting-Toomey, 2009). Interlocutors are expected to protect each other's face (Holtgraves, 2009), thus users interacting with the monolingual chatbot may have felt rejected by its seeming disapproval of their English or non-standard Choctaw.

7 Conclusion and Future Directions

In this work, we tested a novel code-switching Choctaw language chatbot and the impact of code-switching on learning. As the language is endangered, effective revitalization efforts are time-critical. The results of our study indicate that users prefer the code-switching chatbot over the monolingual one based on the survey responses, which could have implications for maintaining long-term learning motivation and interest. Both cohorts demonstrated learning gains from the interaction in the form of a vocabulary and grammar quiz, with the monolingual cohort learning just slightly more but not significantly more. Our contributions include novel insights into the user experience of interacting with a code-switching dialogue system, a chatbot capable of responding to code-switched user input, a schema for chatbot responses using linguistic frameworks and translanguaging techniques, and a corpus of learning users' conversations with the chatbot. Choctaw learners have received little study, and the conversation logs could serve as a meaningful resource for language instructors and linguists.

One possibility for future work is to evaluate the learning gains over a longer period to determine if additional time spent interacting with the chatbot or over several sessions could produce strongly significant results, either on the survey or language test. It is possible that retention would be higher with the group paired with the code-switching chatbot, given the higher survey scores, and with higher retention, the possibility of higher learning. A final consideration is that replication is needed for other language communities to confirm that the results found here are not unique to the Choctaw language.

8 Limitations

One computational limitation of Masheli was that the system could not process some of the unique characters of participants' input. The system was trained using specific ASCII characters but had not been trained on some of the other possible ASCII variations. Additionally, some of the characters did not render correctly for unclear reasons, such as a̠ sometimes presented as å. Participants were encouraged during the experiment to use alternative spellings if the system could not process their original statement; however, this may have impacted user satisfaction.

9 Ethics

This work was completed with consultation and review from the Choctaw Nation of Oklahoma (see Section 4.1 for more details). All of the collected data from this research was requested to be archived at the Choctaw Nation's Cultural Center archives to ensure that the tribe would continue to benefit from this effort.

References

Emily Ahn, Cecilia Jimenez, Yulia Tsvetkov, and Alan W Black. 2020. What code-switching strategies are effective in dialog systems? In *Proceedings of the Society for Computation in Linguistics 2020*, pages 213–222.

Tarmo Ahvenainen. 2021. Language proficiency face-work and perceptions of language proficiency face in l2 interaction. *JYU dissertations*.

Dee H Andrews, Thomas D Hull, and Jennifer A Donahue. 2009. Storytelling as an instructional method: Descriptions and research questions. *The Interdisciplinary Journal of Problem-based Learning• volume*, 3(1):6–28.

Peter Auer. 1995. The pragmatics of code-switching: a sequential approach. In Leslie Milroy and Pieter Muysken, editors, *One speaker, two languages*, chapter 6, pages 115–135. University of Cambridge.

Jacqueline Brixey, Eli Pincus, and Ron Artstein. 2018. Chahta anumpa: A multimodal corpus of the Choctaw language. In *Proceedings of LREC 2018*, Miyazaki, Japan.

Jacqueline Brixey and David Traum. 2021. Masheli: A Choctaw-English bilingual chatbot. In *Conversational Dialogue Systems for the Next Decade*, pages 41–50. Springer.

Wolfgang Butzkamm and John AW Caldwell. 2009. *The bilingual reform: A paradigm shift in foreign language teaching*. Narr Francke Attempto Verlag.

Cyrus Byington. 1915. *A Dictionary of the Choctaw Language*. US Government Printing Office. Edited by John R. Swanton and Henry S. Halbert. Smithsonian Institution Bureau of American Ethnology Bulletin 46.

Suresh Canagarajah. 2011. Translanguaging in the classroom: Emerging issues for research and pedagogy. *Applied linguistics review*, 2(1):1–28.

Gina P Cantoni. 1999. Using tpr-storytelling to develop fluency and literacy in native american languages. *Revitalizing Indigenous Languages*, page 53.

Morgan Cassels and Chloë Farr. 2019. Mobile applications for indigenous language learning: Literature review and app survey. *Working Papers of the Linguistics Circle*, 29(1):1–24.

Jasone Cenoz and Durk Gortegaorter. 2017. Minority languages and sustainable translanguaging: Threat or opportunity? *Journal of Multilingual and Multicultural Development*, 38(10):901–912.

Molly J Champlin. 2016. *Translanguaging and bilingual learners: A study of how translanguaging promotes literacy skills in bilingual students*. Ms thesis, St. John Fisher College.

Chih-Yueh Chou, Tak-Wai Chan, and Chi-Jen Lin. 2003. Redefining the learning companion: the past, present, and future of educational agents. *Computers & Education*, 40(3):255–269.

Tyne Crow and David Parsons. 2015. A mobile game world for māori language learning. In *International Conference on Mobile and Contextual Learning*, pages 84–98. Springer.

Jessica Dougherty. 2021. Translanguaging in action: Pedagogy that elevates. *ORTESOL Journal*, 38:19–32.

Alan Firth. 1996. The discursive accomplishment of normality: On 'lingua franca'english and conversation analysis. *Journal of pragmatics*, 26(2):237–259.

Luke Fryer and Rollo Carpenter. 2006. Bots as language learning tools. *Language Learning & Technology*, 10(3):8–14.

Ofelia García. 2009. Education, multilingualism and translanguaging in the 21st century. In *Social justice through multilingual education*, pages 140–158. Multilingual Matters.

Jonathan Gratch, Ning Wang, Jillian Gerten, Edward Fast, and Robin Duffy. 2007. Creating rapport with virtual agents. In *Intelligent Virtual Agents: 7th International Conference, IVA 2007 Paris, France, September 17-19, 2007 Proceedings 7*, pages 125–138. Springer.

Michael Haugh. 2009. Face and interaction. In Michael Haugh and Francesca Bargiela-Chiappini, editors, *Face, communication and social interaction*, chapter 1, pages 1–30. Equinox London.

Jack Healy and Victor J. Blue. Tribal elders are dying from the pandemic, causing a cultural crisis for American Indians. *The New York Times*.

Thomas Holtgraves. 2009. Face, politeness and interpersonal variables: implications for language production and comprehension. In Michael Haugh and Francesca Bargiela-Chiappini, editors, *Face, communication and social interaction*, chapter 10, pages 192–207. Equinox London.

Gemma Karstens-Smith. B.C. Teen creates app to help revive fading Indigenous language. *Toronto Star*.

Elizabeth A Kickham. 2015. *Purism, Prescriptivism, and privilege: Choctaw language ideologies and their impact on teaching and learning*. Ph.D. thesis, UNIVERSITY OF OKLAHOMA.

Anton Leuski and David Traum. 2011. Npceditor: Creating virtual human dialogue using information retrieval techniques. *Ai Magazine*, 32(2):42–56.

Patsy M Lightbown and Nina Spada. 2013. *How Languages are Learned 4th edition-Oxford Handbooks for Language Teachers*. Oxford University Press.

Chris Lowman, Tangimai Fitzgerald, Patsy Rapira, and Rahera Clark. 2007. First language literacy skill transfer in a second language learning environment: Strategies for biliteracy. *Set*, 2:24–28.

Megan Lukaniec and Kayla Palakurthy. 2022. Additional language learning in the context of indigenous language reclamation. In *The Routledge handbook of second language acquisition and sociolinguistics*, pages 341–355. Routledge.

Leketi Makalela. 2015. Translanguaging as a vehicle for epistemic access: Cases for reading comprehension and multilingual interactions. *Per Linguam: a Journal of Language Learning= Per Linguam: Tydskrif vir Taalaanleer*, 31(1):15–29.

Rosamond Mitchell, Florence Myles, and Emma Marsden. 2013. *Second Language Learning Theories*. Routledge.

Christopher Moseley. 2010. *Atlas of the World's Languages in Danger*. Unesco.

David Novick and Iván Gris. 2014. Building rapport between human and eca: A pilot study. In *Human-Computer Interaction. Advanced Interaction Modalities and Techniques: 16th International Conference, HCI International 2014, Heraklion, Crete, Greece, June 22-27, 2014, Proceedings, Part II 16*, pages 472–480. Springer.

Lourdes Ortega. 2014. *Understanding second language acquisition*. Routledge.

Arja Piirainen-Marsh. 1995. Face in second language conversation. *JYU dissertations*.

Mike Rogers. Choctaw Nation members talk about impact of losing native speakers to COVID-19. *KXII.com*.

Corinne A Seals and Vincent Olsen-Reeder. 2020. Translanguaging in conjunction with language revitalization. *System*, 92:102277.

Bayan Abu Shawar and Eric Atwell. 2007. Fostering language learner autonomy through adaptive conversation tutors. In *Proceedings of the The fourth Corpus Linguistics conference*.

Gary F. Simons and Charles D. Fennig, editors. 2018. *Ethnologue: Languages of the World*, twenty-first edition. SIL International, Dallas, Texas.

Helen Spencer-Oatey. 2007. Theories of identity and the analysis of face. *Journal of pragmatics*, 39(4):639–656.

The Choctaw Nation of Oklahoma Dictionary Committee. 2016. *Chahta Anumpa Tosholi Himona: New Choctaw Dictionary*, 1st edition. Choctaw Print Services.

Stella Ting-Toomey. 2009. Facework collision in intercultural communication. In Michael Haugh and Francesca Bargiela-Chiappini, editors, *Face, communication and social interaction*, chapter 12, pages 227–249. Equinox London.

David Traum, Andrew Jones, Kia Hays, Heather Maio, Oleg Alexander, Ron Artstein, Paul Debevec, Alesia Gainer, Kallirroi Georgila, Kathleen Haase, and 1 others. 2015. New dimensions in testimony: Digitally preserving a holocaust survivor's interactive storytelling. In *International Conference on Interactive Digital Storytelling*, pages 269–281. Springer.

Ning Wang, W Lewis Johnson, Richard E Mayer, Paola Rizzo, Erin Shaw, and Heather Collins. 2008. The politeness effect: Pedagogical agents and learning outcomes. *International journal of human-computer studies*, 66(2):98–112.

Frederick White. 2006. Rethinking native american language revitalization. *American Indian Quarterly*, 30(1/2):91–109.

A hybrid approach to low-resource machine translation for Ojibwe verbs

Tran Minh Nguyen, Christopher Hammerly
Department of Linguistics
University of British Columbia
Vancouver, B.C., Canada
minhngca@student.ubc.ca, chris.hammerly@ubc.ca

Miikka Silfverberg
Independent
mpsilfve@iki.fi

Abstract

Machine translation is a tool that can help teachers, learners, and users of low-resourced languages. However, there are significant challenges in developing these tools, such as the lack of large-scale parallel corpora and complex morphology. We propose a novel hybrid system that combines LLM and rule-based methods in two distinct stages to translate inflected Ojibwe verbs into English. We use an LLM to automatically annotate dictionary data to build translation templates. Then, our rule-based module performs translation using inflection and slot-filling processes built on top of an FST-based analyzer. We test the system with a set of automated tests. Thanks to the ahead-of-time nature of the template-building process and the light-weight rule-based translation module, the end-to-end translation process has an average translation speed of 70 milliseconds per word. The system achieved an average ChrF score of 0.82 and a semantic similarity score of 0.93 among the successfully translated verbs in a test set. The approach has the potential to be extended to other low-resource Indigenous languages with dictionary data.

1 Introduction

Ojibwe is an Indigenous language of North America in the Algonquian family spoken in both the US and Canada. There are approximately 25,440 (Statistics Canada, 2023) in Canada, and likely not more than a few thousand speakers in the US. It is important to document and revitalize the language for the benefit of the Indigenous community and the learners. As recently discussed by (Littell et al., 2018), machine translation has the potential to help learners and reduce the workload of teachers.

However, it is a difficult task, because Ojibwe is a morphologically complex language, and there is not enough parallel data for modern neural machine translation. Similar in spirit to recent work by (Zhang et al., 2024), we propose a novel combination of advanced neural architecture such as LLM (Large Language Model) to annotate the dictionary data of Ojibwe to create translation templates, and from that, using rule-based translation computer program, to construct good English translations of inflected Ojibwe verbs. The present work was designed to overcome the challenges of not having enough data to build neural translation systems, while keeping the precision and speed of rule-based translations. The purpose is to help learners, teachers, and researchers.

There are currently no machine translation systems available for the Ojibwe language. Many of the current translation projects for lower-resourced languages like Ojibwe are rule-based (Littell et al., 2018), though there are exceptions such as the recent translation system developed by Google for Inuktitut (Caswell, 2024) and Meta's NLLB (Koishekenov et al., 2022). We know of one rule-based system for machine translation of an Algonquian language – Plains Cree – which has been integrated into the *itwêwina* dictionary (Arppe et al., 2022).

One important type of rule-based system, which can provide at least a partial solution for machine translation, are finite-state transducers (FSTs) or morphological parsers more generally (Zhang et al., 2024). Like all rule-based systems, FSTs have the advantage of only requiring meta-linguistic knowledge of morphophonological forms and rules and a dictionary of stems to get off the ground — there is no need for large collections of training data.[1] As such, FSTs are now relatively commonplace for

[1] It should be noted that, for some languages, even meta-linguistic descriptions in the form of grammars and dictionaries is uncommon. At the extreme, such languages could be seen not just as low-resourced, but unresourced when it comes to documentation and description. For these languages, it is still true that the task of creating a set of rules and collecting word lists is a far more tractable task than creating parallel corpora on the order of millions of tokens.

Proceedings of the Fifth Workshop on NLP for Indigenous Languages of the Americas (AmericasNLP), pages 18–26
May 4, 2025

North American Languages (e.g. Harrigan et al., 2017; Bowers et al., 2017; Forbes et al., 2021; Hammerly et al., 2025). However, these systems generally produce abstract tags, rather than direct translations to another language such as English. In this paper, we show how these tags can be used as an intermediary form to guide rule-based translations.

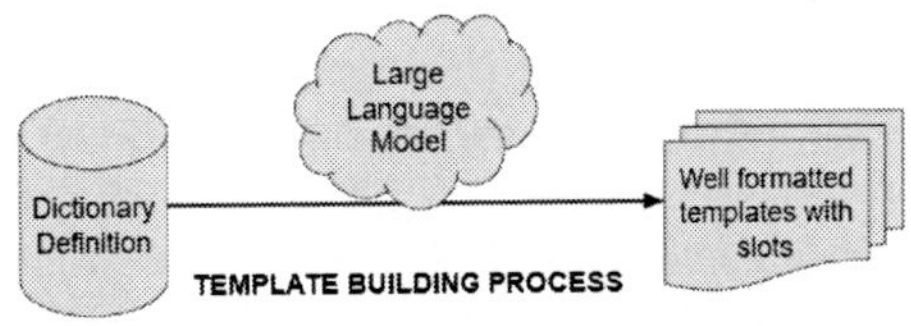

Figure 1: Template Building Process

2 Translation Approach

The system contains two main components: the Template Building module and the Translation module. The code for this project is publicly available in the OjibweTranslation repository (ELF-Lab, 2025).

2.1 Template Building module

The Template Building module has the main task of analyzing Ojibwe dictionary data, which is based on the Ojibwe People's Dictionary (OPD; Nichols, 2012). This data is openly available for use and adaptation by researchers and educators for non-commercial use under a Creative Commons license (Attribution-NonCommercial-ShareAlike 3.0 Unported License), with the explicit goal "to make the dictionary content available as a tool for Ojibwe language revitalization, academic scholarship and cultural awareness". Note, we have only released a limited set of verbs in the public version of the source code at the request of the editors of the OPD.

Our basic process is schematized in Figure 1. We took dictionary data including the English-language definition and used an LLM to build templates with relevant slots. For example, the Ojibwe verb *waabam* defined in English as "**see h/**" (where "h/" means "him/her") becomes "**{{subject}} see {{object}}**". The purpose of building templates is to make it easier for the Translation module to replace these slots with appropriate pronouns or other information, according to the inflected verb.

Verbs in Ojibwe are separated into four basic types based on valency and animacy. Valency refers to whether a verb is intransitive (only a subject) or transitive (both a subject and object). Animacy restricts certain arguments of the verb based on grammatical noun class. All nouns in Ojibwe are grammatically categorized as "animate" or "inanimate", a roughly conceptual split that puts humans, animals, and most plants into one class (animate), and everything else into the other (inanimate). Animate Intransitive (AI) verbs have an animate subject, Inanimate Intransitive (II) verbs have an inanimate subject, Transitive Animate (TA) verbs have an animate object (but the subject can be any animacy), and finally transitive inanimate (TI) verbs have an inanimate object (and again, subjects can have any animacy).

In an early stage of the project, we attempted to use a rule-based approach to create templates. However, we quickly found that the significant inconsistencies in the way dictionary entries were formatted made such an approach untenable. While such inconsistencies do not at all get in the way of normal use – this is not a critique of the dictionary in general – this was a barrier for creating a simple set of rules that could work across all 15,000 verbs in our set. We therefore opted for an LLM approach, which allowed for more flexibility by creating examples and prompts, rather than hard-and-fast rules.

Our ultimate implementation used the Groq API provider, with a model named "**llama3-70b-8192**" based on Meta's Llama3. This particular approach also has the advantage of ensuring data is not passed on to a third party such as Meta (Groq does not use or retain data from prompts), which could potentially violate the license of the dictionary, or more generally afoul of Indigenous data sovereignty. In our case, the LLM is nothing more than a tool to get a specific job done: the annotation of thousands of dictionary entries. This job is not possible to complete with a purely rule-based approach (see above), and discussed later in the section, would be multiple of orders of magnitude less efficient if completed via purely human annotation.

We used the few-shot prompt strategy. The prompt included: (i) The initial instruction to ask the LLM analyze the context, subject and object; (ii) 10 to 20 human written examples; and (iii) A command to process new data. A sample prompt used for processing VTA verbs is in Appendix 5.

For example, with the same definition "see h/", we produce a transitive template "{{subject}} see {{object}}". Using slots such as {{subject}} and {{object}} makes it possible to build more complex sentences in the subsequent steps.

If the lemma definition has multiple meanings or glosses we instructed the LLM to split the definition into multiple templates. For example, with the word **niimaakwa'**, which have the definition "**pick it (animate) up or hold it (animate) out with something stick-like**", the system will produce the following templates:

- verbs: ['pick', 'hold'],
- templates:
  - "{{subject}} pick {{object}} up"
  - "{{subject}} hold {{object}} out with something stick-like"

It is important to emphasize that, while our Template Building module requires an LLM to extract and build templates, it is an ahead-of-time operation, meaning that we need to build the dictionary templates only once and export the templates to a computer-readable data format (such as csv). We do not need to run the template building process every time we do translation. We only need the exported data, which is stored locally, for translation in the subsequent steps. This increases the efficiency of translation.

Template building took about 3 seconds per example, which means about 12 hours of processing time for about 15,000 verbs. In comparison, if the task is to be done with a human annotator, it would take about 5 minutes per example, or about 1,250 hours of working time—a process that would also lead to high numbers of typos and other errors and inconsistencies. The LLM-based template building therefore resulted in an efficiency ratio of about 100 times, while maintaining favorable output quality.

2.2 Translation Module

The Translation module is a pipeline to transform the input (an inflected Ojibwe verb) through several steps to complete the final English translations. The process is schematized in Figure 2.

Important to note is that verbs in Ojibwe are morphologically marked for the person, animacy, and number of all arguments (using up to four distinct morphological slots), whether the predicate has a positive or negative polarity, and an aspectual distinction known as mode. The verb complex also contains certain morphologically dependent tense prefixes. All of these elements are part of the target

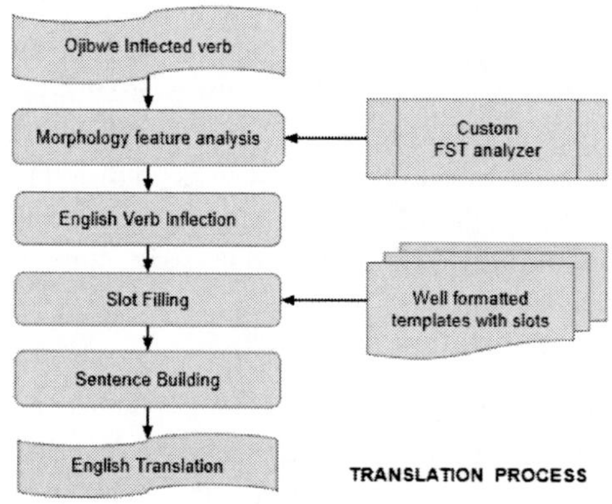

Figure 2: Translation Process

Paradigms	VTA, VTI, VAI(O), VII
Order	Independent, Conjunct, Imperative
Mode	Neutral, Preterit, Dubitative
Tense	Present, Definitive future, Past, Future/wish
Negation	Positive, Negative

Table 1: Supported verb properties. For each paradigm, all possible argument combinations are supported.

for our translation. A summary of the verb properties that can be handled by the translation model is given in Table 1.

Our translation module uses the following data sources:

- The dictionary and template data, built from previously mentioned Template Building Module.
- The FST binary file (in ".att" or ".fomabin" format) contains the rules for Ojibwe inflection, so that a FST parser can analyze the inflected input.

At the core of the Translation module are then the following operations:

- **Morphological feature analysis**: the Ojibwe verb is parsed by the FST to analyze and extract morphological features. It returns all important linguistics information such as the lemma, order, mode, subject, object, tense, negation, etc. in the list-of-tags format. For example, for the verb "giwaabamin" ("I see you" in

English), the FST parser returns the tag waabam+VTA+Ind+Pos+Neu+1SgSubj+2SgObj, which indicates the lemma "waabam" ("to see somebody" in English), the verb paradigm "VTA", the order "Independent", the polarity "Positive", the mode "Neutral", the subject "1st Singular", the object "2nd Singular". The FST parser is integrated into the translation system through a Python library called "fst_runtime"(CultureFoundry, 2025) made by CultureFoundry. The fst_runtime library uses compiled binary data of OjibweMorph (Hammerly et al., 2025) to process the Ojibwe input word and returns the analyses back to the translation system.

- **Verb inflection**: the inflection step considers the main English verb (of the English definition) in the infinitive form and the input Ojibwe FST context, which contains the subject, the mode, the tense and polarity. Then a set of custom rules is implemented in Python code to convert the infinitive English verb to the corresponding inflected English verb, which will be used in the subsequent slot-filling step. The sequence of FST tags to process English verb inflection is generally tense, then mode, then polarity (negation), then subject. To transform an infinitive verb, including irregular verbs, into different tenses such as past or perfect tense, it is done through a Python package called "pyInflect"(Jascob, 2023). Some examples of how a verb might be transformed depending on the context are given in Appendix C, Table 4.

- **Slot filling**: based on the subject and object of the sentence structure, it will replace the slots with relevant information, for example {{subject}} → "he/she" for 3SgSubj, and {{object}} → "me" for 1SgObj . The slot-filling process is illustrated in Figure 3.

- **Sentence building**: This builds a complete sentence from the template, using verb inflection and slot-filling operations. For example, the template "{{subject}} see {{object}}" → "He/she will not see me" for 3rd Singular subject, 1st Singular object, future tense, negative polarity, neutral mode, independent order.

Again, the translation pipeline is entirely rule-based, so it does not require direct use of LLMs.

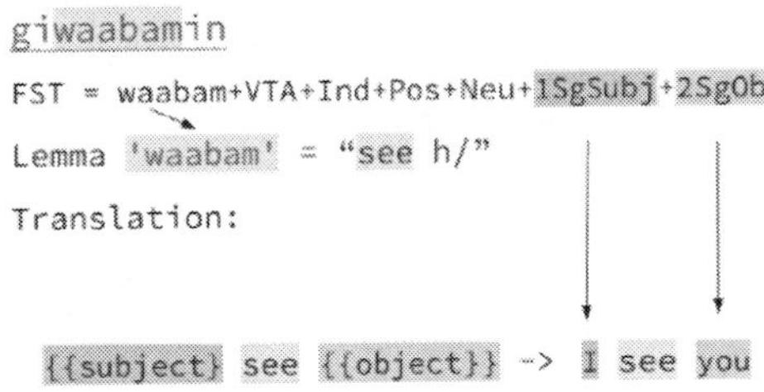

Figure 3: Slot-Filling Illustration

As such, the system produces transparent and predictable results and we can easily modify the rules to suit specific needs. A sample of translations is provided in Appendix B.

3 Evaluation

We completed two types of tests: Speed tests and translation accuracy tests.

3.1 Speed tests

For speed, our system processed a batch of 10 words for translation with an average speed of around 700 millisecond / batch, which means about 70 millisecond / word. The hardware used is a laptop with 24GB RAM and AMD Ryzen 7 5800H CPU, without using GPU (Graphical Processing Unit). That our system can run on standard hardware with limited computing power is a major benefit to making the tool accessible.

Because Ojibwe is a morphologically complex language and a single verb in Ojibwe can be translated into a full sentence in English. If the definition has multiple meanings, the output can contain several sentences or phrases in English. Therefore, the processing speed implies one Ojibwe verb input and one or more English sentences output, rather than one Ojibwe input word and one corresponding English output word.

3.2 Translation accuracy tests

We created a test set of inflected Ojibwe verbs, along with gold translations, from the University of Toronto Ojibwe Textbook (Meltzer et al., 2022-2023), available under the BY-NC-SA 2.5 CA. We selected only inflected verbs from the provided word list and performed simple data cleaning and normalization on the gold translations, including:

- changing abbreviations such as "s/he" to "he/she", etc.

Number of verbs in test set	214
Number of successful translated verbs	200
Percentage of successful translation	93%
Mean ChrF score	0.82
Mean Semantic Similarity score	0.93

Table 2: Evaluation scores

- removing punctuation
- removing extra information inside parentheses, such as "(ani.)", "(inc.)"
- keeping only one translation if there are multiple translations.

There are 214 inflected verbs included in the test set—a small, but reasonable, number due to the low-resource nature of Ojibwe. Our system was able to provide a translation for 200 of the 214 verbs (93%). Some verbs cannot be translated because of missing definition or stem in the database from the dictionary. Examples of comparisons between system and gold translations are illustrated in Appendix D, Table 5

We first calculated the ChrF score (Popović, 2015). The score is a real number between 0.0 (no overlap between translations) and 1.0 (perfectly matched translations). We used NLTK sentence_chrf function with parameters min_length=1 (unigram) and max_length=3 (3-gram) to calculate ChrF score between system and gold translation. If the system generates multiple translations, the translation with highest score was selected. Among the verbs that were successfully translated, the average score is 0.82, as summarized in Table 2.

We also performed a semantic similarity comparison between the system and the gold translations through the Sentence-BERT package (Reimers and Gurevych, 2019). and the LaBSE (Language-agnostic BERT Sentence Embedding) (Feng et al., 2020) embeddings model. Semantic similarity is useful in scenarios where the system and gold translations use synonyms, for example, "we will **enjoy** the taste of **things**" versus "we will **like** the taste of **something**". In this case, the semantic similarity score would be high, while the ChrF score could be considerably lower.

The semantic similarity score between two sentences is a real number between 0.0 (completely unrelated meanings) to 1.0 (perfectly aligned meanings). If the system produces multiple translations, the highest score was selected. Out of the successfully translated verbs, the average semantic similarity score is 0.93, as summarized in Table 2.

4 Applications

The translation package will be used in various settings and purposes, which include:

- Ojibwe language learners, teachers, and schools via a free web interface to analyze and understand complex inflected verbs.
- Researchers to produce an automated translation of Ojibwe verbs for downstream tasks, such as neural machine translation.

In addition to a ready-to-use Python package that can be easily integrated into current popular NLP pipelines, we also included a web application (see Figure 4 in Appendix A) built on the NiceGUI framework, so users such as teachers and students can use it easily without coding, making it more approachable to the general audience. We have yet to widely and systematically test this interface, but such testing is an aim of future work.

5 Future directions

There are a number of avenues for future work. First, the current system only works at the individual word level, so cannot yet handle full sentences. One potential rule-based way to augment the current system to handle full sentences is through the use of a constraint grammar to identify overt subject and object nouns, which could be fed to our rule-based translation module. Second, we are not yet able to translate from English to Ojibwe, nor from Ojibwe to a language other than English. Expanding the system for rules that work in the other direction, or for other languages, is another priority. Third, there is a small set of low-frequency verb forms not yet handled by the system, as well as the more general system of so-called lexical preverbs (which behave much like adverbs) that are not yet handled. Adding support for some of the most common lexical preverbs and expanding remaining tenses and modes in the functional domain is another direction for our future work. Finally, while the data from the Ojibwe People's Dictionary is robust, adding more words and definitions to improve coverage will be an ongoing task.

6 Ethics Statement

The present work was conducted in the context of a larger body of work by our research group to build computational tools relevant to language revitalization of Ojibwe. Our team includes a member of the Ojibwe community with linguistic training, and we have engaged in both formal and informal community consultation about our tools, including elders and teachers. We are committed to striking the balance between practicing open science and generating work that may find uses beyond the immediate community we are serving on one hand, while ensuring the integrity of the data and respecting the elders and community members who have created resources such as the Ojibwe People's Dictionary.

7 Limitations

The current system, although covered a wide range of Ojibwe paradigms and various grammar aspects such as order, mode, tense, etc., it still has some notable limitations such as:

- It works at word level, in particular Ojibwe verbs only. It does not yet have capability to translate other word types such as nouns, adjectives, etc. It is also not able to translate at sentence level, i.e. a full Ojibwe sentence to a full English sentence.
- Because of the diverse and potentially inconsistent format of the Ojibwe People's Dictionary definitions, some of the templates might not be extracted and built properly. We have not yet performed an exhaustive check on all template data. Some unusual definitions can lead to unusual templates, and in extreme case, we can not rule out templates that are not grammatically correct or do not make sense. It has the potential to produce inaccurate or ungrammatical translations in these cases. However, it is still likely to yield some meaningful text in the translations in these cases.
- Because of rule-base translation process, and it is not a neural translation model, therefore, it does not remember or learn all dictionary definitions. It requires external template data to do translation.
- The current system can translate Ojibwe to English, but is not yet able to translate English to Ojibwe.
- It can translate Ojibwe to English as the target language, but another target language, such as French, is not yet supported.
- Although the system supports an extensive grammar range of Ojibwe verbs, it does not fully cover all aspects of the verbs yet. For example, such as preterit-dubitative, which means uncertainty about a past completed event (Valentine, 2001) is not yet supported.
- Due to the low-resource nature of the Ojibwe language, we have not yet built a larger gold-standard test set to better evaluate the performance and quality of the system.

References

Antti Arppe, Jolene Poulin, Eddie Antonio Santos, Andrew Neitsch, Atticus Harrigan, Katherine Schmirler, Daniel Hieber, Ansh Dubey, and Arok Wolvengrey. 2022. Towards a morphologically intelligent and user-friendly on-line dictionary of Plains Cree – next next round. In *Presentation at the 54th Algonquian Conference, Boulder, CO*.

Dustin Bowers, Antti Arppe, Jordan Lachler, Sjur Moshagen, and Trond Trosterud. 2017. A morphological parser for Odawa. In *Proceedings of the 2nd Workshop on the Use of Computational Methods in the Study of Endangered Languages*, pages 1–9.

Isaac Caswell. 2024. Google translate learns inuktut. Accessed: 2024-11-05.

CultureFoundry. 2025. fst-runtime. `https://github.com/CultureFoundryCA/fst-runtime`. Accessed: 2025-03-01.

ELF-Lab. 2025. Ojibwe translation repository. Accessed: 2025-03-28.

Fangxiaoyu Feng, Yinfei Yang, Daniel Cer, Naveen Arivazhagan, and Wei Wang. 2020. Language-agnostic bert sentence embedding. *arXiv preprint arXiv:2007.01852*.

Clarissa Forbes, Garrett Nicolai, and Miikka Silfverberg. 2021. An FST morphological analyzer for the Gitksan language. In *Proceedings of the 18th SIGMORPHON Workshop on Computational Research in Phonetics, Phonology, and Morphology*, pages 188–197.

Christopher Hammerly, Nora Livesay, Antti Arppe, Anna Stacey, and Miikka Silfverberg. 2025. Ojibwe-morph: An approachable finite-state transducer for Ojibwe (and beyond). *Preprint Submitted to Language Resources and Evaluation*.

Atticus G Harrigan, Katherine Schmirler, Antti Arppe, Lene Antonsen, Trond Trosterud, and Arok Wolvengrey. 2017. Learning from the computational modelling of Plains Cree verbs. *Morphology*, 27:565–598.

Brad Jascob. 2023. pyinflect: A python module for word inflections designed for use with spacy. `https://github.com/bjascob/pyinflect`.

Yeskendir Koishekenov, Alexandre Berard, and Vassilina Nikoulina. 2022. Memory-efficient nllb-200: Language-specific expert pruning of a massively multilingual machine translation model. *arXiv preprint arXiv:2212.09811*.

Patrick Littell, Anna Kazantseva, Roland Kuhn, Aidan Pine, Antti Arppe, Christopher Cox, and Marie-Odile Junker. 2018. Indigenous language technologies in Canada: Assessment, challenges, and successes. In *Proceedings of the 27th International Conference on Computational Linguistics*, pages 2620–2632.

Jed Meltzer, Michael Sullivan Juvenal Ndayiragije Lindsay Morcom Marie-Odile Junker Inge Genee John-Paul Chalykoff Callie Hill Maureen Buchanan Perry Bebamash, with contributions from Gordon Jourdain, and Conor Quinn. 2022-2023. Ojibwe textbook: Downloadable resources. Funded by SSHRC Partnership Development Grant between Rotman Research Institute at Baycrest Hospital, University of Toronto, and Kingston Indigenous Languages Nest. Accessed: 2025-03-27.

John D. Nichols. 2012. Ojibwe People's Dictionary.

Maja Popović. 2015. chrF: character n-gram F-score for automatic MT evaluation. In *Proceedings of the Tenth Workshop on Statistical Machine Translation*, pages 392–395, Lisbon, Portugal. Association for Computational Linguistics.

Nils Reimers and Iryna Gurevych. 2019. Sentence-BERT: Sentence embeddings using siamese BERT-networks. *arXiv preprint arXiv:1908.10084*.

Statistics Canada. 2023. Indigenous languages in Canada, 2021.

Randy Valentine. 2001. *Nishnaabemwin reference grammar*. University of Toronto Press.

Kexun Zhang, Yee Choi, Zhenqiao Song, Taiqi He, William Yang Wang, and Lei Li. 2024. Hire a linguist!: Learning endangered languages in LLMs with in-context linguistic descriptions. In *Findings of the Association for Computational Linguistics ACL 2024*, pages 15654–15669.

Acknowledgments

We acknowledge Scott Parkhill from CultureFoundry for advice and guidance on code quality and organization, and Antti Arppe from the University of Alberta for comments on early versions of this project. This work was supported by a SSHRC Insight Grant (435-2023-0474) awarded to Hammerly and Silfverberg.

A Web Application interface

A screenshot of the built-in Web Application interface Figure 4.

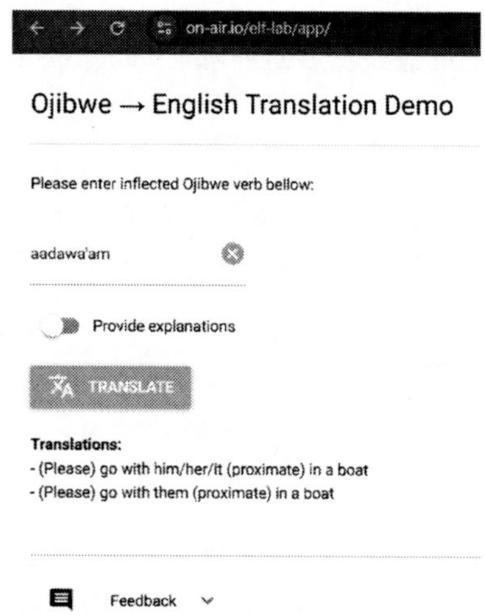

Figure 4: Web Application Interface

B Translation examples

Examples of Ojibwe verb inputs and their corresponding translations are provided in Table 3

Ojibwe verb	English translation
odaadawa'amaan	he/she (proximate) goes with him/her/it (obviative) in a boat
	he/she (proximate) goes with them (obviative) in a boat
aadawa'am	(Please) go with him/her/it (proximate) in a boat
	(Please) go with them (proximate) in a boat
abweninjii	he/she (proximate) has a sweaty hand
gaawiin gii-abweninjiisiin	he/she (proximate) did not have a sweaty hand

Table 3: Translation examples

English verb	Context	Inflected verb
be	3rd Singular Subject ("He/she"), present tense, positive polarity	(he/she) is
be	1st Plural subject ("We"), past tense, negative polarity	(we) were not
be	1st Singular subject ("I"), future/wish tense, positive polarity	(I) want to be
dance	3rd Plural subject ("They"), Dubiative mode, past tense, positive polarity	(They) might have danced
dance	2nd Singular subject ("You"), neutral mode, future tense, negative polarity	(You) will not dance
dance	1st Singular subject ("I"), preterit mode, past tense, positive polarity	(I) used to dance

Table 4: Verb inflection examples

C English verb inflection examples

Examples of how some English verbs are transformed and inflected according to the input Ojibwe FST context (subject, tense, mode, negation, etc) are provided in Table 4

D System versus Gold translation examples

Examples of system (hypothesis) translations compared with gold (reference) translations of inflected Ojibwe verbs are included in Table 5. Note that extra information inside parentheses was removed in both gold and system translations before calculating ChrF and semantic similarity scores.

E Prompt used for VTA verbs

A screenshot of the prompt used to create templates for VTA verbs, with LLM model "llama3-70b-8192" can be found in Figure 5.

Ojibwe verb	Gold translation	System translation	ChrF score	Semantic Similarity score
nimbakade	I am hungry	I am hungry	1.0	1.0
gibakade	you are hungry	you are hungry	1.0	0.99
apatoo	he/she runs	he/she (proximate) runs in a certain way	0.87	0.69
nimindid	I am big	I am big	1.0	0.99
wii-wiisini	he/she want/will eat	he/she (proximate) wants to eat	0.65	0.95
izhaa	he/she is going to a certain place	he/she (proximate) goes to a certain place	0.75	0.99
niwaabamaag	I see them	I see them (proximate)	1.0	1.0
nindizhaa	I am going to a certain place	I go to a certain place	0.71	0.99

Table 5: Gold versus System translations

```
prompt_template = """A given definition example: d = "smudge, cense h/; smoke h/ (for preservation)".
Analyze the definition d. What is subject and object? Rewrite definition by replacing subject and object by literal `{{subject}}` and `{{object}}`.
Replace verbs to infinitive form (e.g. wants -> want, is -> be, gets -> get).
Answer in form {"verbs":[], "templates":[]}. Split the definition for each main verb.
Note the words like "something" or "(it)", don't parse them as "{{object}}", keep them as literal.
Translate "h/ or it" to "{{object}}".
Extract the main verbs only, if the sentence is in passive voice, the main verb is "be". The answer for definition d should be in JSON format
output = {verbs:["smudge", "cense", "smoke"],"templates":["{{subject}} smudge {{object}}", "{{subject}} cense {{object}}", ""{{subject}} smoke {{object}} (for preservation)"]}.
Do not invent new verbs. Keep the new definitions literally close as the original definition. Keep things in brackets as literal, e.g. (it), (something) or (by someone).

Bellow are more examples:

Definition = pull h/ aboard
Output = {'verbs': ['pull'], 'templates': ['{{subject}} pull {{object}} aboard']}
--------------------
Definition = fix, repair (it) for h/
Output = {'verbs': ['fix', 'repair'], 'templates': ['{{subject}} fix (it) for {{object}}', '{{subject}} repair (it) for {{object}}']}
--------------------
Definition = throw h/ aboard
Output = {'verbs': ['throw'], 'templates': ['{{subject}} throw {{object}} aboard']}
--------------------
Output = {'verbs': ['cool'], 'templates': ['{{subject}} cool {{object}} with water']}
--------------------
Definition = cook it (animate)
Output = {'verbs': ['cook'], 'templates': ['{{subject}} cook {{object}} (animate)']}
--------------------
Definition = throw (it) here to h/
Output = {'verbs': ['throw'], 'templates': ['{{subject}} throw (it) here to {{object}}']}
--------------------
Definition = cut it (animate; sheet-like) short
Output = {'verbs': ['cut'], 'templates': ['{{subject}} cut {{object}} ((animate; sheet-like) short ']}
--------------------
Definition = cut it (animate) so wide
Output = {'verbs': ['cut'], 'templates': ['{{subject}} cut {{object}} (animate) so wide']}
--------------------
Definition = staunch h/ bleeding
Output = {'verbs': ['staunch'], 'templates': ['{{subject}} staunch {{object}} bleeding']}
--------------------
Definition = ride mounted on top of h/; sit astride h/
Output = {'verbs': ['ride', 'sit'], 'templates': ['{{subject}} ride mounted on top of {{object}}', '{{subject}} sit astride {{object}}']}
--------------------
Definition = warm something (liquid) up for h/
Output = {'verbs': ['warm'], 'templates': ['{{subject}} warm something (liquid) up for {{object}}']}
--------------------
Definition = warm something for h/ at the fire
Output = {'verbs': ['warm'], 'templates': ['{{subject}} warm something for {{object}} at the fire']}
--------------------
Definition = warm h/ foot or feet
Output = {'verbs': ['warm'], 'templates': ['{{subject}} warm {{object-possessive}} foot or feet']}
--------------------
Definition = catch up to h/ following h/ tracks or trail
Output = {'verbs': ['catch'], 'templates': ['{{subject}} catch up to {{object}} following {{object-possessive}} tracks or trail']}
--------------------
Definition = dye, color h/ or it (animate)
Output = {'verbs': ['dye', 'color'], 'templates': ['{{subject}} dye {{object}} (animate)', '{{subject}} color {{object}} (animate)']}
--------------------
Definition = dye, color (it) for h/
Output = {'verbs': ['dye', 'color'], 'templates': ['{{subject}} dye (it) for {{object}}', '{{subject}} color (it) for {{object}}']}
--------------------

Now process a new definition
"""
```

Figure 5: Prompt used for VTA templates

Advancing Uto-Aztecan Language Technologies: A Case Study on the Endangered Comanche Language

Jesus Alvarez C, Daua D. Karajeanes, Ashley Celeste Prado, John Ruttan, Ivory Yang, Sean O'Brien, Vasu Sharma, Kevin Zhu
Algoverse AI Research
ivory.yang.gr@dartmouth.edu, kevin@algoverse.us

Abstract

The digital exclusion of endangered languages remains a critical challenge in NLP, limiting both linguistic research and revitalization efforts. This study introduces the first computational investigation of Comanche, an Uto-Aztecan language on the verge of extinction, demonstrating how minimal-cost, community-informed NLP interventions can support language preservation. We present a manually curated dataset of 412 phrases, a synthetic data generation pipeline, and an empirical evaluation of GPT-4o and GPT-4o-mini for language identification. Our experiments reveal that while LLMs struggle with Comanche in zero-shot settings, few-shot prompting significantly improves performance, achieving near-perfect accuracy with just five examples. Our findings highlight the potential of targeted NLP methodologies in low-resource contexts and emphasize that visibility is the first step toward inclusion. By establishing a foundation for Comanche in NLP, we advocate for computational approaches that prioritize accessibility, cultural sensitivity, and community engagement.

1 Introduction

The decline of endangered languages represents not only a linguistic loss (Low et al., 2022) but also the erosion of invaluable cultural, historical, and ecological knowledge (Tulloch, 2006; Cámara-Leret and Bascompte, 2021; Sallabank and Austin, 2023). Despite growing advancements in language technology, computational efforts overwhelmingly favor widely spoken languages, leaving endangered languages largely unsupported (Meighan, 2021; Yang et al., 2025a; Jerpelea et al., 2025). Over 88% of the world's languages have minimal to no representation in mainstream language technologies, exacerbating their digital marginalization (Rangel, 2019). This exclusion hinders linguistic research and deepens the digital divide (Valijärvi and Kahn, 2023; Yang et al., 2025b), complicating preservation and revitalization efforts. Among these, Comanche, an Uto-Aztecan language, faces imminent extinction, with fewer than 50 fluent speakers remaining (Chaika et al., 2024).

Contact other authors at: jalvarezc@my.canyons.edu, d.d.karajeanes@student.tue.nl, aprad054@fiu.edu, jruttan3@uwo.ca, seobrien@ucsd.edu, vasus@andrew.cmu.edu

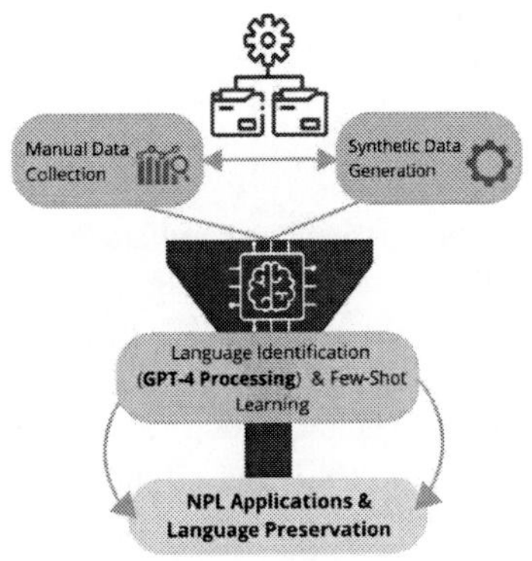

Figure 1: Stylized overview of our exploration of NLP applications for the endangered Comanche language.

We present a case study on the Comanche language, demonstrating that with minimal cost and computational resources, it is possible to achieve what large corporations and academic institutions have largely neglected. As shown in Figure 1, we contribute (1) a manually curated dataset, (2) synthetic data generation pipeline for resource expansion, and (3) an empirical evaluation of GPT-4o and GPT-4o-mini in zero-shot and few-shot language identification. Our findings highlight the potential of large language models (LLMs) in low-resource settings, offering insights into their applicability for endangered language preservation. **This work marks the first-ever introduction of Comanche into the NLP domain, laying groundwork for future research and linguistic equity**.

Proceedings of the Fifth Workshop on NLP for Indigenous Languages of the Americas (AmericasNLP), pages 27–37
May 4, 2025 ©2025 Association for Computational Linguistics

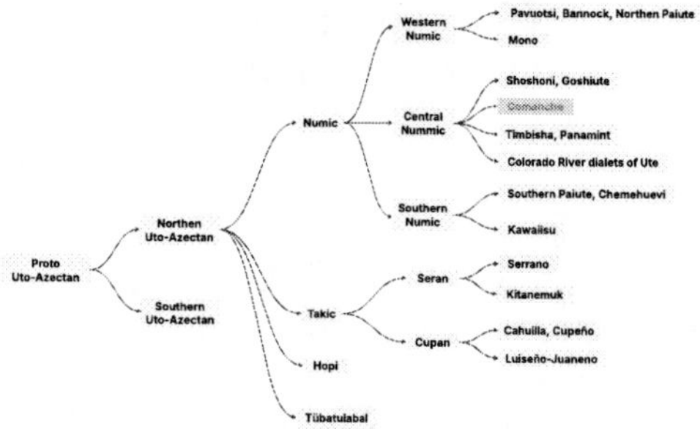

Figure 2: Family tree for Uto-Aztecan Languages, with Comanche highlighted.

2 Related Work

Efforts to preserve endangered languages, particularly Native American languages, date back to at least the early 20th century (Charney, 1993), with early approaches relying heavily on linguistic documentation and literary preservation (Schwartz and Dobrin, 2016). While these foundational efforts paved the way, they were hindered by the scarcity of available datasets and standardized benchmarks, leading researchers to explore alternative strategies for text processing (Lorenzo et al., 2024; Spencer and Kongborrirak, 2025). Despite these advancements, modern computational linguistics continues to face significant challenges when working with polysynthetic languages such as Comanche and Apache, due to their intricate orthographic and morphological structures (Kelly, 2020). In recent years there have been promising community-led revitalization initiatives, including immersive education programs, digital archives, and collaborations with computational linguists (of Indian Affairs, 2023; Schwartz et al., 2021).

Data scarcity remains a fundamental challenge in NLP (Glaser et al., 2021). Unlike widely spoken languages with abundant corpora, low-resource languages lack annotated datasets, limiting the effectiveness of LLMs for preservation (Zhong et al., 2024; Dinh et al., 2024). Few-shot prompting has emerged as a promising solution, allowing LLMs to generate synthetic data from minimal examples (Zhang et al., 2021), though its success hinges on data quality. Transfer learning (Adimulam et al., 2022) has also been explored to improve low-resource NLP, but without robust evaluation frameworks tailored for Indigenous languages (Shu et al., 2024), achieving meaningful generalization remains a challenge (Mager et al., 2023).

3 Native American Language Landscape

The linguistic diversity of Native American languages is vast, spanning multiple language families with distinct phonetic, morphological, and syntactic properties. Despite this richness, many of these languages are critically endangered, with fluency declining due to historical policies of forced assimilation, boarding schools, and sociopolitical marginalization (Krauss, 1992). Language documentation efforts have attempted to counteract this loss, but computational resources remain scarce, and mainstream NLP models are ill-equipped to process these languages effectively (Blasi et al., 2022). The lack of digital resources further exacerbates the challenge, preventing these languages from benefiting from advances in language technologies (U.S. Department of the Interior, 2022).

Comanche belongs to the Uto-Aztecan language family, one of the largest language families in the Americas, encompassing over 60 languages spoken across the western United States, Mexico, and Central America (Opler, 1943). While some Uto-Aztecan languages, such as Nahuatl (Andrews, 2003), have relatively larger speaker populations and a degree of digital presence, others, including Comanche, face imminent extinction. As shown in Figure 2, Comanche developed as a distinct language after diverging from Shoshone in the 18th century, evolving unique phonological and lexical features (Casagrande, 1955). Today, with fewer than 50 fluent speakers, Comanche lacks sufficient linguistic resources for computational modeling.

4 Data

4.1 Manual Data Collection

To construct a foundational dataset for Comanche, we conducted a systematic review of linguistic resources, including academic literature, digital archives, and historical records. Given the scarcity of publicly available corpora, we aggregated and curated data from 15 distinct domains (Appendix B), ensuring consistency through transcription and standardization. To enhance data reliability, we cross-referenced linguistic materials with community-driven documentation efforts, validating authenticity and linguistic accuracy. This structured dataset of 412 Comanche phrases, the first digitalized dataset of its kind, serves as a crucial resource for both language preservation and computational linguistic research in Comanche.

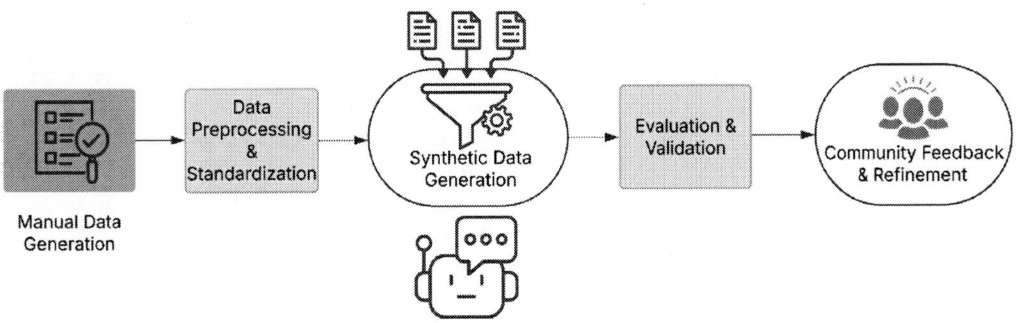

Figure 3: Data pipeline.

4.2 Synthetic Data Generation

Given the extreme scarcity of parallel Comanche–English text, we leveraged few-shot prompting with GPT-4o to generate synthetic translations. Using a manually curated dataset of 100 Comanche–English sentence pairs, we split the data into an 80% training set and a 20% test set. During training, GPT-4o was provided examples from the training subset and then prompted to generate translations for the test set (Appendix C). The generated outputs were evaluated using normalized Levenshtein similarity, ensuring a minimum quality threshold of 0.1[1] before incorporation into the dataset. This controlled expansion strategy maintained linguistic integrity while demonstrating that even minimal data can be effectively leveraged to create valuable resources for endangered language NLP. While the pipeline shown in Figure 3 is in early stage, it underscores the potential of leveraging NLP for endangered language documentation and expansion. As data scarcity persists, synthetic augmentation offers a scalable approach to bridge resource gaps and support revitalization efforts.

Figure 4: GPT-4o achieves a remarkable improvement in language identification performance, with the help of few-shot examples.

5 Language Identification

While data collection and synthetic expansion are crucial aspects of language preservation, identification is equally essential. Despite supporting over 200 languages, Google's LangID system (Caswell et al., 2020) does not include a single Native American language, including Comanche, highlighting the systematic exclusion of these languages from mainstream computational resources. This absence not only limits automatic language identification capabilities, but also further marginalizes endangered languages in digital spaces, making their preservation even more challenging.

While LLMs have demonstrated remarkable proficiency in high-resource language tasks, their ability to identify low-resource languages remains a critical challenge. In our zero-shot prompting experiments using a dataset of 412 Comanche entries, GPT-4o achieved only 13.5% accuracy, correctly identifying 56 instances. These results highlight the broader issue that without explicit guidance, even state-of-the-art models struggle to recognize endangered languages. To address this limitation, we introduced few-shot prompting with both Comanche and English samples, training the model to actively identify features of the Comanche language. For this experiment, we used a sample of 100 randomly

[1]Given that Comanche has never been explored in NLP, we set a baseline threshold of 0.1 due to the difficulty of the task. As the pipeline matures, we will refine our evaluation criteria and increase the required similarity score.

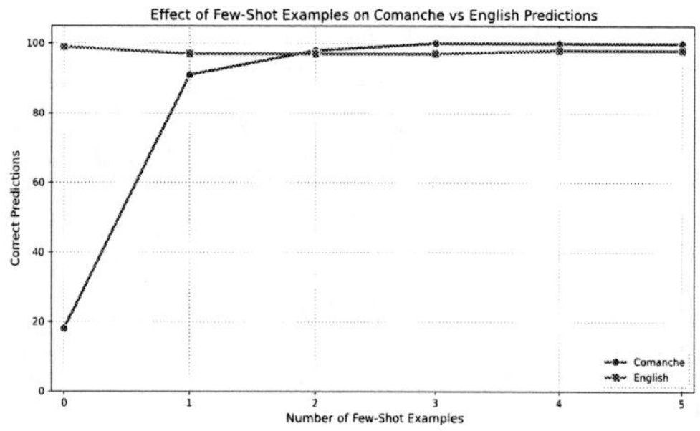

Figure 5: Effect of Few-Shot Examples on Comanche Prediction Accuracy.

selected entries from our original dataset. Each few-shot pair included one Comanche phrase and a randomized English entry from the dataset, as shown in Figure 4. With just one Comanche example, GPT-4o achieved 91% accuracy in identification of Comanche. Extending to a three-shot strategy consistently yielded 100% accuracy, as shown in Figure 5. Notably, English identification accuracy remained consistently high (97-100%) across all experimental conditions. These findings underscore the limitations of default language identification systems and demonstrate that even minimal targeted prompting can significantly enhance recognition capabilities. The stark performance gap between Comanche and English underscores the model's inherent bias toward high-resource languages when tasked with identification. Our results provide a scalable, low-resource approach for integrating endangered languages into NLP systems, offering a pathway toward more inclusive computational language technologies.

6 Community Feedback

To ensure that our approach to NLP-driven language preservation is both transparent and respectful, we engaged with a community member of Comanche and Rarámuri heritage through a semi-structured interview. The interview provided insights into the lived experiences of individuals connected to endangered languages, highlighting both the cultural significance of linguistic preservation and the challenges posed by data scarcity.

The interviewee shared that although the Comanche and Rarámuri languages were not passed down to him, he maintains a profound connection to his Native American heritage. He recounted a childhood experience in which he struggled to communicate with members of a Rarámuri community in Chihuahua, Mexico, due to language barriers[2]. His reflections highlight the critical role that digital resources and computational methods can play in language preservation. While exposure to artificial intelligence and NLP technologies remains limited in many Indigenous communities, the potential for these tools to support language revitalization is immense. Our study emphasizes that responsible NLP research must engage directly with affected communities, ensuring that technological interventions align with cultural needs and ethical considerations.

7 Future Work

Future efforts will focus on expanding the manually curated Comanche dataset, refining the synthetic data generation pipeline, and developing a real-time language identification demo. Given the largely oral nature of Comanche, we will also investigate audio-based approaches to support speech recognition and transcription, as well as exploring learning (Wang and Guo, 2019; Mangar et al., 2025) and reading comprehension tasks (Zhang et al., 2024). Additionally, we will actively engage with more Comanche community members to ensure our work remains aligned with their needs and perspectives. We hope to eventually secure the resources to conduct a deeper analysis of Comanche and other indigenous languages—work that has largely been limited to high-resource languages—examining dimensions such as linguistic features (Lee et al., 2024), implicit versus explicit expression (Wang et al., 2025), persuasive strategies (Wang et al., 2024; Yang et al., 2024) and intellectual humility (Guo et al., 2024).

8 Conclusion

This study represents the first computational effort to integrate Comanche into the NLP landscape, addressing critical gaps in language documentation and technological accessibility. Through manual data collection, synthetic data expansion, and empirical evaluations of LLM-based language identification, we demonstrate that even minimal resources can yield meaningful improvements in language modeling for endangered languages. While this work marks an initial step, continued collaboration

[2]The interviewee recalled attempting to explain to local Rarámuri residents that his disposable camera differed from a Polaroid and would not produce an immediate photograph. This miscommunication left a lasting impression on him, reinforcing the importance of language technologies.

with Comanche speakers, expansion into audio-based methods, and refinement of evaluation metrics will be essential to advancing these efforts. We advocate for a NLP research paradigm that actively includes Indigenous and low-resource languages, ensuring that they are not only preserved but empowered through computational advancements.

Limitations

Despite the contributions of this study, several limitations must be acknowledged. Firstly, the manually curated Comanche dataset remains small, constraining both model performance and generalizability. Future work must expand this dataset to improve model robustness and alignment (Zeng et al., 2025), as well as to prevent biases (Guan et al., 2025). In addition, while synthetic data augmentation offers a promising avenue for resource expansion, the quality of generated translations is inherently dependent on the prompting strategy (Jian et al., 2022) and the capabilities of the underlying language model. Further refinements to the pipeline and more rigorous evaluation methodologies are necessary to ensure linguistic accuracy. Moreover, our experiments focus primarily on text-based language identification, overlooking the oral tradition of Comanche. Future research should incorporate audio-based approaches, such as automatic speech recognition, to better align with the language's natural form. Lastly, our engagement with community members, while valuable, represents only an initial step. Sustained collaboration with Comanche speakers and language advocates will be essential to ensuring that computational interventions align with community priorities and ethical considerations.

Ethics Statement

Our research adheres to ethical principles that prioritize Indigenous data sovereignty, cultural sensitivity, and responsible engagement. We collected Comanche words, affixes, and phrases exclusively from publicly available sources, ensuring transparency in our data practices and proper attribution of all resources. All relevant citations for the manual dataset can be found in Appendix D. Consistent with the principles outlined by Schwartz (2022), we acknowledge that Indigenous languages are deeply tied to cultural identity, historical continuity, and community sovereignty. We explicitly recognize the Comanche Nation as the rightful stewards of their language and are committed to ensuring that our work aligns with their goals of preservation and revitalization. Our research seeks not only to document but to actively contribute to the accessibility and visibility of Comanche within the computational linguistics community. We emphasize the importance of relational engagement with Indigenous communities, acknowledging that linguistic data is not merely an artifact for academic study but also a living expression of cultural heritage (Appendix A).

Finally, we uphold ethical obligations of cognizance, beneficence, accountability, and non-maleficence. We remain committed to avoiding harm, ensuring that our findings and datasets serve as tools for language empowerment rather than extraction. Future work will continue to involve direct engagement with Comanche speakers, fostering a collaborative research framework that respects community agency and cultural priorities. In the spirit of transparent and ethical research, our full dataset and code have been made available at (`https://github.com/comanchegenerate/ComancheSynthetic`).

References

Thejaswi Adimulam, Swetha Chinta, and Suprit Kumar Pattanayak. 2022. Transfer learning in natural language processing: Overcoming low-resource challenges. *International Journal of Enhanced Research In Science Technology & Engineering*, 11:65–79.

James Richard Andrews. 2003. *Introduction to classical Nahuatl*, volume 1. University of Oklahoma Press.

Damian Blasi, Antonios Anastasopoulos, and Graham Neubig. 2022. Systematic inequalities in language technology performance across the world's languages. In *Proceedings of the 60th Annual Meeting of the Association for Computational Linguistics (Volume 1: Long Papers)*, pages 5486–5505, Dublin, Ireland. Association for Computational Linguistics.

Rodrigo Cámara-Leret and Jordi Bascompte. 2021. Language extinction triggers the loss of unique medicinal knowledge. *Proceedings of the National Academy of Sciences*, 118(24):e2103683118.

Joseph B Casagrande. 1955. Comanche linguistic acculturation iii. *International Journal of American Linguistics*, 21(1):8–25.

Isaac Caswell, Theresa Breiner, Daan van Esch, and Ankur Bapna. 2020. Language id in the wild: Unexpected challenges on the path to a thousand-language web text corpus. In *Proceedings of the 28th International Conference on Computational Linguistics*, pages 6588–6608.

O. Chaika, N. Sharmanova, and O. Makaruk. 2024. Revitalising endangered languages: Challenges, successes, and cultural implications. *Futurity of Social Sciences*, 2(2):38–61.

Jean Ormsbee Charney. 1993. *A Grammer of Comanche*. University of Nebraska Press.

Nguyen Dinh, Thanh Dang, Luan Thanh Nguyen, and Kiet Nguyen. 2024. Multi-dialect vietnamese: Task, dataset, baseline models and challenges. In *Proceedings of the 2024 Conference on Empirical Methods in Natural Language Processing*, pages 7476–7498.

Ingo Glaser, Shabnam Sadegharmaki, Basil Komboz, and Florian Matthes. 2021. Data scarcity: Methods to improve the quality of text classification. In *ICPRAM*, pages 556–564.

Xin Guan, Nate Demchak, Saloni Gupta, Ze Wang, Ediz Ertekin Jr, Adriano Koshiyama, Emre Kazim, and Zekun Wu. 2025. Saged: A holistic bias-benchmarking pipeline for language models with customisable fairness calibration. In *Proceedings of the 31st International Conference on Computational Linguistics*, pages 3002–3026.

Xiaobo Guo, Neil Potnis, Melody Yu, Nabeel Gillani, and Soroush Vosoughi. 2024. The computational anatomy of humility: Modeling intellectual humility in online public discourse. In *Proceedings of the 2024 Conference on Empirical Methods in Natural Language Processing*, pages 5701–5723.

Alexandru-Iulius Jerpelea, Alina Radoi, and Sergiu Nisioi. 2025. Dialectal and low resource machine translation for aromanian. In *Proceedings of the 31st International Conference on Computational Linguistics*, pages 7209–7228.

Yiren Jian, Chongyang Gao, and Soroush Vosoughi. 2022. Contrastive learning for prompt-based few-shot language learners. In *Proceedings of the 2022 Conference of the North American Chapter of the Association for Computational Linguistics: Human Language Technologies*, pages 5577–5587.

Kevin Kelly. 2020. *An Evaluation of Parallel Text Extraction and Sentence Alignment for Low-Resource Polysynthetic Languages*. Ph.D. thesis, University of Groningen.

Michael Krauss. 1992. The world's languages in crisis. *Language*, 68(1):4–10.

Dongryeol Lee, Yerin Hwang, Yongil Kim, Joonsuk Park, and Kyomin Jung. 2024. Are llm-judges robust to expressions of uncertainty? investigating the effect of epistemic markers on llm-based evaluation. *arXiv preprint arXiv:2410.20774*.

Abelardo Carlos Martínez Lorenzo, Pere-Luís Huguet Cabot, Karim Ghonim, Lu Xu, Hee-Soo Choi, Alberte Fernández Castro, and Roberto Navigli. 2024. Mitigating data scarcity in semantic parsing across languages: the multilingual semantic layer and its dataset. In *The 62nd Annual Meeting of the Association for Computational Linguistics (ACL 2024)*.

Dylan Scott Low, Isaac Mcneill, and Michael Day. 2022. Endangered languages: A sociocognitive approach to language death, identity loss, and preservation in the age of artificial intelligence. *Sustainable Multilingualism*, 21(1):1–25.

Manuel Mager, Arturo Oncevay, Annette Rios, Jamshidbek Mirzakhalov, and Katharina Kann. 2023. The role of computational linguistics in indigenous language revitalization: Challenges and opportunities. In *Proceedings of the 1st Workshop on Computation for Indigenous Languages (C3NLP)*, pages 23–31.

Ravindra Mangar, Cesar Arguello, David Inyangson, Tina Pavlovich, Karen Gareis, and Tushar M Jois. 2025. Engaging students from under-represented groups to pursue graduate school in computer science and engineering. In *Proceedings of the 56th ACM Technical Symposium on Computer Science Education V. 1*, pages 742–748.

Paul J Meighan. 2021. Decolonizing the digital landscape: The role of technology in indigenous language revitalization. *AlterNative: An International Journal of Indigenous Peoples*, 17(3):397–405.

Bureau of Indian Affairs. 2023. Native language revitalization literature review.

Marvin K Opler. 1943. The origins of comanche and ute. *American Anthropologist*, 45(1):155–158.

Jhonnatan Rangel. 2019. Challenges for language technologies in critically endangered languages. In *UNESCO International Conference Language Technologies for All (LT4All)*, Paris, France. ⟨hal-02917830⟩.

Julia Sallabank and Peter K Austin. 2023. Endangered languages. In *The Routledge handbook of applied linguistics*, pages 362–373. Routledge.

Lane Schwartz. 2022. Primum Non Nocere: Before working with Indigenous data, the ACL must confront ongoing colonialism. In *Proceedings of the 60th Annual Meeting of the Association for Computational Linguistics (Volume 2: Short Papers)*, pages 724–731, Dublin, Ireland. Association for Computational Linguistics.

Lane Schwartz, Emily Chen, Hyunji Hayley Park, Edward Jahn, and Sylvia L.R. Schreiner. 2021. A digital corpus of st. lawrence island yupik. *arXiv preprint*.

Saul Schwartz and Lise M Dobrin. 2016. The cultures of native north american language documentation and revitalization. *Reviews in Anthropology*, 45(2):88–123.

Peng Shu, Junhao Chen, Zhengliang Liu, Hui Wang, Zihao Wu, Tianyang Zhong, Yiwei Li, Huaqin Zhao, Hanqi Jiang, Yi Pan, et al. 2024. Transcending language boundaries: Harnessing llms for low-resource language translation. *arXiv preprint arXiv:2411.11295*.

Piyapath T Spencer and Nanthipat Kongborrirak. 2025. Can llms help create grammar?: Automating grammar creation for endangered languages with in-context learning. In *Proceedings of the 31st International Conference on Computational Linguistics*, pages 10214–10227.

Shelley Tulloch. 2006. Preserving dialects of an endangered language. *Current Issues in Language Planning*, 7(2-3):269–286.

U.S. Department of the Interior. 2022. Federal Indian Boarding School Initiative Investigative Report. Accessed: 2025-03-04.

Riitta-Liisa Valijärvi and Lily Kahn. 2023. The role of new media in minority-and endangered-language communities. *Endangered Languages in the 21st Century. Abingdon, Oxon, England: Routledge*, pages 139–157.

Chixiang Wang and Junqi Guo. 2019. A data-driven framework for learners' cognitive load detection using ecg-ppg physiological feature fusion and xgboost classification. *Procedia computer science*, 147:338–348.

Yuxin Wang, Ivory Yang, Saeed Hassanpour, and Soroush Vosoughi. 2024. Mentalmanip: A dataset for fine-grained analysis of mental manipulation in conversations. In *Proceedings of the 62nd Annual Meeting of the Association for Computational Linguistics (Volume 1: Long Papers)*, pages 3747–3764.

Yuxin Wang, Xiaomeng Zhu, Weimin Lyu, Saeed Hassanpour, and Soroush Vosoughi. 2025. Impscore: A learnable metric for quantifying the implicitness level of sentences. In *The Thirteenth International Conference on Learning Representations*.

Ivory Yang, Xiaobo Guo, Sean Xie, and Soroush Vosoughi. 2024. Enhanced detection of conversational mental manipulation through advanced prompting techniques. In *Eighth Widening NLP Workshop (WiNLP 2024) Phase II*.

Ivory Yang, Weicheng Ma, and Soroush Vosoughi. 2025a. Nüshurescue: Reviving the endangered nüshu language with ai. In *Proceedings of the 31st International Conference on Computational Linguistics*, pages 7020–7034.

Ivory Yang, Weicheng Ma, Chunhui Zhang, and Soroush Vosoughi. 2025b. Is it navajo? accurate language detection in endangered athabaskan languages. *arXiv preprint arXiv:2501.15773*.

Hongchuan Zeng, Senyu Han, Lu Chen, and Kai Yu. 2025. Converging to a lingua franca: Evolution of linguistic regions and semantics alignment in multilingual large language models. In *Proceedings of the 31st International Conference on Computational Linguistics*, pages 10602–10617.

Ningyu Zhang, Luoqiu Li, Xiang Chen, Shumin Deng, Zhen Bi, Chuanqi Tan, Fei Huang, and Huajun Chen. 2021. Differentiable prompt makes pre-trained language models better few-shot learners. *arXiv preprint arXiv:2108.13161*.

Yuhong Zhang, Shilai Yang, Gert Cauwenberghs, and Tzyy-Ping Jung. 2024. From word embedding to reading embedding using large language model, eeg and eye-tracking. In *2024 46th Annual International Conference of the IEEE Engineering in Medicine and Biology Society (EMBC)*, pages 1–4. IEEE.

Tianyang Zhong, Zhenyuan Yang, Zhengliang Liu, Ruidong Zhang, Yiheng Liu, Haiyang Sun, Yi Pan, Yiwei Li, Yifan Zhou, Hanqi Jiang, et al. 2024. Opportunities and challenges of large language models for low-resource languages in humanities research. *arXiv preprint arXiv:2412.04497*.

A Appendix A

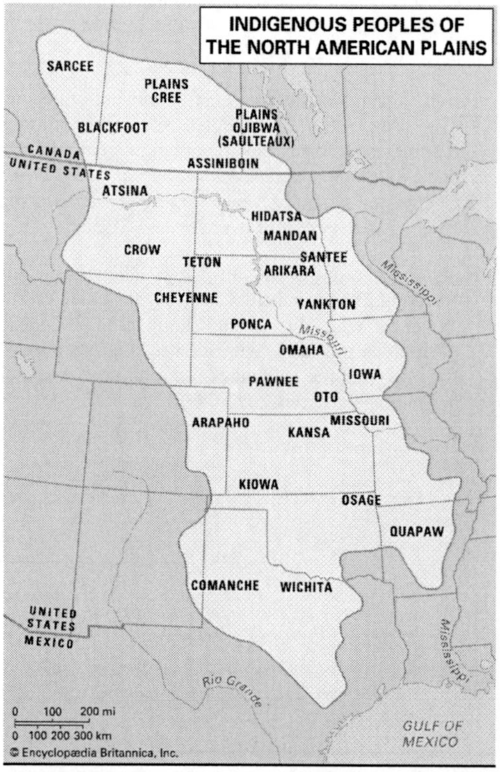

Figure 6: Map showing approximate locations of Indigenous peoples of the Great Plains prior, to displacement in the 19th century. Comanche territory is depicted in the bottom-left region. Source:https://www.britannica.com/place/Great-Plains#/media/1/243562/330.

Figure 7: Comanche cultural artifacts.

Figure 8: Lloyd Heminokeky, Jr., Language Consultant for the Comanche Nation Language Department, hosts an event honoring Comanche Code Talkers, including his grandfather, Technician Fifth Grade Wellington Mihecoby, whose distinguished service is highlighted in the portrait beside him. Source: https://youtu.be/M_JO8C63Ins?si=uc8JzAiAX7sCrF9A.

B Appendix B

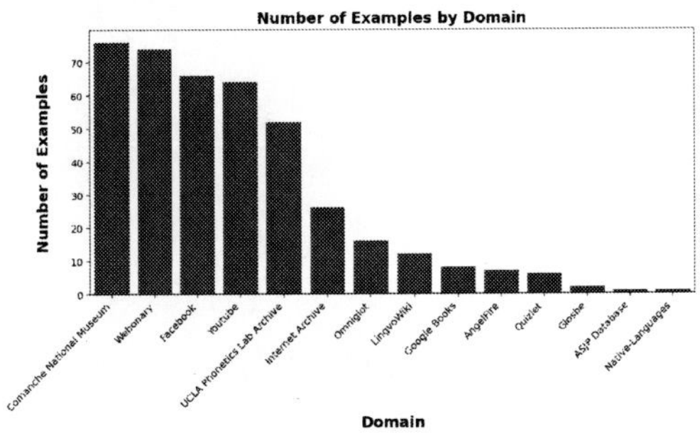

Figure 9: Distribution of manually collected Comanche-English phrases across 15 sources. The Comanche National Museum, Webonary, and Facebook (via the Comanche Nation Language Department) contributed the highest number of examples. This distribution underscores the variability in available linguistic resources for Comanche.

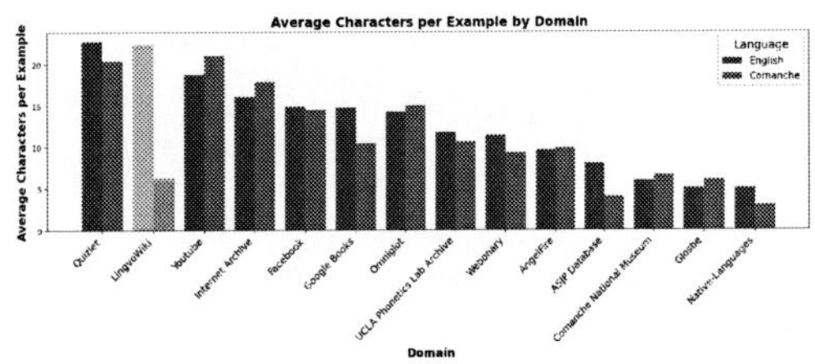

Figure 11: Comparison of average characters per example across various sources of English and Comanche. Notably, the Comanche data from LingvoWiki appears unusually short due to the presence of affixes in the collected samples, which artificially lowers the character count for that source.

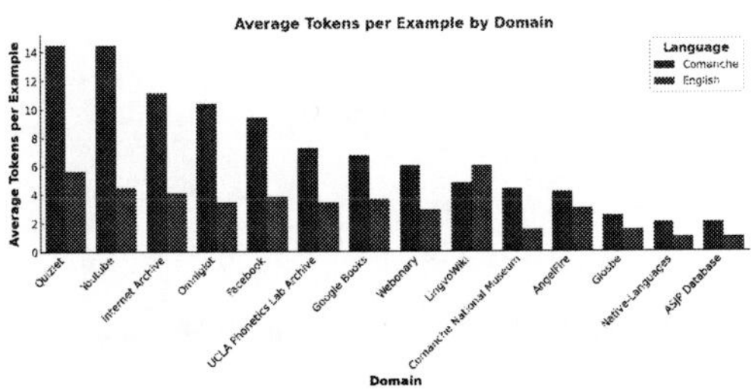

Figure 10: The average token length per example differs notably between Comanche (blue) and English (red). Some sources, such as Quizlet and Youtube, contain significantly longer Comanche phrases, while others, such as LingvoWiki, show an inverse pattern due to the presence of affixes and bound morphemes. These variations highlight source-specific differences, particularly in how morphology and translation conventions impact token length.

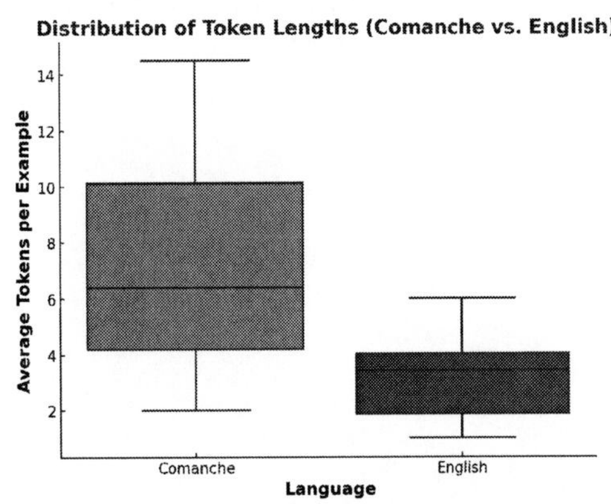

Figure 12: Box plot distribution of token lengths in Comanche and English phrases. Comanche phrases exhibit a wider range of token lengths, with a median of around 6 tokens per example, and an extended upper quartile value, reflecting its polysynthetic structure. English translations, by contrast are more compact with less variability.

C Appendix C

English	Real Comanche	GPT Comanche	Levenshtein Similarity
Everyday speak Comanche.	Oyo?tabeni nʉmʉtekwa	Oyotabeni nʉmʉ tekwapʉ̲	69.23%
I see a bird	huutsu?a nʉ puni	huutsuu nʉ puni	72.22%
I lost my money that I had put in a can	nʉ buhiwi hta nʉ' narohtʉma kʉ nʉ rʉki 'ih a watsi kʉ'	Nʉ wana nʉ ʉnʉmʉ̲ ʉ hʉpi nʉ puni	31.48%
I don't understand you	ke nʉ ʉ naki̲supana?itʉ	Keta nʉ naki̲supana?itʉ nʉ	64.29%
We dance for our People	Nʉnʉ̲se taanahnʉmʉnʉʉ?a nʉhkakʉrʉ	Taanʉmʉnʉʉ?a?nani̲sutaikʉrʉ̲	36.36%

Figure 13: Comparison of English sentences with their corresponding Real Comanche translations and GPT-generated Comanche translations.

D Appendix D

Table 1: Online sources referenced to construct the Comanche-English dataset.

Cite Key	Author (Year)	Title	URL
omniglotwriting	Omniglot (n.d.)	Comanche language, alphabet and pronunciation	https://www.omniglot.com/writing/comanche.htm
omniglotphrases	Omniglot (n.d.)	Comanche phrases	https://www.omniglot.com/language/phrases/comanche.htm
ucla1992	UCLA Phonetics Lab Archive (1992)	Comanche word lists (1992)	https://archive.phonetics.ucla.edu/Language/COM/
angelfire	Angelfire (n.d.)	Comanche language page	https://www.angelfire.com/creep2/fracod/comanche.html
rosettaproject	Internet Archive (n.d.)	rosettaproject_com_morsyn-1	https://archive.org/details/rosettaproject_com_morsyn-1/page/n3/mode/2up
cnlanguagefb	Comanche Nation Language Dept. (n.d.)	Facebook videos	https://www.facebook.com/CNLanguage/videos/
comanchemuseum	Comanche National Museum and Cultural Center (n.d.)	Comanche dictionary	https://www.comanchemuseum.com/dictionary.html
nativelang	Native Languages of the Americas (n.d.)	Comanche language: Word sets	https://www.native-languages.org/comanche_words.htm
glosbecomanche	Glosbe (n.d.)	English–Comanche dictionary	https://glosbe.com/en/com
asjpcomanche	ASJP (n.d.)	COMANCHE	https://asjp.clld.org/languages/COMANCHE
webonarycomanche	Comanche Dictionary Project (n.d.)	Comanche webonary	https://www.webonary.org/comanche/
lingvoforum	LingvoForum (n.d.)	Comanche dictionary (LingvoForum Wiki)	https://wiki.lingvoforum.net/wiki/Comanche_dictionary
quizletcomanche	Quizlet (n.d.)	Comanche phrases flashcards	https://quizlet.com/718424723/comanche-phrases-flash-cards/
youtubecn	Comanche Nation Language Dept. (n.d.)	CNLanguage YouTube channel	https://www.youtube.com/@CNLanguage/videos

Py-Elotl: A Python NLP package for the languages of Mexico

Ximena Gutierrez-Vasques[1,5] **Robert Pugh**[2,4,5] **Victor Mijangos**[1,5]
Diego Alberto Barriga Martínez[1,5] **Paul Aguilar**[5] **Mikel Segura**[1,5] **Paola Innes**[1,5]
Javier Santillan[5] **Cynthia Montaño**[3,5] **Francis M. Tyers**[2,4,5]
[1]UNAM, México [2]Indiana University, Bloomington [3]University of California, Berkeley
[4]Kaltepetlahtol, A.C. [5]Comunidad Elotl
contacto@elotl.mx

Abstract

This work presents Py-Elotl, a suite of tools and resources in Python for processing text in several indigenous languages spoken in Mexico. These resources include parallel corpora, linguistic taggers/analyzers, and orthographic normalization tools. This work aims to develop essential resources to support language pre-processing and linguistic research, and the future creation of more complete downstream applications that could be useful for the speakers and enhance the visibility of these languages. The current version supports language groups such as Nahuatl, Otomi, Mixtec, and Huave. This project is open-source and freely available for use and collaboration[1].

```
from utils import format_feats
from elotl.nahuatl.morphology import Analyzer

analyzer = Analyzer("nhi")

tokens = analyzer.analyze("otechinmacaya xocomeh")

for token in tokens:
    print(f"Form: {token.wordform}")
    print(f"  POS: {token.pos}")
    print(f"  LEMMA: {token.lemma}")
    print(f"  FEATS: {format_feats(token)}")
# >> Form: otechinmacaya
# >>   POS: VERB
# >>   LEMMA: maca
# >>   FEATS: Aspect=Impf|Number[dat]=Plur|...|Tense=Past
# >> Form: xocomeh
# >>   POS: NOUN
# >>   LEMMA: xocotl
# >>   FEATS: Number=Plur
```

Figure 1: Example of a morphological analysis (Nahuatl) performed using Py-Elotl.

1 Introduction

Language technologies have become an integral part of daily life for many people around the world. We regularly interact with automatic translators, voice assistants, AI agents, and writing tools, to name a few. These advanced NLP technologies (downstream applications) have only been possible due to the gradual and systematic creation of foundational resources and tools (upstream tasks). This includes the creation of training corpora, linguistic taggers/analyzers, and orthographic normalization tools, among others, all of which play a crucial role in enabling more sophisticated language technology applications.

For many hegemonic languages, these fundamental upstream tasks may appear to have already been solved or are of lesser research interest. As a result, efforts often shift toward advancing more sophisticated technologies, such as large language models (LLMs) capable of generating text, as in commercial assistants like ChatGPT (OpenAI) or Gemini (Google). However, for many other languages, there are still no tools that cover the most basic upstream tasks, so the landscape of language technologies remains uneven (Joshi et al., 2020; Hedderich et al., 2021; Ducel et al., 2022; Blasi et al., 2022).

In order to advance toward a more linguistically-diverse language technology landscape and enable more comprehensive applications for under-resourced languages, it is crucial to start with the fundamental building-blocks, or "upstream tasks".

To that end, this work presents a suite of tools and resources for processing text in several indigenous languages spoken in Mexico. Py-Elotl, an open-source Python library, supports several upstream tasks such as parallel corpus loading, orthographic normalization, and morphological analysis (see Figure 1). The name *elotl* comes from the Nahuatl word for "ear of fresh maize".

This collaborative initiative aims to develop essential resources to support language preprocessing, linguistic research, and the future creation of more downstream applications that could be useful for the speakers and enhance the visibility of these languages.

[1]https://github.com/ElotlMX/py-elotl

Proceedings of the Fifth Workshop on NLP for Indigenous Languages of the Americas (AmericasNLP), pages 38–47
May 4, 2025 ©2025 Association for Computational Linguistics

2 Related work

Although over 7,000 languages are spoken worldwide, most remain largely overlooked in NLP research (Magueresse et al., 2020). The Americas, in particular, are home to immense linguistic diversity, where most of the indigenous languages in the region face varying degrees of endangerment (Moseley and Nicolas, 2010).

In recent years, the NLP community has increasingly focused on the languages of the Americas, promoting specialized forums (Mager et al., 2021b) and shared tasks to advance machine translation, the automatic creation of educational resources, and other applications (Mager et al., 2021a; Chiruzzo et al., 2024). These languages often exhibit high internal diversity and a lack of standardization traditions due to sociopolitical factors, along with other linguistic phenomena that make them particularly challenging to process (Mager et al., 2018).

Previous works have shown that tokenization, data normalization, and cleaning, as well as high-quality corpora, are very important for developing systems for these languages, including machine translation (Vázquez et al., 2021; Attieh et al., 2024). However, it is not that common to find preprocessing tools readily available and easy to use.

Some Python libraries specialize in languages spoken in the Americas. For example, *Chana*[2] is a Natural Language Processing (NLP) toolkit for the Shipibo-Konibo language of Peru, offering tasks such as lemmatization, Named Entity Recognition (NER), and Part-of-Speech (POS) tagging. Another example is *nahuatl-tools*[3], a Python package that supports partial morphological analysis and orthographic normalization for at least one Nahuatl dialectal variant. Furthermore, Apertium (Forcada et al., 2011), an open-source tool for rule-based NLP tasks, provides repositories for several under-resourced languages of the Americas[4], including Guarani, Tzeltal, K'iche', Cusco Quechua, Apurimac Quechua, Nahuatl, Otomi and Huave. The morphological analyzers described in Section 4.3 are also published in Apertium.

Regarding commercial downstream applications, machine translation systems have recently begun supporting some Indigenous languages spoken in the Americas. Google Translate now includes varieties of Zapotec, Nahuatl, Quechua, Guarani, Aymara, Yucatec Maya, Q'eqchi', and Inuktut. Meanwhile, Bing Translator supports translation for a variant of Otomi and Yucatec Maya.

[2]https://pypi.org/project/chana/

[3]https://pypi.org/project/nahuatl-tools/

[4]https://github.com/apertium/apertium-languages

2.1 Digital adoption

The internet, and the digital technologies that underlie it, has become an essential tool for communication, with over 65 % of people in the Americas now using it, and the digital divide between the U.S. and Latin America shrinking rapidly (Martínez-Domínguez and Mora-Rivera, 2020).

While internet adoption has been slow in Mexico, particularly in rural areas, there are indications of a sharp increase in usage. Recent initiatives have pledged to increase the availability of fiber-optic internet access to all municipalities, and cellular service is expanding in rural communities. Given the high concentration of indigenous language speakers in these areas, this growth suggests that a significant and increasing number of indigenous language speakers are gaining access to the internet. These facts highlight the importance of prioritizing language technology research and applications for Mexican indigenous languages.

3 Languages supported by Py-Elotl

Mexico's linguistic landscape. Besides Spanish, the languages spoken in Mexico belong to 11 linguistic families and 68 language groups. All 68 of these groups hold the status of "national languages" alongside Spanish. Despite this linguistic diversity, education and mass media are predominantly in Spanish, which places significant pressure on indigenous languages. All of the indigenous languages of Mexico can be considered at risk of being lost (INALI, 2012b).

Speakers of each language group are immersed in distinct cultural contexts and particularities. However, they share similar conditions that represent a technological challenge for NLP, i.e., significant regional variations at many levels, including a lack of consensus in the orthographic conventions.

In its current version, Py-Elotl provides various functionalities for four language groups: Nahuatl, Otomi, Mixtec, and Huave. The first three are among the most widely spoken in the country; however, many of their varieties face varying degrees of endangerment (INALI, 2012a). Figure 2 illustrates their geographical distribution. Next, we introduce their characteristics and current status.

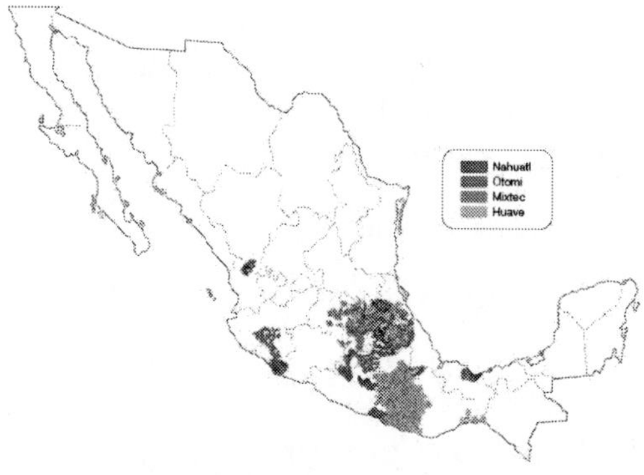

Figure 2: Geographical distribution of Nahuatl, Otomi, Mixtec, and Huave in Mexico.

Nahuatl is a group of languages present in several regions of Mexico (around 1.6 million speakers in total). It belongs to the Nahuan branch of the Uto-Aztecan (or Yuto-Nahua) linguistic family. This language family covers a vast territory; it distributes across the USA, Mexico, and El Salvador. Nahuatl is the Uto-Aztecan language with the most southern geographical distribution, and is spoken in 16 states of Mexico. Some sources recognize 30 dialectal variations (INALI, 2008), while others 28 (Lewis, 2009). Nahuatl has a rich concatenative morphology with polysynthetic and agglutinative tendencies. In particular, verbs can agglutinate many affixes to encode, for example, person and number of subject and objects, tense, aspect, directionality, and reverence.

Mixtec is a group of languages spoken in central and southern Mexico (~500,00 speakers). It belongs to the Mixtecan branch of the Oto-Manguean linguistic family. Mixtec is spoken in three states of Mexico: Oaxaca, Puebla and Guerrero.

This language exhibits the biggest dialectal variation in the country. According to INALI (2008), it has 81 dialectal variants, while Ethnologue (Lewis, 2009) recognizes 52. Due to this, Mixtec is sometimes considered as a 'macro-language'.

One of its main characteristics is the presence of tones. Most varieties distinguish three tones, while some even four (Méndez-Hord, 2017; Mendoza Ruiz, 2016; Palancar, 2016). Its morphology is usually considered isolating/analytic. However, it has the peculiarity that it actually marks many grammatical distinctions, but they are encoded at the suprasegmental level employing the tones.

Otomi is a group of languages spoken in central Mexico (around 300,000 speakers).[5] It belongs to the Oto-Pamean branch of the Oto-Manguean linguistic family (Barrientos López, 2004; Valiñas, 2020). Otomi is spoken in eight states of Mexico, including Guanajuato, Querétaro, Hidalgo, Puebla, Veracruz, Michoacán, Tlaxcala and Estado de México (Lastra, 2001).

INALI (2008) recognizes nine dialectal variants. Ethnologue (Lewis, 2009) recognizes the same number of variants; however, the reported variants are not exactly the same as noted by Valiñas (2020).

Otomi has rich morphophonological phenomena and an elaborated system of inflectional classes (Palancar, 2004). Phonologically, it features a complex vowel system with nine oral vowels and five nasal vowels, as well as a three-tone distinction (low, high, and ascending). Most of the observed orthographic variations occur within the vowel system.

Huave is a language spoken in the coastal region of Oaxaca, near the Isthmus of Tehuantepec. It is a language isolate classified within the Huavean language family and has approximately 37,000 speakers (Valiñas, 2020).

Sources differ on the number of dialectal variations, identifying between two and four distinct varieties. Typologically, Huave exhibits tonal phenomena, although tones are not as productive as in other tonal languages. It is an agglutinative language, where meaning is primarily conveyed through the combination of stems with prefixes and suffixes (Tyers and Castro, 2023).

4 Description of Py-Elotl

In this section we summarize the key components that are currently available in Py-Elotl.

4.1 Corpus loader

The toolkit includes a parallel corpus loader for three of the languages mentioned above. A parallel corpus consists of sentences in a source language paired with their corresponding translations in a target language. This kind of corpus is essential for developing translation technologies and conducting comparative linguistic studies.

In Py-Elotl, the parallel corpora always include Spanish as one of the languages, as it is relatively common to find translations to and from Spanish

[5] http://cuentame.inegi.org.mx/hipertexto/todas_lenguas.htm.

when accessing digital resources for Mexico's indigenous languages.

This module enables users to load a given parallel corpus directly into a Python data structure, allowing for easy manipulation and analysis of parallel sentences. Additionally, each parallel sentence includes metadata about its source document and the dialectal variety in which it is written.

In all cases, the parallel corpora encompass various dialectal varieties, orthographic conventions, and sources. Below, we describe the characteristics of each corpus.

Spanish-Nahuatl. The data come from the *Axolotl* parallel corpus (Gutierrez-Vasques et al., 2016), one of the largest Spanish-Nahuatl parallel corpora that is also available through a web search interface [6]. It compiles texts from diverse sources, including short stories, history books, and recipe books, among others. These sources cover several dialectal variations, with Classical Nahuatl (nci) being the most common. Additionally, it includes Highland Puebla Nahuatl (azz), Morelos Nahuatl (nhm), Central Nahuatl (nhn), Western Huasteca Nahuatl (nhw), and Eastern Huasteca Nahuatl (nhe). It is important to note that some sources are currently classified as "unknown" (unk) for various reasons, such as the combination of multiple dialects or difficulties in identification.

Spanish-Otomi. This parallel data comes from the *Tsunkua* corpus[7], which consists primarily of translations from history books, dialogues, grammars, and educational materials. Currently, the corpus includes sources written in three dialectal variations: Hñähñu/Mezquital Otomi (ote), Otomi del Estado de México (ots), and Ixtenco Otomi (otz), with the first being the most prominent.

Spanish-Mixtec The parallel corpus for this language pair was built from educational sources, grammars, and short stories. Although relatively small, it encompasses a wide range of dialectal variations, including Chalcatongo Mixtec (mig), Magdalena Peñasco Mixtec (xtm), Ocotepec Mixtec (mie), Tezoatlán Mixtec (mxb), San Jerónimo Xayacatlan Mixtec (mit), Northern Tlaxiaco Mixtec (xtn). This corpus, named *kolo*, is also available through a web search interface[8].

For a more comprehensive overview of the size and distributions in the parallel corpora, see Table 1 and Figure 4. Additionally, see Figure 3 for an example of using this feature in the Python library.

Corpus	#Parallel sentences	Dialects (ISO-639-3)
Axolotl (Spanish-Nahuatl)	16K	nci, azz, nhm, nhn, nhw
Tsunkua (Spanish-Otomi)	5K	ots, ote, otz
Kolo (Spanish-Mixtec)	2K	mig, xtm, mie, mxb, mit, xtn

Table 1: Parallel corpora currently available in Py-Elotl

```
import elotl.corpus

kolo = elotl.corpus.load("kolo")

for row in kolo:
    print(f"l1={row[0]}")
    print(f"l2={row[1]}")
    print(f"variant={row[2]}")
    print(f"doc={row[3]}")


# >> l1=cuajilote
# >> l2=chite
# >> variant=Mixteco de Magdalena Peñasco (xtm)
# >> doc=Algunos dichos y creencias
#         tradicionales de Magdalena Peñasco
```

Figure 3: Example of the parallel corpus loader in Py-Elotl

4.2 Orthographic normalization

Orthographic normalization is the process of converting written text into a standardized form within a language. While this is not a major issue for languages with well-established writing conventions, it poses a significant challenge for many other languages. Documents written in languages like Nahuatl and Otomi often have multiple orthographic tendencies in use, leading to spelling variation alongside dialectal differences.

Orthographic normalization in Py-Elotl has been implemented explicitly[9] for Nahuatl and Otomí. In both cases, finite-state transducers (FSTs) are used to convert a non-normalized input string, which may or may not conform to a particular orthographic standard, first to a phonemic representation, and subsequently to a user-specified orthographic norm for the language. Therefore, in all cases, this is a two-step process: mapping source text to a phonetic alphabet (IPA) and then generat-

[6]https://axolotl-corpus.mx/

[7]https://tsunkua.elotl.mx/

[8]https://kolo.elotl.mx/

[9]For Huave, there is no explicit orthographic normalization, but the morphological analyzer supports some orthographic flexibility in its input.

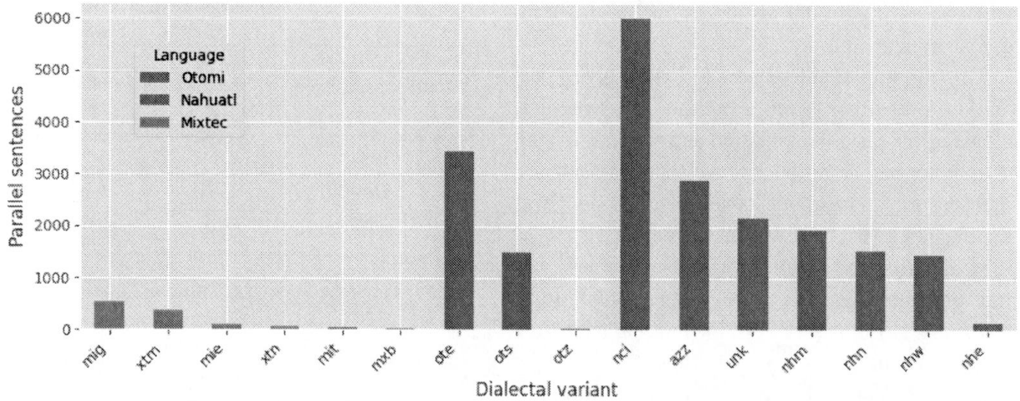

Figure 4: Distribution of dialects for each of the three parallel corpora available in Py-Elotl.

ing the target orthography.

For **Nahuatl**, the input is expected to either follow some combination of the existing writing norms (e.g. k, c or qu for the phoneme /k/), or common patterns observed in Nahuatl writing (e.g. grapheme y for phoneme /i/ word-finally). For the normalized output, four orthographic norms are currently supported, including the orthography often employed by the National Institute of Indigenous Languages (INALI) (INALI, 2018) and the ACK orthography commonly used by academics to write colonial-era Nahuatl (Karttunen, 1992). It is important to note that, given the large amount of linguistic variation within Nahuatl's many variants, a true "phonemic" representation is not possible. Instead, we opt for a generic, approximate phonemic transcription that serves as input for the various output orthographies.

Similarly, in the case of **Otomi**, the system takes input text in a potential source orthographic norm and should be able to convert it to any target orthographic norm. Currently, this module supports four orthographic standards. The transduction rules were informed by a linguist's expertise and existing documentation (Hernández-Green, 2016). Mezquital Otomi (Hñahñu) is the most widely spoken variant and forms the basis of the writing standard proposed by (INALI, 2014). See Figure 5 for an example of using the normalizer in the Python library.

Adding other output orthographies is relatively straightforward, and requires creating an FST that maps the phonemic representation to the norm of interest, and committing the FST in .att format. See Table 3 and Table 2 for a more detailed description of the available norms.

To get a sense of the **performance** of the Nahuatl orthographic normalizer, we used the Universal Dependencies treebank for Western Sierra Puebla Nahuatl, which for each token includes the original orthography and a version written in the INALI norm. We manually converted the normalized forms to the other three output orthographies, deduplicating the original forms[10], and excluding punctuation, Spanish words, and named entities. We then compared the manually-normalized words to the output of the Py-Elotl normalizer given the treebank's original forms. The normalizer correctly normalizes 98% of the 2,142 unique words for all four of the output orthographies.

In the case of Otomi, as a preliminary evaluation, we collected 1,282 word types written in the OTQ and the OTS norm, respectively. Using Py-Elotl, we converted them to the INALI norm: OTS→INALI , OTQ→INALI . We then compared the results to a gold standard, finding that the normalizers correctly processed 81% of word types on average. Performance was affected by code-switching and ambiguity in the dataset, as the current rule set does not yet cover these phenomena.

Given that the presence of named-entities and/or code-switching may mean that certain words should not be normalized or should undergo a different process for normalization. As a first step to support this potential complexity, the orthographic normalizers in Py-Elotl offer the option to provide an exceptions list in the form of a dictionary that maps a

[10]We deduplicate the original forms in order to avoid inflated performance due to the frequent repetition of easy-to-normalize common words such as the determiner/subordinator *in* or the antecessive clitic *o*.

Norm	Description
INALI	Norm used by the National Institute of Indigenous Laguages of Mexico
Ref.	INALI (2018); Flores Nájera (2019),
SEP	Norm used previously by the Secretary of Public Education and for Indigenous Education
Ref.	Various
ACK	Orthography popularized by Nahuatl scholars J. Richard Andrews, Joseph Campbel, and Frances Karttunen
Ref.	Andrews (1975); Karttunen (1992)
ILV	Norm developed by the community of San Miguel Tenango (Western Sierra Puebla Nahuatl) in collaboration of the Summer Institute of Linguistics.
Ref.	Márquez Hernández and Schroeder (2005)
Norm	**Example sentence**
INALI	[...]ihkwak walas mitsitas
SEP	[...]ijkuak ualas mitsitas
ACK	[...]ihcuac hualaz mitzitaz
ILV	[...]ihcuac ualas mitzitas
Phones	[...]iʔkʷak walas mitsitas

Table 2: A description of currently-supported orthographic norms for Nahuatl.

set of words to their preferred normalizations. One possible application of this functionality is to pass a list of common Spanish words so that they maintain the Spanish orthography.

4.3 Finite-state morphological analyzers

The use of finite-state transducers for morphological analysis has a long and rich history in the field of NLP (Kornai, 1996; Beesley and Karttunen, 2003), and is a particularly good option when there is little annotated data with which to train data-driven approaches such as deep neural networks, and can even be useful as a means for generating training data for such approaches (Moeller et al., 2018).

Py-Elotl aggregates free and open-source finite-state transducer morphological analyzers, and currently supports five indigenous Mexican languages: Three variants of Nahuatl (Classical Nahuatl[11], the analyzer for which comes from Tyers et al. (2023) (which in turn leverages the extensive lexicon in Escobar Farfan and Jonathan Irvine Israel (2019)), Highland Puebla Nahuatl (Tyers and Pugh, 2023), and Western Sierra Puebla Nahuatl (Pugh et al., 2021)), San Mateo del Mar Huave (Tyers and Castro, 2023), and Otomí[12].

While it is by no means a requirement, currently all of the Py-Elotl morphological analyzers are part of the Apertium project, and are regularly updated to reflect recent changes. The package supports stand-alone FST morphological analyzers as .att files. Since the aggregation of analyzers may result in differing tagsets, we unify tagsets via a rule-based mapping of each analyzer's output to the universal part-of-speech tags and universal morphological features used in the Universal Dependencies project (Nivre et al., 2020).

```
from elotl.otomi.orthography import Normalizer

sentence = "Hindí tsi ra chuni"
# Available norms: ["inali", "ots", "otq", "ref"]
ots_normalizer = Normalizer("ots")
otq_normalizer = Normalizer("otq")

print(f"OTS: {ots_normalizer.normalize(sentence)}")
print(f"OTQ: {otq_normalizer.normalize(sentence)}")

# >> OTS: jindí tsi ra chuni
# >> OTQ: hindí tsi ra txuni
```

Figure 5: Example of orthographic normalization using Py-Elotl. This functionality is currently available for Otomí and Nahuatl. Not featured in the figure is the .to_phones method that return the intermediate, phonemic representation.

Norm	Description
INALI	Norm designed by the National Institute of Indigenous Laguages of Mexico
Ref.	(Inali, 2014)
OTS	Standard used in some texts from variants in the State of Mexico
Ref.	(De la Vega, 2017)
OTQ	Standard proposed mainly for Querétaro variants
Ref.	(Hekking and de Jesús, 1989)
RFE	A phonetic alphabet developed for Spanish. Some Otomi transcriptions follow this standard.
Ref.	(Lastra, 1997)
Norm	**Example sentence**
INALI	[...]bijúgígó escuela pero ndichichithóhó
OTQ	[...]bijúgígó escuela pero nditxitxithóhó
OTS	[...]bikjúgígó escuela pero ndichichitjójó
RFE	[...]bikhúgígó escuela pero ndičičithóhó
Phones	[...]bikhúgígó eskwéla pero ndɨtʃitʃithóhó

Table 3: A description of currently-supported orthographic norms for Otomi.

[11] "Classical Nahuatl" is the name commonly used for the historical literary variety of Nahuatl spoken in central México during the early colonial period.

[12] https://github.com/apertium/apertium-ote

Language group	Parallel Corpus	Orthographic Normalizer	Morphological Analyzer
Nahuatl	🌽	🌽	🌽
Huave	-	-	🌽
Otomí	🌽	🌽	(🌽)
Mixtec	🌽	-	-

Table 4: An overview of the different NLP resources and tools available for each language supported in Py-Elotl. The parentheses around the elote emoji for the Otomí morphological analyzer is used to indicate the "prototype" status of the system, since the coverage and performance of this analyzer has not been published.

5 Free Software

Py-Elotl is freely available as a Python package, allowing users to integrate it into their workflow. Additionally, they can collaborate and contribute through open repositories. As a Free Software tool, it grants users and communities the freedom to run, copy, distribute, study, modify, and improve it. The source code and builds are publicly accessible on GitHub. Table 4 shows an overview of the current functionalities supported.

Releasing source code, models, and data is considered good practice in areas like NLP to ensure reproducibility. Some argue that this is especially important when working with endangered languages due to the ethical implications, i.e., the risk of doing cultural or linguistic appropriation of vulnerable groups (Hämäläinen, 2021; Washington et al., 2021).

Along a similar line, Aguilar Gil (2020) reflects on how the practices of cooperation that the indigenous communities have carried out as means of survival could influence the development of technologies. It should not be a matter of vulnerable groups receiving technology passively but encouraging an intercultural dialogue in how we do technology. She coins the term "tequiologias" compatible with the free and open-source software philosophy.

6 Conclusions

We introduced a suite of tools and resources focused on facilitating text processing for various under-resourced languages spoken in Mexico. This toolkit integrates: a) three parallel corpora with representation of different dialectal variations within the language groups; b) Orthographic normalization tools where we took on the task of identifying the main orthographic tendencies and wrote FST technology to convert across different standards automatically; c) Morphological analyzers for several dialectal variants that are also available through Apertium.

Currently, we support the following language groups: Nahuatl, Otomi, Mixtec, and Huave. However, adding resources and features for more languages is relatively straightforward. The toolkit is available as a Python package, and the code is openly accessible in public repositories to encourage the development of open and collaborative technologies.

The current scope of Py-Elotl focuses on upstream NLP tasks, including rule-based approaches, as neural and statistical methods are often not entirely applicable. To foster a more linguistically diverse landscape in language technologies and support under-resourced languages, we believe it is essential to first establish strong foundational resources.

Limitations

While we present this Python toolkit as a resource for the languages of Mexico, our coverage is not exhaustive. We currently focus on a few language groups, some with large speaker populations within Mexico. However, many other indigenous languages and dialectal variations remain underrepresented in this release. Expanding coverage to include a broader range of languages and dialects is an important goal for future development, requiring further linguistic collaboration, data collection, and community involvement

The morphological analyzers and orthographic normalization modules used in this work are rule-based, which may limit their flexibility to handle phenomena such as code-switching, ambiguous cases, and non-standard language use, which constitute the linguistic reality many speakers of these languages face.

Finally, the development of technology for underrepresented groups should not only focus on applying the latest NLP techniques but also encouraging diverse groups of work, in a way that the resulting technologies and resources are really aligned with the necessities and context of the speakers.

Acknowledgments

This work was partially funded by the projects PAPIIT TA100924 and TA100725 at UNAM, Mexico, and by the National Science Foundation Proposal #23192462319247, "Collaborative Research: Syntactically-annotated corpora for endangered languages in areal contact." We thank the reviewers for the relevant comments on our work.

References

Yasnaya Elena Aguilar Gil. 2020. A modest proposal to save the world. https://restofworld.org/2020/saving-the-world-through-tequiology/.

J.R. Andrews. 1975. *Introduction to Classical Nahuatl*, 2nd edition. University of Texas Press.

Joseph Attieh, Zachary Hopton, Yves Scherrer, and Tanja Samardžić. 2024. System description of the NordicsAlps submission to the AmericasNLP 2024 machine translation shared task. In *Proceedings of the 4th Workshop on Natural Language Processing for Indigenous Languages of the Americas (AmericasNLP 2024)*, pages 150–158, Mexico City, Mexico. Association for Computational Linguistics.

Guadalupe Barrientos López. 2004. *Otomíes del Estado de México*. Comisión Nacional para el Desarrollo de los Pueblos Indígenas.

Kenneth R Beesley and Lauri Karttunen. 2003. Finite-state morphology: Xerox tools and techniques. *CSLI, Stanford.*

Damian Blasi, Antonios Anastasopoulos, and Graham Neubig. 2022. Systematic inequalities in language technology performance across the world's languages. In *Proceedings of the 60th Annual Meeting of the Association for Computational Linguistics (Volume 1: Long Papers)*, pages 5486–5505, Dublin, Ireland. Association for Computational Linguistics.

Luis Chiruzzo, Pavel Denisov, Alejandro Molina-Villegas, Silvia Fernandez-Sabido, Rolando Coto-Solano, Marvin Agüero-Torales, Aldo Alvarez, Samuel Canul-Yah, Lorena Hau-Ucán, Abteen Ebrahimi, Robert Pugh, Arturo Oncevay, Shruti Rijhwani, Katharina von der Wense, and Manuel Mager. 2024. Findings of the AmericasNLP 2024 shared task on the creation of educational materials for indigenous languages. In *Proceedings of the 4th Workshop on Natural Language Processing for Indigenous Languages of the Americas (AmericasNLP 2024)*, pages 224–235, Mexico City, Mexico. Association for Computational Linguistics.

Lázaro Margarita De la Vega. 2017. Aprendiendo otomí (hñähñu). *Ciudad de México, Comisión Nacional para el Desarrollo de los Pueblos Indígenas.*

Fanny Ducel, Karën Fort, Gaël Lejeune, and Yves Lepage. 2022. Do we name the languages we study? the# benderrule in lrec and acl articles. In *Proceedings of the Thirteenth Language Resources and Evaluation Conference*, pages 564–573.

Escobar Farfan and Jonathan Irvine Israel. 2019. *Nahuatl contemporary writing : studying convergence in the absence of a written norm.* Ph.D. thesis, University of Sheffield.

Lucero Flores Nájera. 2019. *La gramática de la cláusula simple en el náhuatl de Tlaxcala.* Ph.D. thesis, Centro de Investigactiones y Estudios Superiores en Antropología Social.

Mikel L Forcada, Mireia Ginestí-Rosell, Jacob Nordfalk, Jim O'Regan, Sergio Ortiz-Rojas, Juan Antonio Pérez-Ortiz, Felipe Sánchez-Martínez, Gema Ramírez-Sánchez, and Francis M Tyers. 2011. Apertium: a free/open-source platform for rule-based machine translation. *Machine translation*, 25:127–144.

Ximena Gutierrez-Vasques, Gerardo Sierra, and Isaac Hernandez Pompa. 2016. Axolotl: a web accessible parallel corpus for Spanish-Nahuatl. In *Proceedings of the Tenth International Conference on Language Resources and Evaluation (LREC'16)*, pages 4210–4214, Portorož, Slovenia. European Language Resources Association (ELRA).

Mika Hämäläinen. 2021. Endangered languages are not low-resourced! *CoRR*, abs/2103.09567.

Michael A Hedderich, Lukas Lange, Heike Adel, Jannik Strötgen, and Dietrich Klakow. 2021. A survey on recent approaches for natural language processing in low-resource scenarios. In *Proceedings of the 2021 Conference of the North American Chapter of the Association for Computational Linguistics: Human Language Technologies*, pages 2545–2568.

Ewald Hekking and Severiano Andrés de Jesús. 1989. *Diccionario español-otomí de Santiago Mexquititlán*, volume 22. Universidad Autónoma de Querétaro.

Nestor Hernández-Green. 2016. Misteriosas figurillas de barro de san jerónimo acazulco. *Tlalocan*, 21:19–48.

INALI. 2008. Catálogo de las lenguas indígenas nacionales: Variantes linguísticas de méxico con sus atodenominaciones y referencias geoestadísticas. https://www.inali.gob.mx/clin-inali/.

INALI. 2012a. Catálogo de las lenguas indígenas nacionales en riesgo de desaparición. https://www.cdi.gob.mx/dmdocuments/lenguas_indigenas_nacionales_en_riesgo_de_desaparicion_inali.pdf/.

INALI. 2012b. *México: Lenguas indígenas nacionales en riesgo de desaparición.* Instituto Nacional de Lenguas Indígenas, México.

INALI. 2014. *Njaua Nt't'ot'i ra Hñähñu Norma de escritura de la lengua Hñähñu (Otomí).* INALI, SEP.

Inali. 2014. *Njaua nt'ot'i ra hñähñu. Norma de escritura de la lengua hñähñu (otomí) de los estados de Guanajuato, Hidalgo, Estado de México, Puebla, Querétaro, Tlaxcala, Michoacán y Veracruz.* Instituto Nacional de Lenguas Indígenas (inaLi), SEP, Mexico.

INALI. 2018. Breviario: Norma ortográfica del idioma náhuatl, méxico. (conforme al avance preliminar de la norma de escritura de la lengua náhuatl a nivel nacional).

Pratik Joshi, Sebastin Santy, Amar Budhiraja, Kalika Bali, and Monojit Choudhury. 2020. The state and fate of linguistic diversity and inclusion in the NLP world. In *Proceedings of the 58th Annual Meeting of the Association for Computational Linguistics*, pages 6282–6293, Online. Association for Computational Linguistics.

Frances E Karttunen. 1992. *An analytical dictionary of Nahuatl.* University of Oklahoma Press.

András Kornai. 1996. Extended finite state models of language. *Natural Language Engineering*, 2(4):287–290.

Yolanda Lastra. 1997. *El otomí de Ixtenco.* UNAM.

Yolanda Lastra. 2001. *Unidad y Diversidad de la Lengua: Relatos otomíes.* UNAM.

M. Paul Lewis, editor. 2009. *Ethnologue: Languages of the World*, sixteenth edition. SIL International, Dallas, TX, USA.

Manuel Mager, Ximena Gutierrez-Vasques, Gerardo Sierra, and Ivan Meza-Ruiz. 2018. Challenges of language technologies for the indigenous languages of the Americas. In *Proceedings of the 27th International Conference on Computational Linguistics*, pages 55–69, Santa Fe, New Mexico, USA. Association for Computational Linguistics.

Manuel Mager, Arturo Oncevay, Abteen Ebrahimi, John Ortega, Annette Rios, Angela Fan, Ximena Gutierrez-Vasques, Luis Chiruzzo, Gustavo Giménez-Lugo, Ricardo Ramos, Ivan Vladimir Meza Ruiz, Rolando Coto-Solano, Alexis Palmer, Elisabeth Mager-Hois, Vishrav Chaudhary, Graham Neubig, Ngoc Thang Vu, and Katharina Kann. 2021a. Findings of the AmericasNLP 2021 shared task on open machine translation for indigenous languages of the Americas. In *Proceedings of the First Workshop on Natural Language Processing for Indigenous Languages of the Americas*, pages 202–217, Online. Association for Computational Linguistics.

Manuel Mager, Arturo Oncevay, Annette Rios, Ivan Vladimir Meza Ruiz, Alexis Palmer, Graham Neubig, and Katharina Kann, editors. 2021b. *Proceedings of the First Workshop on Natural Language Processing for Indigenous Languages of the Americas.* Association for Computational Linguistics, Online.

Alexandre Magueresse, Vincent Carles, and Evan Heetderks. 2020. Low-resource languages: A review of past work and future challenges. *Preprint*, arXiv:2006.07264.

Marlen Martínez-Domínguez and Jorge Mora-Rivera. 2020. Internet adoption and usage patterns in rural Mexico. *Technology in society*, 60:101–226.

Esteban I Méndez-Hord. 2017. *Tone in Acatlán Mixtec Nouns.* The University of North Dakota.

Juana Mendoza Ruiz. 2016. Fonología segmental y patrones tonales del tu'un savi de alcozauca de guerrero. *Ciudad de México: Centro de Investigaciones y Estudios Superiores en Antropología.*

Sarah Moeller, Ghazaleh Kazeminejad, Andrew Cowell, and Mans Hulden. 2018. A neural morphological analyzer for Arapaho verbs learned from a finite state transducer. In *Proceedings of the Workshop on Computational Modeling of Polysynthetic Languages*, pages 12–20.

Christopher Moseley and Alexander Nicolas, editors. 2010. *Atlas of the World's Languages in Danger*, 3 edition. UNESCO, Paris.

Elizabeth Márquez Hernández and Petra Schroeder. 2005. *Pequeño diccionario ilustrado*, Second edition. Instituto Lingüístico de Verano, A.C., Mexico.

J. Nivre, M.-C. de Marneffe, F. Ginter, J. Hajič, C. D. Manning, S. Pyysalo, S. Schuster, F. Tyers, and D. Zeman. 2020. Universal Dependencies v2: An evergrowing multilingual treebank collection. In *Proceedings of the 12th Conference on Language Resources and Evaluation (LREC 2020)*, pages 4027–4036.

Enrique L Palancar. 2004. Verbal morphology and prosody in otomi. *International journal of American linguistics*, 70(3):251–278.

Enrique L Palancar. 2016. A typology of tone and inflection: A view from the oto-manguean languages of mexico. In *Tone and Inflection*, pages 109–140. De Gruyter Mouton.

Robert Pugh, Francis Tyers, and Marivel Huerta Mendez. 2021. Towards an open source finite-state morphological analyzer for zacatlán-ahuacatlán-tepetzintla nahuatl. In *Proceedings of the 4th Workshop on the Use of Computational Methods in the Study of Endangered Languages Volume 1 (Papers)*, pages 80–85.

Francis Tyers and Samuel Herrera Castro. 2023. Towards a finite-state morphological analyser for san mateo huave. In *Proceedings of the Sixth Workshop on the Use of Computational Methods in the Study of Endangered Languages*, pages 30–37.

Francis Tyers and Robert Pugh. 2023. A finite-state morphological analyser for highland puebla nahuatl. In *Proceedings of the Workshop on Natural Language Processing for Indigenous Languages of the Americas (AmericasNLP)*, pages 103–108.

Francis Tyers, Robert Pugh, and Valery Berthoud. 2023. Codex to corpus: Exploring annotation and processing for an open and extensible machine-readable edition of the Florentine Codex. In *Proceedings of the Workshop on Natural Language Processing for Indigenous Languages of the Americas (AmericasNLP)*, pages 19–29.

Leopoldo Valiñas. 2020. *Lenguas originarias y pueblos indígenas de México: familias y lenguas aisladas*. Academia Mexicana de la Lengua.

Raúl Vázquez, Yves Scherrer, Sami Virpioja, and Jörg Tiedemann. 2021. The Helsinki submission to the AmericasNLP shared task. In *Proceedings of the First Workshop on Natural Language Processing for Indigenous Languages of the Americas*, pages 255–264, Online. Association for Computational Linguistics.

Jonathan Washington, Felipe Lopez, and Brook Lillehaugen. 2021. Towards a morphological transducer and orthography converter for western tlacolula valley zapotec. In *Proceedings of the First Workshop on Natural Language Processing for Indigenous Languages of the Americas*, pages 185–193.

Analyzing and generating English phrases with finite-state methods to match and translate inflected Plains Cree (*nêhiyawêwin*) word-forms

Antti Arppe
Alberta Language Technology Lab
Department of Linguistics, University of Alberta
arppe@ualberta.ca

Abstract

This paper presents two finite-state transducer tools, which can be used to analyze or generate simple English verb and noun phrases, that can be mapped with inflected Plains Cree (*nêhiyawêwin)* verb and noun forms. These tools support fetching an inflected Cree word-form directly with an appropriate plain English phrase, and conversely providing a rough translation of an inflected Cree word-form. Such functionalities can be used to improve the user friendliness of on-line dictionaries. The tools are extendable to other similarly morphologically complex languages.

1 Introduction

Exemplifying with the pairing of a morphologically complex Indigenous language spoken on the Western plains of Canada and the corresponding morphologically simpler majority language, namely Plains Cree (*nêhiyawêwin*; ISO: crk) and English, this paper presents computational tools using finite-state transducer (FST) technology for analyzing and generating basic English phrases, as if they were complex inflected word-forms. When paired with an already existing FST computational morphological model for Plains Cree, these computational tools allow for 1) providing an inflected Plains Cree word-form that roughly matches the meaning and morphosyntactic features of a simple English phrase, and 2) generating a simple English phrase that matches the meaning and morphosyntactic features of an inflected Cree word-form.

For analyzing and generating English phrases, both tools make use the FOMA compiler (Hulden 2009) for Xerox-style finite-state transducer (FST) specifications (Beesley and Karttunen 2003). [1] These FSTs are applied on the English definitions of Plains Cree entries in three bilingual Cree-to-English dictionaries. These dictionaries are 1) *nêhiyawêwin : itwêwina / Cree : Words* (CW: Wolvengrey 2001), 2) *Maskwacîs Dictionary of Cree Words* (MD: Maskwachees Cultural College 2009), and 3) *Alberta Elders' Cree Dictionary* (AECD: LeClaire and Cardinal 2002). For analyzing and generating Plains Cree word-forms, we use the already existing finite-state morphological model (Snoek et al. 2014; Harrigan et al. 2017), which has been compiled with the Helsinki FST compiler (HFST: Lindén et al. 2011).

The first tool noted above provides an alternative to presenting the results of analyzing a morphologically complex Cree word-form by presenting the morphosyntactic analysis tags, whether as is or in relabeled form (into plain English or plain *nêhiyawêwin* labels), as has been the standard previously in intelligent on-line dictionaries (e.g. Arppe et al. 2022: 22-23, 59-61). The second tool provides an alternative to finding an inflected word-form with the appropriate morphosyntactic features by looking up that form in a paradigm table, often quite daunting in their extent (Arppe et al. 2022: 19-24). These tools are already integrated to provide these two functionalities in the on-line Plains Cree – English dictionary, *itwêwina* (`itwewina.altlab.app`) (Arppe et al. 2022; Arppe et al. 2023; see also Appendix E in this paper), built with the open source *morphodict* intelligent dictionary platform, developed in the *21st Century Tools for Indigenous Languages* (21C) project hosted by the Alberta Language Technology Lab (ALTLab). [2]

[1] Source: `https://github.com/giellalt/lang-crk/tree/main/src/fst/transcriptions`

[2] `https://morphodict.readthedocs.io/en/latest/index.html`

Proceedings of the Fifth Workshop on NLP for Indigenous Languages of the Americas (AmericasNLP), pages 48–62
May 4, 2025 ©2025 Association for Computational Linguistics

Nevertheless, one should note that mapping the English features with Cree features, and finding the Cree entry matching the English lexical content requires software modules that are not covered in this paper.[3] As far as we are aware of, *itwêwina* is the only implementation of a combined integration of both simple English phrase analysis and generation in an on-line dictionary, at the same time effectively implementing the only translation system to/from Cree, though in a very restricted form. General machine translation solutions have been developed, of course, for majority and other languages, in particular well-resourced ones. However, the current state-of-the-art approaches that such MT systems rely on require large amounts of parallel corpus data; the closest to this in the North American context that one has come for Indigenous and polysynthetic languages has been for the pairing of Inuktitut and English (Littell et al. 2018; Knowles et al. 2020; Le and Sadat 2020; Microsoft Translator 2021; Caswell 2024).

Originally, the morphosyntactic features that are covered in the above two tools were based on those included in the so-called extended paradigms for nouns and verbs, as specified for the online *itwêwina* dictionary[4]. For nouns, these are based on unpublished complete paradigm layouts provided by Arok Wolvengrey (p.c.); for verbs, these are also largely based on published paradigms provided by Wolvengrey (2011: 393ff, Appendices A and B). For nouns, these extended paradigms include all the possible inflectional features, namely singular, plural, obviative, locative and distributive forms, for the non-possessed word-forms as well as with all possible possessors. For verbs, these extended paradigms include all the possible person and number combinations for subjects, as well as objects, when applicable (only for transitive animate verbs). For all possible subject-object combinations, the most common cases of tense/aspect/mood (expressed by prefixes known as *preverbs*) are included, namely the unmarked case (often referred to as the present tense, usually translated as "s.t. **happens**" or "s/he **does** s.t."), the past (*kî-*, "s/he **did** s.t."), future definite (*ka-*, "s/he **will** do s.t."), future prospective (*wî-*, "s/he **is going to** do s.t."), and the infinitive/irrealis (*ka-* and *ta-*, "**for** s.o. **to** do s.t.") tenses/moods. In addition, all subjunctive, *aka* future conditional forms (translated usually as "**when** s.o. does s.t."), as well as imperative forms in both the immediate and delayed cases are included (translated as "(you) do something **now**" or "(you) do s.t. **later**", respectively).

Later on, the set of morphosyntactic features has been expanded (only for English verb phrase generation) to include, not only those that are relevant for Plains Cree, but also other languages in the Algonquian and Dene language families. This has led to covering negated ("s/he does **not** do s.t.") and progressive forms as well as dual (e.g. "we **both**") and distributed plural (e.g. "**each and every one of us** does s.t.") and indirect object arguments (e.g. "s/he gives s.t. **to us**" or "s/he does s.t. **for us**") for verbs.[5] Nevertheless, one should note that the English phrase types that can be analyzed and generated by the tools presented here are only a small and quite restricted subset of the entire set of possible English constructions, even though the selected subset can be considered as the most common of English simple construction types, with the highest relevance for the most common inflected Cree noun and verb word-forms.

2 Implementation – Analysis

2.1 Analysis of English verb phrases

The analysis (and generation) of English verb phrases, relies on two factors. Firstly, English personal pronouns indicating subjects, objects, and possessors are mostly distinct from each other, with the exception of the second person *you* and third person neuter *it*. This allows for the identification of these arguments and their relevant syntactic roles in simple phrases with a single predicate; when one or more of such verbal arguments can be identified, that is interpreted to indicate a verbal phrase to be matched with a Plains Cree verb form.

---

[3] https://github.com/UAlbertaALTLab/morphodict/tree/main/src/morphodict/phrase_translate

[4] https://github.com/UAlbertaALTLab/morphodict/tree/main/src/morphodict/paradigm/layouts

[5] The English verb phrase generator can be extended to other languages, provided that their morphosyntactic features can be mapped to available English auxiliary constructions, and the English dictionary definitions follow a templatic structure similar to the three Cree lexical resources referred to in this paper. E.g. for Tsuut'ina (ISO: srs; Dene language family), its Imperfective, Perfective, and Progressive verbal aspects can be mapped to the English Future Definite, Past, and Present Progressive tenses, respectively, and the Repetitive subaspect to the English Repetitive adverbial construction (with "again and again"). We have initially explored this with encouraging results.

Tense/aspect/modality feature(s)	Initial zone	Subject/ Existential	Predicate zone	Object/ Reflexive	Final zone
Present		we	help>0	you	
Past		we	help>ed	you all	
Future+Definite		we	will help	you	
Future+Prospective		we	are going to help	you all	
Imperative+Immediate / Delayed	let	you and us	help	him	now/later
Imperative+Immediate+Negation	do not let	you and us	help	her	now
Infinitive	for	us	to help	you	
(Future) Conditional	when	we	help	you all	
Present (Existential)		there	is	light	
Present+Negation (Existential)		there	is not	light	
Present (Copula)		it	is red		
Present+Negation		we	do not help	you	
Present (Copula)		we	are ready		
Present+Negation (Copula)		we	are not ready		

Table 1. Examples of various English verb constructions, split into the various templatic zones with the help of subject/existential and object (reflexive) markers (in blue). The parts of the Predicate zone indicating Tense/Mood are marked in red. Analyses of the above verb phrases are shown in Appendix A.

Secondly, combined with the relatively strict word order of English, these subject and object personal pronouns allow for the partitioning of English phrases into a *templatic structure* with an initial, predicate, and final zone.

In the *predicate* zone, immediately after the subject pronoun (or existential marker) and before the object pronoun, when available, usually the first word is either 1) an auxiliary verb (e.g. *will* or *do*, *does*, or *did*, or the copula *am/is/are/was/were*, by itself or as part of an auxiliary phrase, e.g. *am/are/is/was/were going to*), or 2) a finite verb form (e.g. *help*, *helps*, or *helped*). This enables the determination of the tense, aspect, and modality of a phrase. The *initial* zone, preceding the first appearance of a personal pronoun indicating the subject, enables the identification of imperative/permissive constructions (and their negation), future conditional, and infinitival constructions, indicated by the initial elements *let*, *when*, and *for*, respectively. Generally, the initial personal pronoun would be in subject form, e.g. "**I** do s.t." or "when **we** do s.t.", but in the case of an initial zone preposition *for* or the auxiliary verb *let*, the initial personal pronoun will take the object form, in e.g. "**for me** to do s.t." or "**let us** do s.t.". The final zone is mainly used for the identification of the immediate or delayed subtypes of imperative constructions introduced above, as well as repetitive forms, indicated by the adverb constructions *again and again* or *repeatedly*. Examples of elements in these zones for the verb phrase template, with their linguistic analyses for tense/aspect/modality, are provided in Table 1 above.

In this current implementation, personal pronouns and certain other nominal expressions (i.e. 'someone' and 'people' for unspecified subjects in Plains Cree) which are identified as arguments are converted into flag diacritics, of the P-flag type that only sets the value of a flag diacritic variable, without checking for any constraints. These flags will then each represent a subject, direct object, indirect object, or reflexive feature. An example of this for the regular subject pronouns is given below in (1).

One may firstly notice that for certain multiword subject expressions, such as ones corresponding to the Plains Cree *further obviative* feature (sometimes referred to as the 5th person), alternative versions are recognized. Secondly, longer subject constructions are attempted to be matched before shorter ones in separate regular expressions that are then composed together, to ensure only a single maximal match. Thirdly, the targeted subject constructions are expected to be demarcated with boundary characters defined as the regular expression `Bx`, consisting of phrasal punctuation characters, the space character, and the input boundary (both initial and final). Finally, we apply a convention where the second person pronoun "you" is interpreted as singular (`+2Sg`) when occurring by itself, and, when occurring with "all" as "you all", as the (exclusive) plural (`+2Pl`).

(1)
```
regex [ {yet another} | {yet others} | {he/she/they over there} | {he or she or they over there} | {she or he or they over there} | {he, she, or they over there} | {she, he, or they over there} -> "@P.subject.5Sg/Pl@" || Bx _ Bx ]
```

```
.o. [ {another} | {others} | {he over
there} | {she over there} | {they over
there} | {he/she/they} | {he or she or
they} | {she or he or they} | {he, she, or
they} -> "@P.subject.4Sg/Pl@" || Bx _ Bx
]
.o. [ {it} -> "@P.object.0Sg@" || Bx _ "
" .#. ]
{you all} -> "@P.subject.2Pl@" || Bx _ Bx
,,
{you} -> "@P.subject.2Sg@" || Bx _ Bx ,,
...
{it} -> "@P.subject.0Sg@" || Bx _ Bx ,,
... ];
define Subject
```

Furthermore, matched elements in the initial zone are converted into P-type flag diacritics representing the associated modality features. In the predicate zone, matched auxiliary verbs and auxiliary phrases as well as the negative adverb *not* are similarly converted into P-type flag diacritics. Sometimes, the interpretation of the subject pronouns is combined with a scrutiny of relevant elements in the initial zone, a fragment of which is exemplified below in (2) for the infinitival phrases, initiated with "for …".

(2)
```
regex [ ...
[ {for you all to} -> "@P.subject.2Pl@"
"@P.tense.Inf@" || .#. _ " " ,,
{for you and us to} | {for you and we to}
| {for you and me to} | {for us and you
to} | {for we and you to} | {for me and
you to} -> "@P.subject.21Pl@"
"@P.tense.Inf@" ,
... ] .o.
[ {for me to} -> "@P.subject.1Sg@"
"@P.tense.Inf@" || .#. _ " " ,,
{for you to} -> "@P.subject.2Sg@"
"@P.tense.Inf@" || .#. _ " " ,,
... ];
define ReverseSubject
```

All these conversions result in removing the function words from the output, and leaving only the lexical content words that will be used in the subsequent English-to-Cree search. In conjunction with this, finite non-auxiliary verb forms that occur in the very beginning of the predicate zone are analyzed as to their tense (present, past, or infinitive) and an appropriate P-type flag diacritic is added, with the verb standardized into the bare infinitive form. Here, for irregular verbs a set of 155 tuplets of past tense and the corresponding infinitive forms are used (specified as `input:output` pairs in a LEXC file); all other, regular verb forms are analyzed using regular expressions recognizing the regular suffixes *-(e)s*, *-(e)d*, and *-ing*, and removing such suffixes to provide the bare infinitive/stem form.

Overall, the English verb phrase analyzer consists of a number of constituent regular expressions such as the ones for `Subject` and `ReverseSubject` presented above, as well as regular expressions for standardizing the input. These are then composed together in a specific order, which is intended to result in appropriate matches. For verb phrases, the ordering is presented below (3). For the most part, this is self-explanatory, in particular for identifying the various argument elements and analyzing the predicate zone. Nevertheless, one first specifies 1) the alphabet on which the English phrase analyzer operates on (which applies for both verbal and nominal phrase types), followed by 2) the insertion of an additional final space to satisfy the boundary requirements for many of the argument-marking component regular expressions, and then 3) the standardization of certain forms as well as masking apostrophes in possessed forms, before 4) undoing contractions such as "don't" as "do not", followed by 4) the resurrection of the apostrophe for possessed word-forms.

(3) Letters+ → InsertFinalSpace → Standardization → Contractions → ResurrectApostrophe → Negation → Past → ReverseSubject → Reciprocal → Subject → Reflexive → Object → 1DuO → 2SgO → 2DuO → 2PlO → 3SgO → 3DuO → 4SgPlO → 5SgPlO → 0SgO → XO → XPlO → Tense → Imperative → Progressive → Repetitive → VerbClass → VerbAnalysis

The next constituent regular expressions from `Negation` through `Repetitive` should be self-explanatory, except for the rule sequence `1DuO → 2SgO → 2DuO → 2PlO → 3SgO → 3DuO → 4SgPlO → 5SgPlO → 0SgO → XO → XPlO`, which concerns the reinterpretation of certain ambiguous argument types as an object, if the argument in question is already preceded in the phrase by a subject argument. Furthermore, the next-to-last regular expression uses the occurrence or absence of identified subject and object arguments and their semantic types to determine the Plains Cree verbal part-of-speech corresponding to the English phrase, based on transitivity of the predicate and animacy of the arguments (as an II, AI, TI, or TA type of verb). This allows for matching the correct type of Cree verb entry for the English phrase.

Finally, all the aforementioned P-type flag diacritics determine the generation of corresponding analysis tags. In fact, all the theoretically possible analysis combinations are generated, but the correct analysis is filtered by matching R-type (for *Require*) flags; the resultant tags are output after the standardized lexical content words using the final regular expression `VerbAnalysis`. A simplified example of the structure of the input and output and the intervening intermediate form with the P-type flags is shown in (4a). After that, the English analysis output is converted into input matching the tags used by the Cree generator FST, resulting in an inflected Cree word-form approximating the original English phrase (4b).

(4a) `I am going to` **see** `you all`
→ `@P.subject.1Sg@ @P.tense.Fut@` **see**
`@P.object.2Pl@`
→ **see +V+TA**`+Fut+1Sg+2PLO`

(4b) → `PV/wî+`**wâpamêw+V+TA**`+Ind+1Sg+2PLO`
→ `kiwî-wâpamitinâwâw`

One should note that mapping the English tags into Cree ones and finding the Cree entry matching the English lexical content makes use of a *morphodict* software module and specifications that are not covered here.[6]

2.2 Analysis of English noun phrases

Similar to verbs, the analysis (and generation) of English noun phrases relies on a relatively fixed word order for the nominal head and locative prepositions, and otherwise on certain identifiable modifiers. The maximally complex noun phrase that we try to analyze is limited by what can be mapped to an inflected Plains Cree nominal word-form, examples of which are presented in Table 2.

The noun which is the head of the noun phrase is expected to be found at its end, identifiable by an immediately following punctuation character understood as separating multiple noun phrases, or a string final boundary; A Plains Cree noun can express either the singular or plural number or obviation, but not both. For the purposes of English noun phrase analysis, plural number can be expressed either morphologically with the suffix *–(e)s* on the final word interpreted as a noun, or with several attributes ("many", "few", "several", or "couple of") occurring as the first element of the noun phrase, while initial articles or indefinite pronouns ("a", "an", or "one") are used to denote a singular number. Obviation can be expressed by adding the phrase "over there" after the final noun, which will override any preceding expression of number. In addition, a noun phrase can be initiated with an optional locative preposition, either "in" or "on", or the optional *distributive* locative preposition "among", both of which in Plains Cree are again mutually exclusive with singular or plural number or obviation. In addition, one can indicate an optional possessor with English possessive pronouns, or certain nouns ("someone's" or "people's") standing in for the unspecified possessor. Furthermore, one can optionally signal a diminutive form by using any of the modifying attributes "little", "lesser", "smaller", or "younger", though currently this is not used to create corresponding Cree noun forms.

Locat-ive	Possess-or	Num-ber	Dimin-utive	Noun head	Obv-iation
		one		**bear**	
		many		**bear>s**	
	another			**bear**	over there
	my	one		**book**	
	my		little	**book**	
in		a		**book**	
among				**bear>s**	
in	my	many		**book>s**	
	my other		little	**tree**	over there

Table 2. A sample of English noun phrases corresponding to Plains Cree noun forms, and their templatic structure. Analyses are shown in Appendix B.

Similar to verbs, the English noun analyzer consists of a number of constituent regular expressions that are applied in a sequence shown below (5). The first regular expression `NounPl2Sg` analyzes the final word of the phrase expecting that to be a noun, and if this appears to be a plural form, either having either of the regular *-s* or *-es* suffixes or being one of the enumerated 79 pairings of irregular plural forms with their singular counterparts, a P-type flag indicating plural number is affixed and the plural form replaced by the corresponding singular form. This is followed by two regular expressions `VerbPhrase` and `NounPhrase`, used to disallow a noun phrase analysis if any of the personal pronouns representing subjects or objects are present. After this, a succession of regular expressions converts various function words into corresponding flags indicating number, obviation,

[6] For the tag mappings between Cree and English, see: `https://github.com/UAlbertaALTLab/morphodict/tree/main/src/crkeng/resources/phrase_translate`

location, diminutivization, and possession, where their actual order in the noun phrase has little role.

As one might well write a phrase combining a locative preposition and any of the markers of number or obviation, as these are converted into P-type flag-diacritics, only the value of the last flag will remain in effect. An exception is implemented with the regular expression `DistrVsPl`, with plural flags deleted after an initial distributive preposition, since that construction is usually translated into English with a plural noun form, e.g. "among the Americans" for *kihci-môhkomâninâhk*, even though the corresponding Cree noun form is underspecified in terms of its number.

The next-to-final regular expression `NounClass` outputs a tag (+N) indicating a noun analysis, whereas the final regular expression `NounAnalysis` outputs analysis tags corresponding to the P-type flag-diacritics generated earlier. Again, all the theoretically possible combinations of noun analysis tags are output, with R-type flags filtering the appropriate correct analysis. One should note that one cannot currently map an English noun phrase to the two Plains Cree animacy types, as English has no such morphosyntactically expressed distinction.

(5) NounPl2Sg → VerbPhrase → NounPhrase → NumberObvLocDistr → Diminutive → Possession → DistrVsPl → NounClass → NounAnalysis

Importantly, the noun analyzer described here is treated as disjunct to the verb analyzer described earlier, resulting in a single finite-state analyzer for English phrases. The (uncompressed) size of the resultant compiled FOMA binary file is 24.4 MB.

3 Implementation – Generation

3.1 English verb phrase generation

The easy identifiability of the subject and object personal pronouns and the associated zones in a simple English verb phrase, as described above in the analysis of such phrases to present a general *templatic* structure, also enables the manipulation of the subject and object pronouns as well as the tense, aspect, and modality of the predicate in such a phrase, allowing for the generation of new phrases matching the morphosyntactic features expressed by an inflected Cree word-form. Indeed, an examination of English definitions in the three bilingual Plains Cree-to-English dictionaries of which we have access to their content in electronic form shows that these all follow particular structures and expressions that support such manipulation. Examples from CW, MD, and AECD for the three Cree entries, *wîcihêw, nisitohtam*, and *mispon*, are given below in (6-8).

(6) *wîcihêw* (to help s.o.)

- s/he helps s.o., s/he assists s.o. (CW)
- s/he provides welfare to s.o. (CW)
- s/he assists s.o. in childbirth, s/he serves as a midwife to s.o. (CW)
- He helps him. (MD)
- He aids him. (MD)
- They help him. (MD)
- s/he assists her/him or them (AECD)
- s/he participates (AECD)

(7) *nisitohtam* (to understand [s.t.])

- s/he understands (CW)
- He understands (MD)
- s/he understands s.t. (CW)
- s/he understands it (AECD)

(8) *mispon* (to snow)

- it snows, it is snowing, there is falling snow, there is a snowfall (CW)
- It is snowing. (MD)
- it snows, or it is snowing (AECD)

While the indication of subjects and objects above, in red and blue, respectively, varies between the three dictionary sources, with "s/he" in CW and AECD vs. "He" in MD for animate subjects, and "it" or "there" throughout for the inanimate subjects/existential marker, and "s.o." in CW vs. "her/him" or "them" in AECD vs. "him" in MD for animate objects (whether for direct or prepositional) and "s.t." in CW vs. "it" in AECD and MD for inanimate objects, the use of specific conventions, e.g. "s/he" or "him/her", in fact makes their identification easier than for the English phrase analysis. Also, the main finite verbs in each of the definitions, underlined above, practically always immediately follow the subject marker, which substantially facilitates their manipulation and/or the insertion of various auxiliary verb constructions immediately after the subject marker, sometimes in conjunction with an additional element appended in the initial zone preceding the subject, to convey a broad range of tense, aspect, and modality features. Finally, in all three sources both commas and semi-colons are almost invariably used only to delineate different senses, further clarifying where the initial zone/subject is to be found in any of the definitions above.

(9) Input → itNonSubjectMarking → Standardization → VerbInflection2 → ModalAuxiliary

→ Tag2FlagConversion → VerbInflection → IrregularVerbs → AuxiliaryPhrase → BeAuxiliaryPhrase → PhrasePrefix → PhraseSuffix → Relativization → BeInflection → IObjectConversion → SubjectConversion → ObjectConversion → ReflexiveConversion → PossessiveConversion → itNonSubjectUnmarking → EngInf2Inf → EngPrt2Prt → EngPrf2Prf → EngProg2Prog → EngPhon → RemoveSuffixBoundary

The actual implementation of the manipulation of the English definitions again consists of a sequence of often quite complex regular expressions, enumerated above in (9). The application of these regular expressions depends on the assumed templatic structure of the base definition phrase, as exemplified earlier above in (6). In general, at various positions in the template the regular expressions either 1) identify elements as particular arguments or modifiers with place-holder markers which are eventually converted into the desired target form, or 2) insert elements to convey the desired tense, modality, and polarity.

As the very first thing, various tags indicating the desired manipulation, in terms of the subject and direct object as well as tense, aspect, and other modalities including negation, are expected to precede the English definition that is to be manipulated. These tags are converted into P-style flag-diacritics that can be used to select and filter the desired manipulation. The order and optionality of the full set of possible tags is enumerated in the first regular expression, named `Input`, shown here in (10) below. A detailed overview of the possible tags available for English verb phrase generation, with their combinatorics and exponents, is presented in Appendix C.

(10)
```
regex [ (Clause | Modality) [
TenseAspect | Auxiliary ] Subject
(DirectObject) (IndirectObject)
(Progressive) (Repetitive) (Negation)
Letters+ ] ;
define Input
```

After this, the regular expression named `Standardization` is used to identify and replace with unambiguous multicharacter symbols the various argument markers for the subject or existential "there", the possessive and reflexive markers that should correspond with the subject, the possible direct object and indirect object markers, and the copula verb "is", so that they cannot be confused with the subsequent manipulations. This is followed by a sequence of regular expressions from `VerbInflection2` through `BeInflection`, which either 1) insert various auxiliary verbs or longer auxiliary constructions, sometimes in co-ordination with an prepended element in the initial zone before the subject/existential marker or at the end of the phrase (before the sense-demarcating punctuation), or 2) convert the finite copula verb or finite regular verb, occurring immediately after the subject marker, into the appropriate forms which are needed for agreement with the auxiliary verb constructions, i.e. present or past tense, present (progressive) or past participle, or the bare infinitive form. Importantly, the entire set of these alternative constructions are always generated, but they are marked with sets of R-type flag diacritics that indicate which initial tag-based P-type flag diacritics they are allowed/required to co-occur with, resulting in (ideally) only one of the generated manipulations getting filtered for final output. To simplify encoding, many P-type and R-type flags, as well as D-type flags (for disallowing contexts) are grouped into named sets that explicitly enumerate the conditions where the particular variant English verb-form is the appropriate one.

Auxiliary Construction	**Flags**
wants to	@R.tense.Int@ @D.neg@ @D.prog@ RsubjectPrs3Sg
want to	@R.tense.Int@ @D.neg@ @D.prog@ DsubjectPrs3Sg
does not want to	@R.tense.Int@ @R.neg.Neg@ @D.prog@ RsubjectPrs3Sg
do not want to	@R.tense.Int@ @R.neg.Neg@ @D.prog@ DsubjectPrs3Sg
wants to be	@R.tense.Int@ @D.neg@ @R.prog.Prog@ RsubjectPrs3Sg
want to be	@R.tense.Int@ @D.neg@ @R.prog.Prog@ DsubjectPrs3Sg
does not want to be	@R.tense.Int@ @R.neg.Neg@ @R.prog.Prog@ RsubjectPrs3Sg
do not want to be	@R.tense.Int@ @R.neg.Neg@ @R.prog.Prog@ DsubjectPrs3Sg

Table 3. The 8 possible realizations of the Future Intentional auxiliary phrase, with associated flags.

Furthermore, in a step beyond the verb phrase analyzer, the various auxiliary verbs and constructions are organized as completely written out sets of constructions following 4-8 patterns, depending on the possible variation arising for each tense/aspect/modality feature and negation; these constructions are then inserted as single "pre-fabricated" chunks between the first subject-marking pronoun and the immediately following predicate zone. Due to diverging patterns between copular and regular finite verbs, two sets of constructions are specified. Crucially, each construction determines what form of the finite verb (or copula) is required (to follow the auxiliary construction). This templating approach turned out absolutely necessary in order to allow for the efficient maintenance of the verb phrase generator, and it has also proven to enable the easy addition of new modalities, in comparison to the jungle of flag-diacritics that arose from initially trying to insert the exponents of various features individually one by one. An example of the set of constructions for various variants of the *future intentional* modality is shown in Table 3 above.

After the generation and insertion of all the possible variants, the various subject, object, and other multicharacter markers are converted with the regular expressions from `IObjectConversion` through `itNonSubjectUnmarking` into the pronouns or nouns specified in the original tags. Then, the regular expressions from `EngInf2Inf` through `EngProg2Prog` provide the correct forms for irregular or regular English verbs occurring in the CW dictionary, while the subsequent regular expression `EngPhon` deals with the orthophonemic variation in the case of all the remaining regular verbs, and the final regular expression `RemoveSuffixBoundary` cleans up the results. An example of the results of English phrase generation, with a first person singular subject and a third person plural object (when applicable), in the future prospective tense, is shown below in (11-13) for the English definitions provided above (in 6-8), with subject/object/existential markers in blue and the inserted auxiliary construction in red.

The FOMA-compiled English verb phrase generator reaches 30.6 MB in (uncompressed) size. One should again note that the full implementation involves a *morphodict* code module, with mappings between Plains Cree word-form analysis tags to English phrase generation tags, which is not discussed here (but see Footnote 7 above).

(11) *niwî-wîcihâwak* (to help s.o.)

- **I** am going to help **them**, **I** am going to assist **them** (CW)
- **I** am going to provide welfare to **them** (CW)
- **I** am going to assist **them** in childbirth, **I** am going to serve as a midwife to **them** (CW)
- **I** am going to help **them**. (MD)
- **I** am going to aid **them**. (MD)
- **I** am going to help **them**. (MD)
- **I** am going to assist **them** (AECD)
- **I** am going to participate (AECD)

(12) *niwî-nisitohtên (to understand [s.t.])*

- **I** am going to understand (CW) (MD)
- **I** am going to understand **something** (CW) (AECD)

(13) *wî-mispon* (to snow)

- **it** is going to snow, **it** is going to be snowing, **there** is going to be falling snow, **there** is going to be a snowfall (CW)
- **It** is going to be snowing. (MD)
- **it** is going to snow, or **it** is going to be snowing (AECD)

3.2 English noun phrase generation

Similar to the verbs, the structure of the English definitions in the three Plains Cree-to-English dictionaries is convergent, with commas/semicolons used to distinguish different senses. But in contrast to verbs, our task is both simpler and more difficult, in that we only need to identify a single anchor word in each noun phrase/sense, namely the noun head, but there is no unambiguous marker word we can rely on throughout; while empirical investigation of the definitions indicate this to be mostly either the word immediately preceding a postmodifying prepositional or relative phrase, or otherwise the final word preceding the sense-demarcating punctuation character or the end of the definition, not all prepositions initiate a postmodifying phrase. An example of English definitions for *okimâw* "chief" is provided below in (14), with the head noun marked underlined in **bold-face**.

(14) *okimâw* "chief":

- **chief**, **leader**, head **person**, **man** of high position (CW)
- **king** (CW)
- **boss** (CW)
- one's **superior** (CW)
- **manager** (CW)
- A **chief**. (MD)
- A **man** in high position. (MD)
- a **leader** on a job site, i.e.: a boss (AECD)
- government **leader**, **manager** (AECD)

Anyhow, the generation of English noun phrases that can be matched with the inflectional features available for Plains Cree noun forms is organized similar to the verb phrase generation described above, but it is overall substantially simpler, and currently has not been partitioned into named constituent regular expressions. One needs only specify one among the mutually exclusive features for either singular or plural number, obviation, locative or distributive form, followed by an optional possessor and optional diminutivization. A detailed overview of the possible tags available for English noun phrase generation with their exponents is presented in Appendix D.

As with the verbs, the tags specifying these features precede the definition to be manipulated, and are first converted into P-type tags. Then, any initial articles or possessive pronouns in the original English definition are removed. After this, an optional modifier "little" indicating a diminutive form can be prepended to the remaining noun phrase, which in turn can be prepended with an optional possessive pronoun, followed by the pronoun "other" in the case of an obviative form. Finally, the possible alternatives among the number/obviation/location complex are added: either the locative or distributive preposition, "in" or "among", is prepended at the very beginning, or an indefinite article for singular number (which combines into "another" in the case of obviation), or the plural suffix *–(e)s* is added to the word at the end of the noun phrase marked by a final string boundary or punctuation separating senses, or if the noun phrase ends with a postmodifying phrase starting with "of", "for", "with", "among", or "who", then to the word immediately preceding these prepositions or relative pronoun. For some 88 irregular English plural nouns the appropriate forms are enumerated, while for the remaining pluralized nouns regular orthophonemic rules are applied. As with the verbs, the complete set of all possible outcomes are generated with associated R-type flags, which allow for the selection of the one desired noun phrase which matches the P-type flags specified by the initial tags. An example of creating plural first-person-singular possessed forms of the definitions above is shown here in (15) (with the incorrect generations ~~struck-through~~). The FOMA-compiled English noun phrase generator reaches 56.9 MB in (uncompressed) size.

(15) *nitokimâmak* "chief":

- my **chief**s, my **leader**s, my head **person**s, my **men** of high position (CW)
- my **king**s (CW)
- my **boss**es (CW)
- ~~my one's **superior**~~s (CW)
- my **manager**s (CW)
- my **chief**s. (MD)
- ~~my **man** in high **position**~~s. (MD)
- ~~my **leader** on a job site~~s, i.e.: my bosses (AECD)
- my government **leader**s, my **manager**s (AECD)

4 Evaluation

To evaluate the English phrase generation, focusing on verbs, with greater complexity, a combination of the extended Plains Cree layouts, a Plains Cree corpus, and the English definitions in the three dictionaries was used to attempt to generate 2253 English phrases corresponding to the Cree morpho-syntactic features for each word-form cell in all these verb paradigms. A quantitative scrutiny showed the English phrase generation was able to generate a manipulated phrase for 2151 (95.5%) of the verb cells, taking 0.457s on a MacBook Pro with an Apple M4 Max CPU. A comprehensive manual evaluation of the generated phrases is under way, but preliminary results for the first 1500 phrases indicate that 1252 (83.5%) are fully well-formed. For evaluating English phrase analysis, we used the aforementioned generations to create 5430 simple English verb phrases, which were then run through the analyzing transducer. For 4268 (78.6%) of these phrases, the transducer provided exactly the same set of morphosyntactic features as were used to generate the phrase.

A qualitative evaluation of the remaining unsatisfactory behavior suggests that this is due to co-ordinated predicate constructions ("Xs and/or Ys") not yet covered by the verb phrase generator, structural ambiguity of some high-frequency verbs (e.g. "lie/lied" vs. "lie/lay"), and missing some orthographical variants of the subject and object markers in the English definitions in the three dictionaries. Another point of improvement concerns the identification and removal of some forms of parenthetical content in the English definitions, usually marked with bracketing, which can confuse the phrase transductors, if missed.

5 Conclusion

This paper presented rule-based finite-state transducers for analyzing and generating simple English phrases, matching the most common inflected Plains Cree verb and noun word-forms. These transducers have been incorporated in the on-line intelligent Plains Cree-English dictionary, *itwêwina*, using the *morphodict* platform (see Appendix E for example screenshots). Combined with a matching Plains Cree morphological transducer and mappings between the English and Plains Cree features, this in effect results in restricted machine translation between the two languages. The morphosyntactic features covered by these English phrase transducers have been extended beyond Cree to cover ones apparent in other Algonquian and Dene languages. While not explored in detail in this paper, this can in principle enable the implementation of the same functionalities for other similar languages.

Limitations

The English phrases that the tools presented in this paper can analyze and generate are restricted to constructions roughly matching the inflected Cree word-forms contained in so-called extended paradigms. One must keep in mind that these recognized constructions are only a very small subset of all possible constructions in English; while the most common Cree word-forms are covered, many rarer inflected word-forms are not. Perhaps more importantly, the generated English phrases should be considered only as rough approximate translations of the corresponding Cree word-forms, and should **not** be used as a replacement for consulting fluent speakers for translations.

The compiled data structures resulting from the finite-state approach employed in this paper, when combining both the analysis/generation of English phrase structure and of certain English word-forms within these constructions, can end up being prohibitively large (in hundreds of megabytes or even bigger), which will be challenging to integrate within other applications, and may be slow to look up. Features that are necessary, such as keeping track of already seen elements (memory) and the precise identification of word and phrase boundaries, are cumbersome to implement in finite-state specifications, requiring flag-diacritics that are notoriously difficult to parse and debug. Based on some preliminary trials, procedural coding approaches (e.g. with Python) would appear to provide an alternative that can implement all the desired features incorporated in the finite-scale models discussed in this paper, and beyond, while at the same time being sufficiently fast and not exploding required memory.

Ethics Statement

The on-line Plains Cree-English dictionary described in this paper has been developed in order to support the explicit objectives of Cree language communities to support their language instruction, maintenance, and revitalization activities. The functionality presented in this paper has been fine-tuned based on feedback from various individuals in Cree-speaking communities.

Acknowledgments

The English phrase analysis and generation tools presented in this paper are greatly facilitated by the systematic structure of the English definitions in the three Plains Cree-English dictionaries that we have received access to, courtesy of Dr. Earle Waugh (AECD), the Maskwacîs Education Schools Commission (MD), and Dr. Arok Wolvengrey (CW). I am grateful to all their authors and editors for their consistency, and in particular Dr. Wolvengrey, who has also proposed the standard English translation templates for the most common inflected Cree word-forms, forming the basis for the generation of the corresponding English phrases. The initial idea for connecting inflecting Cree word-forms directly with matching English phrases was suggested to me by Dr. Jordan Lachler, while the flag-diacritic approach which allows for keeping the size of the compiled transducers reasonable was suggested and explained to me by Dr. Miikka Silfverberg. The practical integration of the English phrase analyzers as a functionality within *itwêwina* and *morphodict* was implemented and improved in various stages by Andrew Neitsch, Jolene Poulin, and Dr. Felipe Bañados Schwerter. The details of the implementation have evolved based on feedback from Cree and other learners and instructors in the communities and the academia. The current though yet on-going quantitative evaluation of the transducers is based on manual scrutiny by Alexis Ibarra. Finally, this work has been supported by the SSHRC Partnership Grant *21st Century Tools for Indigenous Languages* (895-2019-1012).

References

Antti Arppe, Andrew Neitsch, Daniel Dacanay, Jolene Poulin, Daniel Hieber, and Atticus Harrigan. 2023. Finding words that aren't there: Using word embeddings to improve dictionary search for low-resource languages. *Proceedings of the Workshop on Natural Language Processing for Indigenous Languages of the Americas (AmericasNLP)*, pages 144–155, Toronto, Canada. Association for Computational Linguistics.

Antti Arppe, Jolene Poulin, Eddie Antonio Santos, Andrew Neitsch, Atticus Harrigan, Katherine Schmirler, and Arok Wolvengrey. 2022. Towards a morphologically intelligent and user-friendly on-line dictionary of Plains Cree – next next round. Presentation at the *54th Algonquian Conference*, Boulder, Colorado, October 20-23, 2022. https://altlab.ualberta.ca/wp-content/uploads/2023/03/itwewinaAC54Oct2022.pptx.pdf

Isaac Caswell. 2024. Google Translate learns Inuktut. https://blog.google/intl/en-ca/company-news/technology/google-translate-learns-inuktut/. Accessed: 2024-11-05.

Atticus Harrigan., Katherine Schmirler, Antti Arppe, Lene Antonsen, Trond Trosterud, and Arok Wolvengrey. 2017. Learning from the computational modelling of Plains Cree verbs. *Morphology*, 27, pages 565–598.

Mans Hulden. 2009. Foma: a finite-state compiler and library. *Proceedings of the Demonstrations Session at EACL 2009*, pages 29–32.

Rebecca Knowles, Darlene Stewart, Samuel Larkin, and Patrick Littell. 2020. NRC Systems for the 2020 Inuktitut-English News Translation Task. In *Proceedings of the Fifth Conference on Machine Translation*, pages 156–170. Association for Computational Linguistics.

Tan Ngoc Le and Fatiha Sadat. 2020. Low-Resource NMT: an Empirical Study on the Effect of Rich Morphological Word Segmentation on Inuktitut. In *Proceedings of the 14th Conference of the Association for Machine Translation in the Americas (Volume 1: Research Track)*, pages 165–172. Association for Machine Translation in the Americas.

Nancy LeClaire and George Cardinal, G (compilers); Earle H. Waugh (editor). 2002. *Alberta Elders' Cree Dictionary / alperta ohci kehtehayak nehiyaw otwestamâkewasinahikan*. University of Alberta Press, Edmonton, Alberta.

Krister Lindén, Erik Axelson, Sam Hardwick, Tommi A. Pirinen, and Miikka Silfverberg. 2011. HFST—framework for compiling and applying morphologies. *Systems and frameworks for computational morphology: Second International Workshop, SFCM 2011*, Zürich, Switzerland, August 26, 2011. Proceedings 2, pages 67–85.

Patrick Littell, Anna Kazantseva, Roland Kuhn, Aidan Pine, Antti Arppe, Christopher Cox, and Marie-Odile Junker. 2018. Indigenous language technologies in Canada: Assessment, challenges, and successes. In *Proceedings of the 27th International Conference on Computational Linguistics*, pages 2620–2632, Santa Fe, New Mexico, USA. Association for Computational Linguistics.

Maskwachees Cultural College. 2009. *Maskwacîs Dictionary of Cree Words / Nêhiyaw Pîkiskwêwinisa*. Maskwacîs, Alberta.

Microsoft Translator. 2021. Inuktitut is now available in Microsoft Translator! *Microsoft Translator Blog*. https://www.microsoft.com/enus/translator/blog/2021/01/27/inuktitutis-now-available-in-microsofttranslator/. Accessed: 31-03-2025.

Conor Snoek, Dorothy Thunder, Kaidi Lõo, Antti Arppe, Jordan Lachler, Sjur Moshagen, and Trond Trosterud. 2014. Modeling the noun morphology of Plains Cree. *Proceedings of the 2014 workshop on the Use of Computational Methods in the Study of Endangered Languages (ComputEL)*, Baltimore, Maryland, pages 34–42.

Arok Wolvengrey (editor) 2001. *nêhiyawêwin: itwêwina / Cree: Words*. Canadian Plains Research Center, Regina, Saskatchewan.

Arok Wolvengrey. 2001. *Semantic and pragmatic functions in Plains Cree syntax*. LOT dissertation series 268, LOT, Utrecht, the Netherlands.

Appendix A. Example analyses of English verb phrases in Table 1.

Initial zone + Subject/Existential + Predicate zone + Object/Reflexive + Final zone	English analysis: Lexical	English analysis: Morphosyntax	Cree FST generation tags	Cree verb form
we help>0 you	help	+V+TA+1Pl+2SgO	wîcihêw+V+TA+Ind+1Pl+2SgO	kiwîcihitinân
we help>ed you all	help	+V+TA+Prt+1Pl+2PlO	PV/kî+wîcihêw+V+TA+Ind+1Pl+2PlO	kikî-wîcihitinân
we will help you	help	+V+TA+Def+1Pl+2SgO	PV/ka+wîcihêw+V+TA+Ind+1Pl+2SgO	kika-wîcihitinân
we are going to help you all	help	+V+TA+Fut+1Pl+2PlO	PV/wî+wîcihêw+V+TA+Ind+1Pl+2PlO	kiwî-wîcihitinân
let you and us help him later	help	+V+TA+Del+21Pl+3SgO	wîcihêw+V+TA+Imp+Del+12Pl+3SgO	wîcihâhkahk
do not let you and us help her now	help	+V+TA+Imm+21Pl+3SgO+Neg	namôya+Ipc wîcihêw+V+TA+Imp+Imm+12Pl+3SgO	namôya wîcihâtân
for us to help you	help	+V+TA+Inf+1Pl+2SgO	PV/ka+wîcihêw+V+TA+Cnj+1Pl+2SgO	ka-wîcihitâhk
when we help you all	help	+V+TA+Cond+1Pl+2PlO	wîcihêw+V+TA+Fut+Cond+1Pl+2PlO	wîcihitâhki
there is light	is light	+V+II+0Sg	kîsikâw+V+II+Ind+3Sg	kîsikâw
there is not light	is light	+V+II+0Sg+Neg	namôya+Ipc kîsikâw+V+II+Ind+3Sg	namôya kîsikâw
it is red	is red	+V+II+0Sg	mihkwâw+V+II+Ind+3Sg	mihkwâw
we do not help you	help	+V+TA+1Pl+2SgO+Neg	namôya+Ipc wîcihêw+V+TA+Ind+1Pl+2SgO	namôya kiwîcihitinân
we are ready	is ready	+V+AI+1Pl	kwêyâtisiw+V+AI+Ind+1Pl	nikwêyâtisinân
we are not ready	is ready	+V+AI+1Pl+Neg	namôya+Ipc kwêyâtisiw+V+AI+Ind+1Pl	namôya nikwêyâtisinân

Appendix B. Example analyses of English noun phrases in Table 2.

Number / Locative + Possessor + Diminutive + Noun head + Obviation	English analysis: Lexical	English analysis: Morpho-Syntactic	Cree FST generation tags	Cree noun form
one bear	bear	+N+Sg	maskwa+N+A+Sg	maskwa
many bear>s	bear	+N+Pl	maskwa+N+A+Pl	maskwak
bear over there	bear	+N+Obv	maskwa+N+A+Obv	maskwa
my one book	book	+N+Px1Sg+Sg	masinahikan+N+I+Px1Sg+Sg	nimasinahikan
my little book	book	+Dim+Px1Sg+Pl	masinahikan+N+I+Der/Dim+N+I+Px1Sg+Pl	nimasinahikanisa
in a book	book	+N+Loc	masinahikan+N+I+Loc	masinahikanihk
among bear>s	bear	+N+Distr	maskwa+N+A+Distr	maskonâhk
in my many book>s	book	+N+Px1Sg+Pl	masinahikan+N+I+Px1Sg+Pl	nimasinahikana
my other little tree over there	tree	+N+Dim+Px1Sg+Obv	mîtos+N+A+Der/Dim+N+A+Px1Sg+Obv	nimîcosimisa

Appendix C. A detailed overview of the tags and their exponents for the English verb phrase generator (optional argument types in parentheses).[7] [8]

(Clause)	**Tense Aspect**[9]	**Subject**	**(Direct Object)**	**(Indirect Object)**	**(Progressive)**	**(Repetitive)**	**(Negation)**
Rel+: who; which Cnj+: as	Prs+: -(e)s Prt+: -(e)d Def+: will Fut+: is going to Int+: wants to Cond+:when Inf+: for s.o. to ... Imm+: let s.o. ... now Del+: let s.o. ... later Prf1+: has done s.t. Prf2+: had done s.t.	0Sg+: it 1Sg+: I 2Sg+: you 3Sg+: he/she 1Du+: we both 2Du+: you both 3Du+: they both 1Distr+: each and every one of us 2Distr+: each and every one of you 3Distr+: each and every one of them: 0Pl+: they 1Pl+: we 21Pl+: you and we 2Pl+: you all 3Pl+: they 4Sg+: another 4Pl+: others 4Sg/Pl+: yet an/other(s) 5Sg/Pl+: yet others X+: someone XPl+: people	0SgO+: it 1SgO+: me 2SgO+: you 3SgO+: him/her 1DuO+: us both 2DuO+: you both 3DuO+: them both 1DistrO+: each and every one of us 2DistrO+: each and every one of you 3DistrO+: each and every one of them 0PlO+: them 1PlO+: us 21PlO+: you and us 2PlO+: you all 3PlO+: them 4Sg/PlO+: an/other(s) 5Sg/PlO+: yet an/other(s) XO+: someone XPlO+: people	1SgIO+: to me 2SgIO+: to you 3SgIO+: to him/her 1DuIO+: to us both 2DuIO+: to you both 3DuIO+: to them both 1PlIO+: to us 21PlIO+: to you and us 2PlIO+: to you all 3PlIO+: to them 4Sg/PlIO+: to an/other(s) 5Sg/PlIO+: to yet an/other(s) XIO+: to someone XPlIO+: to people	Prog+: be ... -ing	Rept+: again and again; repeatedly	Neg+: not
(Modality) Obl2+: has to Nec2+: needs to Abl2+: is able to Perm2+: is allowed to Int2+: wants to Hab+: keeps on Init+: starts Fin+: finishes	**Auxiliary** Obl+: must Nec+: needs to Abl+: can Perm+: may Int+: wants to Poss+: could Rec+: should Pred+: would						

[7] The features used for English verb phrase generation are a superset of the features available for English verb phrase analysis. Furthermore, the tags for English verb phrase analysis are similar to the ones for English verb phrase generation, with the analysis tags preceded by a plus sign (e.g. `+1Sg` or `+Prt`) and all the tags following the English core lexical content resulting from the analysis (e.g. "I slept well" → `sleep well +Prt+1Sg`), whereas the generation tags are followed by a plus sign and all the tags precede the English core sentence frame that is to be manipulated (e.g. `Prt+1Sg+s/he sleeps well` → "I slept well").

[8] Example with maximal types of generation tags: `Abl2+Fut+1Sg+2SgO+3PlIO+Prog+Rept+Neg+s/he transfer s.o. to s.b.` → "I am not going to be being able to transfer you to them again and again".

[9] Features for Tense/Aspect and Auxiliary (i.e. simple modality, which consists of auxiliary verbs which cannot be further inflected) are mutually exclusive, whereas features for Tense/Aspect or Auxiliary can be combined with features for Modality (which are periphrastic constructions where the first element is treated as the finite verb that can be fully inflected).

Appendix D. A detailed overview of the tags and their exponents for the English noun phrase generator (optional argument types in parentheses).[10] [11]

Number/ Obviation	(Diminutive)	(Possession)
Sg+: a(n)	Dim+: little	Px1Sg+: my
Pl+: -(e)s		Px2Sg+: your
Obv+: an/other … -s		Px3Sg+: his/her
		Px1Pl+: our
Locative/ Distributive		Px12Pl+: your and our
Loc+: in		Px2Pl+: your
Distr+: among		PxPx3Pl+: their
		Px4Sg/Pl+: another's/others'
		PxX+: someone's

[10] The features used for English noun phrase generation are (currently) equivalent to the features available for English noun phrase analysis. Furthermore, the tags for English noun phrase analysis are similar to the ones for English noun phrase generation, with the analysis tags preceded by a plus sign (e.g. `+Pl` or `+Px1Sg`) and all the tags following the English core lexical content resulting from the analysis (e.g. "my little black books" → `black book +N+Dim+Px1Sg+Pl`), whereas the generation tags are followed by a plus sign and all the tags precede the English core phrase frame that is to be manipulated (e.g. `Pl+Dim+Px1Sg+ a black book` → "my little black books"). Importantly, in noun phrase generation a space character is currently required after the tags, before the phrase to be manipulated. Note also that the order of tags differs between noun phrase analysis, i.e. `(Diminutive) (Possession) Number/Locative`, and noun phrase generation, i.e. `Number/Locative (Diminutive) (Possession)`.

[11] Examples with maximal combinations of generation tags: `Obv+Dim+Px12Pl+ a black book` → "our and our other little black book(s)"; `Loc+Dim+Px4Sg/Pl+ a black book` → "in another's/others' little black book".

Appendix E. Screenshots of *itwêwina*, with the English phrase analysis and generation integrated, exemplified with searches with "I helped you" and its approximate Cree match *kikîwîcihitin* (with inflectional morpheme boundaries marked with middle-dots).

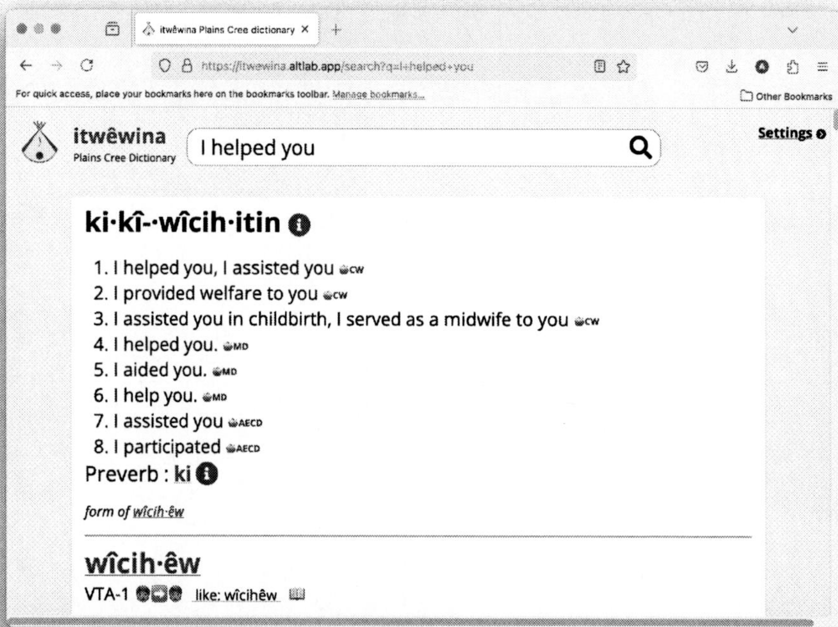

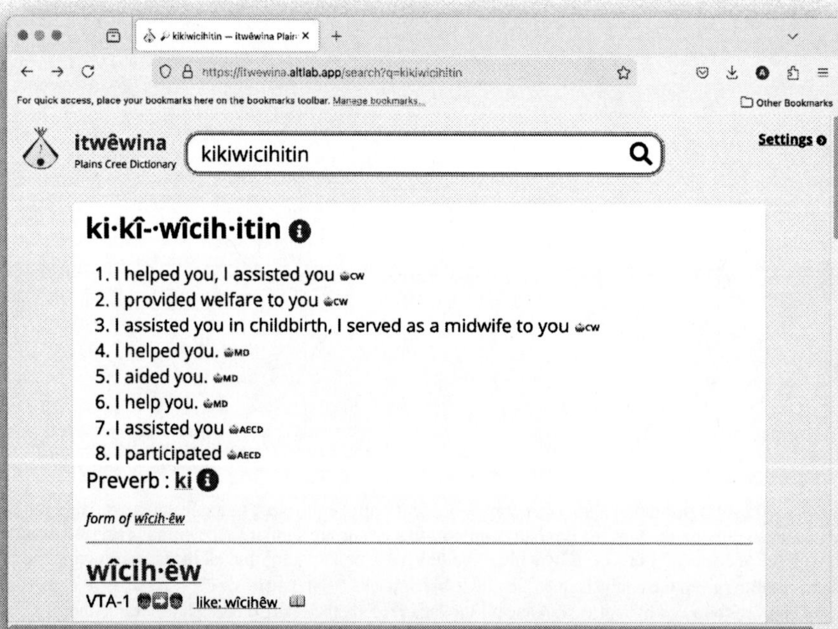

Unsupervised, Semi-Supervised and LLM-Based Morphological Segmentation for Bribri

Carter Anderson
Dartmouth College
carter.d.anderson.26@dartmouth.edu

Mien Nguyen
Dartmouth College
josephinee.nguyen@gmail.com

Rolando Coto-Solano
Dartmouth College
rolando.a.coto.solano@dartmouth.edu

Abstract

Morphological Segmentation is a major task in Indigenous language documentation. In this paper we introduce a novel statistical algorithm called Morphemo to split words into their constituent morphemes, and we compare its performance to five other methods for morphological segmentation, including large language models (LLMs). We use these tools to analyze Bribri, an under-resourced Indigenous language from Costa Rica. Morphemo has better performance than the LLM when splitting multimorphemic words, mainly because the LLMs are more conservative tend to leave words under-analyzed, which gives them an advantage with monomorphemic words. In future work we will use these tools to tag Bribri language corpora, which currently lack morphological segmentation. A Python implementation of Morphemo is publicly available.

Resumen

Segmentación morfológica del Bribri con métodos no-supervisados, supervisados y basados en modelos grandes del lenguaje. La segmentación morfológica es una tarea importante en la documentación de lenguas indígenas. En este artículo presentamos un nuevo algoritmo estadístico llamado Morphemo, que divide las palabras en sus respectivos morfemas. Además, comparamos el desempeño de Morfemo con cinco otro algoritmos, incluyendo modelos grande de lenguaje (LLM). Usamos estas herramientas para analizar el bribri, una lengua indígenas de bajos recursos de Costa Rica. Morphemo tiene mejor rendimiento al dividir palabras multimorfémicas, sobretodo porque los LLMs es más conservadores y dejan más palabras sin analizar, lo que a su vez les da una ventaja al lidiar con palabras monomorfémicas. En el futuro usaremos estas herramientas para anotar corpus de lengua bribri, que en este momento carecen de segmentación morfológica. Finalmente, liberamos una versión en Python de Morfemo, disponible públicamente.

1 Introduction

Natural Language Processing can be a useful tool to accelerate the documentation of Indigenous languages. Numerous 'bottlenecks' make the work considerably more time-consuming than for majority languages (Seifart et al., 2018), and easing these bottlenecks can free up the time of linguists, language teachers and activists to perform their time-critical work towards language teaching, revitalization and reclamation.

In this paper we have two goals. First, we will study how a probability-based statistical algorithm can provide good performance in the task of morphological segmentation. Second, we will also study how Large Language Models (LLMs) perform this task, and their advantages and disadvantages compared to statistical methods.

1.1 Morphological Segmentation in Indigenous Languages

Morphological segmentation is a key aspect of linguistic documentation, and the highest-priority task when performing interlinearized annotation of minority-language data (Moeller, 2025). In Indigenous languages this task is particularly complicated because the paucity of data makes it difficult to train automated segmentation tools.

Much past work on low-resource languages has taken an unsupervised learning approach (Hammarström and Borin, 2011; Kurimo et al., 2010; Khandagale et al., 2022; Eskander et al., 2020). This is often preferred or, in some cases, required because it eschews the need for a labeled corpus of data for training, which is particularly difficult to develop for low-resource languages. Mott et al. (2020) examined the effectiveness of existing unsupervised models (models that only train on unlabeled data) cross a range of low-resource languages with 2000 tokens. They found average F1 scores were generally between 0.2 to 0.6, with a mean be-

Proceedings of the Fifth Workshop on NLP for Indigenous Languages of the Americas (AmericasNLP), pages 63–76
May 4, 2025

low 0.5. However, even this limited success must be tempered by the reality that much of these systems' accuracy derives from their correct prediction of monomorphemic words.[1] Put another way, the system is good at analyzing words without a morpheme boundary, in which the system is correct simply by not segmenting. When performing morphological segmentation, it is imperative that a tool can actually segment a multimorphemic word into its constituent morphemes.

A semi-supervised model trains on both labeled and unlabeled data. This can allow a small set of annotated data to supplement a significantly larger collection of unannotated data. Comprising on the limits of data collection and the need for effective segmentation, recent scholarship has focused on semi-supervised systems (Kohonen et al., 2010; Ruokolainen et al., 2016). For instance, for English, Finnish, and Turkish, a semi-supervised approach achieved F1 scores of 0.8 to 0.9, despite the annotated data comprising less than 1% of the overall dataset (Ruokolainen et al., 2014). Although these datasets have hundreds of thousands of unlabeled tokens, significantly greater than the Bribri corpus that will be used here (see section 2.3 for details), they demonstrate effectiveness with approximately 1000 labeled tokens.

There is some recent work on using LLMs for morphological segmentation (Weissweiler et al., 2023; Ács, 2025), and for segmentation of low-resource languages in particular. For example, ChatGPT-4o (Hurst et al., 2024) has shown morpheme segmentation accuracies between 13% and 50% for languages like Lezgi and Uspanteko (Ginn et al., 2024).

1.2 Bribri Morphology and NLP

Bribri is a Chibchan language spoken in Southern Costa Rica and northern Panama. It has a estimated total of 7000 speakers (INEC, 2011), and it is classified as a vulnerable language (Sánchez Avendaño, 2013), given that many children in the community no longer speak it. The language has a relatively high number of written resources compared to other languages in its family. It has a grammar (Jara, 2018), an online and a print dictionary (Margery, 2005; Krohn, 2021), two textbooks (Constenla et al., 2004; Jara Murillo and García Segura, 2013), an oral corpus (Flores-Solórzano, 2017a,b), and several schoolbooks (Sánchez Avendaño et al., 2021a,b) and books with traditional stories translated into Spanish and English (García Segura, 2016; Jara Murillo and García Segura, 2022).

Bribri is a morphologically inflectional language. Table 1 has examples of nominal, verbal and adjectival suffixes. The first word, *alìnu̲k* 'to be cooked', has suffixes for the middle voice and the infinitive. The second word is the pronoun *ie'pa* 'they', with the plural suffix -pa attached to the 3rd person singular pronoun. The third word, *bua'ë* 'very good', is an adjective with an intensifier suffix.

Word	Morphemes	Meaning
1. *alìnu̲k*	`al+ìn+u̲k`	'to be cooked'
2. *ie'pa*	`ie'+pa`	'they'
3. *bua'ë*	`bua'+ë`	'very good'

Table 1: Examples of Bribri inflectional suffixes for verbs, nouns and adjectives

In addition to inflectional suffixes, Bribri has numerous derivational suffixes (Jara, 2018). Table 2 shows examples of derivation for nouns, verbs and adjectives. The first two are nouns: *bríbriwak* 'Bribri (person)' has the suffix {-wak} 'person'; the second word, *kalö̀io* 'pants' has the noun *kalö̀* 'foot, leg' and the suffix {-io} 'wearable (thing)'. Words #3 and #4 are verbs. The word *shkö̀kka̲* 'to climb' is composed of the verb *shkö̀k* 'to walk' and the directional suffix {-ka̲}, 'upwards', so this word literally means 'to up-walk'. Verb #4, *kù̲kwa̲* 'to find', is made up of the verb *kù̲k* 'to pull' and the directional suffix {-wa̲} 'inwards', and so it literally means 'to in-pull'. Finally, the fifth word is the adjective *dawèie* 'sick', made up of the noun *dawè* 'sickness' plus a suffix that forms adjectives.

Word	Morphemes	Meaning
1. *bríbriwak*	`bríbri+wak`	'Bribri person'
2. *kalö̀io*	`kalö̀+io`	'pants'
3. *shkö̀kka̲*	`shk+ö̀k+ka̲`	'to climb'
4. *kù̲kwa̲*	`k+ù̲k+wa̲`	'to find'
5. *dawèie*	`dawè+ie`	'sick'

Table 2: Examples of Bribri derivational suffixes for nouns, verbs and adjectives

Finally, Bribri exhibits compounding and reduplication as morphological processes. Table 3 shows examples of such words. The word *kalö̀tök*

[1]Monomorphemic words are words with a single identifiable meaningful unit, for example, 'run' in English. Contrast this with multimorphemic words, where multiple meaningful units can be identified, such as 'running' or 'runner' which are each composed of 'run' and some other component ('-ing' or '-er') that indicates tense or a person who does the action.

is a compound of the word *kalö̀* 'foot, leg' and the verb *tö̆k* 'to hit'. The second word, *tsìrtsir* is the plural form of the adjective 'small', and it is a partial reduplication of *tsìr* 'small' (notice how the second part has a different tone). The third word, *máshmash* 'orange (color)', is a partial reduplication of the adjective *màtk* 'red'.

Word	Morphemes	Meaning
1. *kalö̀tök*	kalö̀+t+ök	'to dance'
2. *tsìrtsir*	tsìr+tsir	'small' (pl.)
3. *máshmash*	másh+mash	'orange (color)'

Table 3: Examples of Bribri compounding and partial reduplication

There has been work on Bribri NLP, including speech recognition for Bribri and its sister language Cabécar (Coto-Solano, 2021; Coto-Solano et al., 2024), and forced alignment for Bribri, Cabécar, and Malecu, another Chibchan language (Coto-Solano and Solórzano, 2016; Solórzano and Coto-Solano, 2017; Coto-Solano et al., 2022). There has also been work on machine translation (Feldman and Coto-Solano, 2020; Kann et al., 2022; Jones et al., 2023; Ebrahimi et al., 2024) and the study of semantics through embeddings (Coto-Solano, 2022). There are also tools to extend the usage of the language, such as keyboards (Solórzano, 2010) and digital dictionaries (Krohn, 2020).

Additionally, there has been previous NLP work on Bribri morphology. Chiruzzo et al. (2024) worked on morphological prediction for the creation of language learning tools, and Karson and Coto-Solano (2024) worked with morphological tagging using UFEATS (de Marneffe et al., 2021), reaching a precision of 80%. Flores-Solórzano (2019) used an FST to annotate a corpus (Flores-Solórzano, 2017a). For example, the word *mè̱ke̱ka̱* 'to put (something) in (something in an upward direction)' produces the output a̱me̱+V+Imp1Tran+Imp2+Dir[ascenso]. Here we will focus on segmentation per se, so that we can get an output form like m+è̱+ke̱+ka̱, where the root, the thematic vowel, the imperfect aspect and the directionals are separated automatically.

2 Methodology

In order to test the segmentation of Bribri morphemes, we will compare the performance of our novel, statistical algorithm (Morphemo) to an unsupervised algorithm (BPE), a semi-supervised algorithm (Morfessor), and to direct prompting from a commercial LLM algorithm (Claude 3.7 Sonnet). We will train and test the algorithms using two pre-existing corpora for Bribri.

2.1 Morphological Segmentation Algorithms

We chose byte-pair encoding, or BPE (Gage, 1994) as a baseline due to its completely unsupervised nature. We used a sample of unlabeled Bribri text to train the BPE tokens (more information about this data in section 2.3). We compare this to the semi-supervised method used in Morfessor (Virpioja et al., 2013), where pre-labeled Bribri words were used for the training. For example, Morfessor saw shk+è̱n+a̱ for *shkè̱na̱* 'hello'.

We then selected an LLM-based algorithm to compare these statistical methods with state-of-the-art deep learning techniques. The selection of a specific model was not straightforward, and it will be described further in section 4.3 below, but, after a preliminary exploration of the performance of several models, Claude 3.7 Sonnet (Feb 19, 2025) was selected (Anthropic, 2025).

We used three types of LLM evaluation. (1) In the *Zero shot* condition, we provided the LLM with a file that contained the list of words to split (the test set), and a prompt asking the system to split the words into morphemes (see Appendix A for the prompts). (2) In the *Few shot* condition, we uploaded three files: (a) the unlabeled test set, which contains a list of words to split, (b) the unlabeled training set, a longer list of words, without any morpheme boundaries (e.g. *shkè̱na̱*), and (c) the labeled training set, where the words do have marked boundaries (e.g. shk+è̱n+a̱). We upload this data to provide a suggestion for how to label the words with their morpheme boundaries. Along with this upload, we provided a prompt for the system to try to learn from the training sets and apply that to the test set. (3) Finally, in the *Few shot plus unlabeled* condition, we uploaded the same three files, plus a fourth file with unlabeled, monolingual Bribri text from the AmericasNLP collection (Ebrahimi et al., 2022), with a total of 20 thousand additional words. 20 thousand was the maximum size allowed by the context window. We hypothesize that the added text will allow the LLM to gain further understanding of the patterns in Bribri text and therefore increase its performance.

2.2 Morphemo Algorithm

We will compare the algorithms above to our novel algorithm we are calling *Morphemo*.[2] This semi-supervised, N-gram-based algorithm is geared towards morphological segmentation in low-resource settings. Using Bayesian inferences, it examines each point in the word between two characters. Let's consider a two character sequence with the characters NM. Considering the N-grams both before N and after M at that point, as well as the current number of assigned morpheme boundaries n_b at the time of calculation, an estimate of the likelihood of a non-morpheme boundary is:

$$f_{\mathrm{p}}(NM) = P(M|N) * P(N|M) * P(n_{\mathrm{b}}) \quad (1)$$

This is to say, the probability of a non-boundary is the probability of M following N, multiplied by the probability of N preceding M, multiplied by the probability that a word of the same length as our word will have n_b boundaries.

Then, using a slightly altered formula to consider the likelihood of a morpheme boundary b given N and M, the boundary likelihood is:

$$f_{\mathrm{m}}(NM) = P(b|N) * P(b|M) * P(n_{\mathrm{b}} + 1) \quad (2)$$

This is to say, the probability of a boundary between N and M is the probability of a boundary after N, multiplied by the probability of a boundary before M, multiplied by the probability that, given the length of the word, it would have n_b+1 boundaries. Once these probabilities are calculated, the system can decide to apply a boundary or not.

This dual forward and backward-facing N-gram approach is designed to capture the intuition that a) certain n-grams may disproportionately precede a morpheme boundary and b) certain n-grams may disproportionately follow a morpheme boundary, such as common verbal inflections or derivation and compound suffixes. Lastly, the term at the end of the model is meant to prevent the model from both over- and under-segmentation, by preferring boundary insertion steps toward the average number of morphemes for the given word's length. Admittedly, these are broad generalizations that avoid many nuanced morphological features. But they were chosen to give a system trained on little data the best chance of succeeding.

The model trains on both the unlabeled and labeled data by building frequency tables. The unlabeled data is used to note the occurrence of sequences of n-grams in the language as a whole (this is used for the *P(N|M)* and *P(M|N)* in the above functions). The labeled data is used to generate a similar table but with an additional morpheme boundary character, providing a more specific view into the frequency of certain n-grams near morpheme boundaries (this is used for the P(N|b) and P(b|M) in the above functions). Additionally, the labeled data is used to tabulate the number of morphemes per word (for *P(n_b)*).

2.3 Data and Evaluation

The algorithms described above were trained using two types of data. First, the labeled data came from a set of 1410 words in the Universal Dependencies TreeBank in Coto-Solano et al. (2021). These words (and the sentences they come from) were chosen from the oral corpus (Flores-Solórzano, 2017a) and from the Constenla et al. (2004) and Jara Murillo and García Segura (2013) textbooks, and they represent a realistic distribution of Bribri morphology.

The words were manually segmented into morphemes by the authors of this paper, one of whom is a linguist trained in the Bribri language. A random 80% of the words were used for training (1128 words), and the remaining 20% were left aside for testing (282 words). This procedure was repeated 20 times, so the results are reported for 20 iterations of training/testing of each algorithm. In the case of Morphemo and Claude 3.7, the labeled data was supplemented with unlabeled, monolingual Bribri data from the AmericasNLP machine translation corpus (Ebrahimi et al., 2022). This was 85816 words for Morphemo, and only 20000 due to prompt-size restrictions.

We chose F1, a combination of precision and recall, to represent the results (β=1). For each of the models we calculated three variations of F1: (1) The F1 for all of the words, regardless of how many morphemes they have, (2) the F1 but only for the monomorphemic words in the gold-standard, and (3) the F1 but only for the multimorphemic words in the gold-standard. We do this to distinguish the performance of the system when understanding

[2] A Python implementation of Morphemo can be downloaded at https://github.com/Celsian4/bribri-morphology

more complex morphological configurations.[3]

In the case of BPE, we trained the model using the 80% splits of the TreeBank's unlabeled data, and then evaluated it using the remaining 20% of the TreeBank's (manually labeled) data. For Morfessor, we used the 80% of the labeled data, and the remaining 20% for the evaluation. As for Claude Zero Shot, we only used the 20% evaluation sets, but in Claude Few Shot we gave the model both the labeled training data and the evaluation set, and in the Claude Few shot + Unlabeled, we loaded labeled training data, the evaluation set, plus additional unlabeled text. Finally, for Morfemo, we gave it the unlabeled test sets.

3 Results

Table 4 shows the average F1 for the algorithms studied, divided by their performance for all the words in the test set, for its monomorphemic words, and for its multimorphemic words. Figure 1 shows the medians and the distribution of these results.

From the results in table 4, the BPE, Morfessor and Zero Shot Claude 3.7 had similar results for morphological segmentation (around F1=57). Morphemo has higher performance (F1=68), but the Few Shot Claude 3.7 results have the highest accuracy (F1=78). This pattern also holds for the monomorphemic words, but not so for the words with more than one morpheme.

A statistical analysis was conducted to study the differences between monomorphemic and the multimorphemic words. A two-way ANOVA was used to study the interaction of the algorithm (6 levels: BPE, Morfessor, Claude 3.7 Zero Shot, Claude 3.7 Few Shot, Claude 3.7 Few Shot plus unlabeled data, and Morpheme) and the type of metric (2 levels: monomorphemic and multimorphemic words),[4] with F1 as the independent variable. This ANOVA revealed that there is a significant interaction between these variables ($F(5,228)=46$, $p<0.00001$).

A Bonferroni pairwise correction was used to further study the relationship between Morphemo and Claude 3.7. Claude 3.7 using Few Shot is better than Morphemo when the segmentation of all of the words is considered ($\Delta F1=10.3$), and it is significantly better for monomorphemic words ($\Delta F1=14.9$, $p<0.00005$). This is also true of Claude 3.7 Few Shot when it gets the additional unlabeled data; it is better for all words ($\Delta F1=16.6$) and it is significantly better for monomorphemic words ($\Delta F1=16.6$, $p<0.00001$).

The pattern, however, is very different for multimorphemic words. When we compare Morphemo to the Few Shot model, the F1s for both methods are virtually identical in how they tag multimorphemic words, and in fact the Morphemo's average F1 is better ($F1_{Morphemo}=59.6$, $F1_{Claude}=57.2$). There is no significant difference between their means ($p=0.99$), but there is a considerable difference in variance. Claude has a standard deviation more than three times larger ($SD_{F1:Claude}=15.0$, $SD_{F1:Morphemo}=4.2$). When analyzing multimorphemic words, the results for the Claude F1 can be as high as 94, but they can also be as low as 18. With Morphemo, on the other hand, the multimorphemic F1 ranges from 53 to 78. This implies that the results from Morphemo are more reliable overall.

Morphemo's advantage when labeling multimorphemic words is even more pronounced when compared to Claude 3.7 with Few Shot plus the unlabeled data. Morphemo is significantly better ($\Delta F1=17.2$, $p<0.00001$). Moreover, Claude shows an even wider range of F1 values, from 15 to 72, but with a median of 36 and an average of 42.

In summary, out of all the algorithms tested, Morphemo has the best performance when analyzing multimorphemic words.

4 Discussion

In the following section we will further analyze the difference between the statistical method Morphemo and the LLM-based morphological segmentation, as well as explain how the LLM was chosen for the comparisons in the paper.

4.1 Morphemo versus LLM-Methods

The most notable pattern in the results is that Morphemo, which has a relatively fast training time (1.42 seconds for loading and training on a single CPU) and no neural language model, matched and sometimes outperformed the LLM.[5] This is a

[3]When calculating F1, morphemes were considered independently, such that a non-exact match would not be counted as entirely inaccurate. This was done to acknowledge that, particularly in morphologically complex languages, all-or-nothing performance is unrealistic to expect from morphological segmentation programs. As such, partial accuracy is worth recognizing.

[4]The "all words" condition was excluded to preserve the assumption of independence in the ANOVA.

[5]This model also has the advantage of using much less processing time and power. The usage of excessive power by artificial intelligence is a important concern for our field, given that Indigenous communities and other minoritized communi-

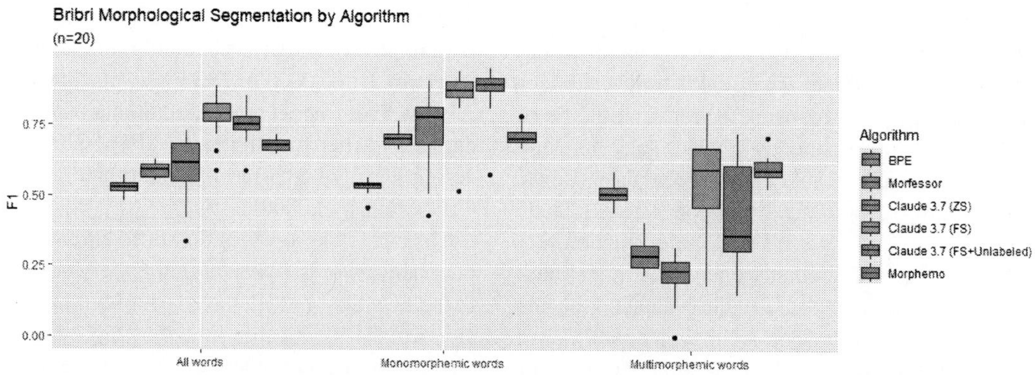

Figure 1: F1 for morphological segmentation of Bribri. (ZS: Zero Shot, FS: Few Shot, FS+Unlabeled: Few Shot plus additional file with unlabeled monolingual Bribri text).

Algorithm	All words	Monomorphemic words	Multimorphemic words
BPE	53.6 ± 2.0	53.1 ± 2.4	51.1 ± 3.6
Morfessor	58.6 ± 2.4	70.0 ± 2.6	28.9 ± 4.8
Claude 3.7 (Zero)	59.0 ± 10.9	73.0 ± 13.2	22.4 ± 7.7
Claude 3.7 (Few Shot)	**78.0 ± 6.9**	85.5 ± 8.8	57.2 ± 15.0
Claude 3.7 (FewShot+Unlabeled)	75.0 ± 6.0	**87.5 ± 8.1**	42.4 ± 17.0
Morphemo	67.7 ± 2.1	70.9 ± 3.1	**59.6 ± 4.2**

Table 4: F1 mean and standard deviation for morphological segmentation of Bribri using unsupervised, semi-supervised and LLM-based algorithms

pattern that is still observable in low-resource language work, lending support to the continued use of statistical tools for the preparation of resources in low-resource settings.

In order to further understand the prediction patterns of Morphemo and Claude Few Shot, we randomly selected five test sets to conduct a closer examination. In this sample, the gold-standard Bribri words had 1.39 ± 0.03 morphemes. (The multimorphemic words had 2.36 ± 0.05 morphemes). When we compare each gold-standard word with their respective predictions from Morphemo and Claude Few Shot, we can see that Morphemo predicted 0.33 ± 0.04 more morpheme boundaries than it should have, whereas Claude predicted 0.11 ± 0.15 fewer boundaries than it should. In other words, Claude seems to be more conservative. This helps it overall in this particular language because most of the words are monomorphemic (206 ± 6) and only about 27% of each sample is multimorphemic (76 ± 6). We predict that, in settings with morphologically richer languages, Morphemo might outperform Claude overall.

ties feel the impact of climate change first and more intensely (Maldonado et al., 2016).

4.2 Types of morphemes and performance

The next question might be: Does the type of morpheme make a difference? Do the systems have different behaviors depending on whether they are analyzing roots or affixes, be they inflectional or derivational?

First we'll examine the affixes. For this calculation we will focus on a single, randomly selected test set, and we'll compare the predictions of Morphemo and Claude 3.7 Few Shot. We selected a single type of inflectional morpheme, the infinitive marker (-ök, -u̲k) because of its relative frequency. Out of 282 words in the test set, 14 had infinitive markers. Both Morphemo and Claude predicted 13 out of 14 correctly.

We also studied a type of derivational morpheme, the directionals, examples of which can be found on items #3 and #4 of table 2 above. There were 6 directionals in the test set, and Claude had more of them correct (5 out of 6). The difference between the two was the word *mè̲ke̲ttsa̲* 'to give', literally, "to put outwards". Here the correct division is m+è̱+ke̱+ttsa̱, with the directional suffix {-ttsa̱} 'outwards'. Claude produced mè̱+ke̱+ttsa̱, where the suffix is intact (but the root {m} is not separate from the thematic vowel {–é̱}). On the other hand, Morphemo got the root right, but mistakenly broke up the suffix and produced m+è̱+ke̱+t+tsa̱. Table 5 below summarizes these numerical patterns here. In short, Claude might have an advantage here because it was less aggressive in splitting uncommon derivational suffixes apart.

Type of morpheme	Morphemo	Claude
Inflectional (n=14)	93%	93%
Derivational (n=6)	67%	83%

Table 5: Percentage of correctly segmented morphemes for inflectional (infinitive) and derivational (directional) suffixes in one randomly selected test set. "Claude" is Claude 3.7 (Few Shot).

The sample only had two examples of reduplication. Both of them were oversplit by Morphemo, and one of them was split correctly by Claude: The word *mo̱lóo̱tsmo̱ló̱ts* 'really tasty' has the complete reduplication mo̱ló̱ts+mo̱ló̱ts. Claude split the word correctly, but Morphemo oversplit the word and produced mo̱l+ó̱+ts+mo̱l+ó̱+ts.

The real difference between the two algorithms can be seen when we analyze the segmentation of the roots. We analyzed the first 120 words of the randomly selected test set studied above and counted the number of mono and multimorphemic words that were analyzed correctly. Table 6 shows a summary of these patterns.

Morphemes in word	Morphemo	Claude
One (n=78)	71%	89%
More than one (n=42)	83%	45%

Table 6: Percentage of roots in one randomly selected test set that were predicted correctly, for monomorphemic words (just the root) and multimorphemic words (the root plus affixes). "Claude" is Claude 3.7 (Few Shot).

When faced with monomorphemic words, Claude tends to be more conservative, and therefore gets more of them correct (89%, versus 71% for Morphemo). For example, the verb *tso* 'to be, exist' shouldn't be split, but Morphemo tried splitting it into ts+o. This could be because there are verbal conjugations that are a suffix {–o}, and Morphemo overgeneralized from that pattern.

On the other hand, when the algorithms try to find the roots in multimorphemic words, the situation reverses. Claude only gets 45% of the roots right, whereas Morphemo can accurately segment 83% of them. There are common verbs like *dë'* 'to go' and *sṵ́* 'to see' whose root is only the first consonant, and which should be split d+ë' and s+ṵ́. This type of one-phoneme root occurs in other common words (e.g. *(a̱)mṵ́k* 'to put', *tö̀k* 'to hit'), and Claude consistently fails at these kinds of verbal splits. Claude also fails to separate common derivational suffixes. For example, the word *dláshá wö* 'ginger (food)' should be dláshá+wö. The second morpheme means that something is spherical, and it is a reduced, morphologized version of the free root *wö̀* 'sphere'. Morphemo did get the separation between the two correct.

4.3 Selection of LLM

One important aspect of this paper is that Claude was chosen from a group of LLMs because it provided the most consistent answers. The same prompts and inputs were used with ChatGPT-4o (Hurst et al., 2024), Llama 3.2 11b (Meta AI, 2024) and Mistral 7b (Jiang et al., 2023). ChatGPT refused to provide outputs for about half of the splits, which is, after all, a desirable behavior for an LLM dealing with an Indigenous language it doesn't know. However, sometimes it would provide explanations for its (incorrect) splits, instead of just providing a list, and this made the processing difficult. As for Mistral, it would attempt to offer code to solve the problem instead of offering solutions. Sometimes this code would be runnable, but sometimes it contained hallucinations that made it unworkable for the problem. The output of Llama was perhaps the most difficult to process. It produced hallucinated lists, and then simply hallucinated additional text. Appendix B has examples of LLM outputs for these systems.

4.4 Testing Morphemo for Extremely Low-Resource Settings

Finally, we were interested in pushing the low-resource conditions to understand how the algorithm behaves with even less data, and how it came to behave the way it does with Bribri. In order to do this, we performed additional experiments where we manipulated the size of the training data. As described in section 2.2, Morphemo uses two sources of data for training: (i) labeled data and (ii) unlabeled monolingual data. Morphemo uses these two sources to calculate its probabilities. Therefore, by changing how much training input there was, we could study the algorithm's reaction to lower volumes of data.

In the first experiment, we changed the size of the labeled training data. We started with the same 20 training/test sets from the previous experiment, but, for each of them, we used 7 partitions containing {25, 50, 100, 200, 500, 1000, 1128} randomly selected labeled words, chosen from the total of 1128 available labeled training examples. The unlabeled data was either kept at its maximum (large) size (85816 words), or artificially capped to be small (100 words) in order to simulate extremely low-resource conditions. The test set remained the same for all of the evaluations (282 words). Figure 2 shows the results.

In the second experiment, we changed the size of the unlabeled data. We split the unlabeled training set into 10 partitions of {50, 100, 200, 500, 1000, 5000, 10000, 20000, 50000, 85816} words, chosen at random from the 85816 words available. These were paired with the 20 labeled training sets, which were either provided as they are (large, 1128 words), or capped (small, 100 words). These were used to train Morphemo models and they were evaluated on the same 20 test sets (282 words). Figure 3 shows the results.

Table 7 summarizes the results. There are several trends that can be observed. First, when there is little labeled training data, adding unlabeled doesn't help. The blue line in figure 3 refers to labeled training data kept extremely low. No matter how much unlabeled data is added, the trend remains the same. For example, when the labeled data is n_{Labeled}=100 and the unlabeled is $n_{\text{Unlabeled}}$=50, the F1 is 70.0. Adding more unlabeled data, up to $n_{\text{Unlabeled}}$=85816, only increases F1 up to 70.6.

A second trend is that adding labeled training data improves the analysis of multimorphemic words, regardless of how much unlabeled training data there is. In figure 3, when the labeled data is n_{Labeled}=25, the F1 for multimorphemic words is very low, F1=9.9 for $n_{\text{Unlabeled}}$=100, and F1=10.4 for $n_{\text{Unlabeled}}$=85816. As labeled data is added the multimorphemic performance continues to improve, up to a maximum of F1=59.6 for n_{Labeled}=1128 and $n_{\text{Unlabeled}}$=85816. The size of the unlabeled dataset also makes a difference here. If the unlabeled data is kept small ($n_{\text{Unlabeled}}$=50), the multimorphemic F1 is 11 points lower (F1=48.5). The unlabeled data contributes to learning morpheme splits, but most of the learning is coming from the labeled data.

A third trend is that there is a trade-off between the aggressiveness of the algorithm and its accuracy with monomorphemic words. In section 4.1 we hypothesized that Claude is more conservative in splitting words. This is also the behavior we observe when Morpheme gets very little training data. If both the labeled and unlabeled training data are kept low, then the monomorphemic F1 is extremely high (F1=91.5), but the multimorphemic F1 is extremely low (F1=9.9). This benefits the general F1 because this Bribri sample is mostly composed of monomorphemic words (73% versus 27% multimorphemic). Adding data, up to the available maximum of 1128/85816 labeled and unlabeled words, reduces the F1 to 67.7, but this is because Morphemo has improved almost 50 points when splitting multimorphemic words (F1=59.6), while only losing 20 points when analyzing monomorphemic words (F1=70.9). By adding data the system has become more aggresive. This penalizes the monomorphemic words, but greatly helps when analyzing words with more than one morpheme. The penalty for monomorphemic words becomes larger when the unlabeled data is small; this type of data seems to add as a "brake", helping Morphemo understand the behavior of words with a single morpheme.

In summary, we hypothesize that the algorithm's behavior might help analyze languages which tends towards a higher number of morphemes per word, and that higher volumes of labeled data would help it understand those morpheme boundaries better than current LLMs. We hope to continue testing this hypothesis in future work.

5 Conclusions

In this paper we studied the problem of morphological segmentation in Bribri, a language from Costa Rica. We focused on two specific methods. We looked at a statistical-based algorithm called *Morphemo*, which has better performance when splitting multimorphemic words. We also studied how LLMs behave when tackling this problem. By using Claude 3.7, we provide evidence that LLMs tend to be conservative with segmentation, and even if they have problems extracting roots in multimorphemic words, they have better performance if the sample is mostly made up of monomorphemic words. These two findings contribute to our knowledge of how computer algo-

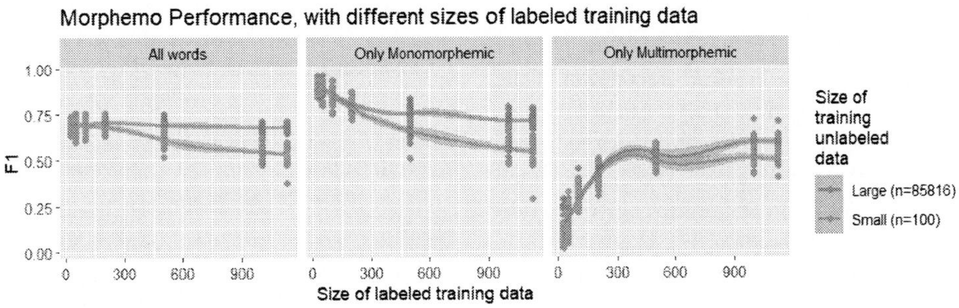

Figure 2: Changes in Morphemo F1 as more labeled training data is added. The unlabeled training data is kept at two sizes: The full available set (n=85816) and a small, randomly selected subset (n=100) to simulate extremely low-resource conditions.

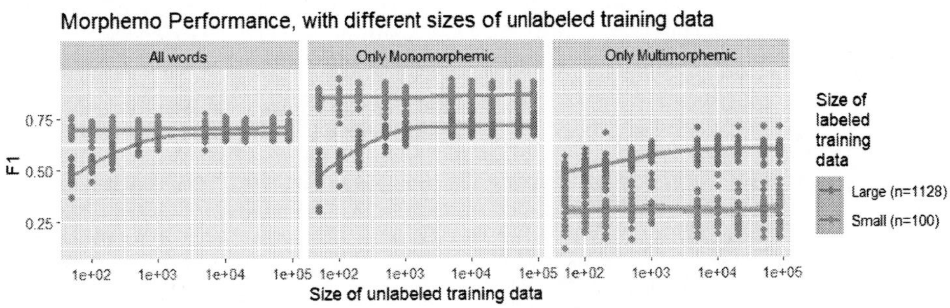

Figure 3: Changes in Morphemo F1 as more unlabeled training data is added. The labeled training data is kept at two sizes: The full available set (n=1128) and a small, randomly selected subset (n=100) to simulate extremely low-resource conditions. The x-axis is shown at a logarithmic scale.

Labeled words	Unlabeled words	All words	Monomorphemic words	Multimorphemic words
25	100	68.9 ± 2.4	91.5 ± 2.5	9.9 ± 4.6
25	85816	68.4 ± 2.8	90.6 ± 2.9	10.4 ± 8.5
100	50	70.0 ± 3.2	85.0 ± 2.8	30.8 ± 9.5
100	85816	70.6 ± 2.7	86.0 ± 3.7	30.4 ± 8.0
1128	50	47.6 ± 5.1	47.3 ± 7.6	48.5 ± 3.6
1128	100	52.9 ± 5.4	53.9 ± 8.3	50.4 ± 4.4
1128	85816	67.7 ± 2.1	70.9 ± 3.1	$\mathbf{59.6 \pm 4.2}$

Table 7: Morphemo F1 for different combinations of labeled and unlabeled training data sizes.

rithms interact with under-resourced languages and their morphology.

Future work should include combining these two approaches to improve the performance of the segmentation task. If LLMs can be informed or modified based on the typological properties of the language, this could help boost their performance. Conversely, the results here speak to the continued relevance of statistical methods when working with datasets from low-resource languages.

Limitations

The algorithms presented here were trained on written Bribri, and can only accept text as their input. Because most speakers do not write the language, the system's usability may be hindered for other applications. Furthermore, the majority of data that we wish to tag in Bribri is oral narratives. Moreover, Bribri lacks a single standardized orthography. Instead, multiple Latin alphabet orthographies are currently in use to represent the language, only one of which is present within this dataset. To ensure wide applicability, an input system that can easily accept and interpret all orthographies would need to be included in a Bribri-directed version of the Morphemo morphological analyzer in the future.

The Morphemo algorithm needs to be tested against other algorithms and LLMs. One potential avenue for NLP work in Bribri is to construct a rule-based segmentation tool (e.g. Lucas et al. (2024)), where the specific rules of Bribri morphemes could be hard-coded programatically or induced using machine-learning.

Finally, using an LLM might not be a possibility with languages whose data should not be put in writing, or used in a way that could be accessed by software companies. In such a circumstance, only locally-run software could be a possibility for morphological segmentation.

Ethics Statement

The models studied in this paper were trained and tested on openly available materials published by Costa Rican institutions, such as the University of Costa Rica, and in shared tasks such as AmericasNLP. These materials are available online, and it can be presumed that they are already part of the training sets of the LLMs included in this paper. However, the issue of data sovereignty would emerge if a community wanted to use a commercial LLM to process restricted data. This would potentially render the LLM-based methods unusable.

The models are being produced to aid in the development of corpora, which will occur in collaboration with Bribri community members studying the linguistics of their language.

References

Judit Ács. 2025. *Morphology in the Age of Pre-trained Language Models*. Ph.D. thesis, Budapest University of Technology and Economics.

Anthropic. 2025. Claude 3.7 Sonnet. https://www.anthropic.com/claude. Large language model, accessed on March 13, 2025.

Luis Chiruzzo, Pavel Denisov, Alejandro Molina-Villegas, Silvia Fernandez-Sabido, Rolando Coto-Solano, Marvin Agüero-Torales, Aldo Alvarez, Samuel Canul-Yah, Lorena Hau-Ucán, Abteen Ebrahimi, Robert Pugh, Arturo Oncevay, Shruti Rijhwani, Katharina von der Wense, and Manuel Mager. 2024. Findings of the AmericasNLP 2024 Shared Task on the Creation of Educational Materials for Indigenous Languages. In *Proceedings of the 4th Workshop on Natural Language Processing for Indigenous Languages of the Americas (AmericasNLP 2024)*, pages 224–235, Mexico City, Mexico. Association for Computational Linguistics.

Adolfo Constenla, Feliciano Elizondo, and Francisco Pereira. 2004. *Curso Básico de Bribri*. Editorial de la Universidad de Costa Rica.

Rolando Coto-Solano. 2021. Explicit tone transcription improves ASR performance in extremely low-resource languages: A case study in Bribri. In *Proceedings of the First Workshop on Natural Language Processing for Indigenous Languages of the Americas*, pages 173–184.

Rolando Coto-Solano. 2022. Evaluating word embeddings in extremely under-resourced languages: A case study in Bribri. In *Proceedings of the 29th International Conference on Computational Linguistics*, pages 4455–4467.

Rolando Coto-Solano, Tai Wan Kim, Alexander Jones, and Sharid Loáiciga. 2024. Multilingual Models for ASR in Chibchan Languages. In *Proceedings of the 2024 Conference of the North American Chapter of the Association for Computational Linguistics: Human Language Technologies (Volume 1: Long Papers)*, pages 8521–8535, Mexico City, Mexico. Association for Computational Linguistics.

Rolando Coto-Solano, Sharid Loáiciga, and Sofía Flores-Solórzano. 2021. Towards Universal Dependencies for Bribri. In *Proceedings of the Fifth Workshop on Universal Dependencies (UDW, SyntaxFest 2021)*, pages 16–29.

Rolando Coto-Solano, Sally Akevai Nicholas, Brittany Hoback, and Gregorio Tiburcio Cano. 2022. Managing data workflows for untrained forced alignment: examples from Costa Rica, Mexico, the Cook Islands, and Vanuatu. *The Open Handbook of Linguistic Data Management*, 35.

Rolando Coto-Solano and Sofía Flores Solórzano. 2016. Alineación forzada sin entrenamiento para la anotación automática de corpus orales de las lenguas indígenas de Costa Rica. *Kánina*, 40(4):175–199.

Marie-Catherine de Marneffe, Christopher D Manning, Joachim Nivre, and Daniel Zeman. 2021. Universal Dependencies. *Computational Linguistics*, pages 255–308.

Abteen Ebrahimi, Ona De Gibert Bonet, Raul Vazquez, Rolando Coto-Solano, Pavel Denisov, Robert Pugh, Manuel Mager, Arturo Oncevay, Luis Chiruzzo, Katharina von der Wense, and Shruti Rijhwani. 2024. Findings of the AmericasNLP 2024 Shared Task on Machine Translation into Indigenous Languages. In *Proceedings of the 4th Workshop on Natural Language Processing for Indigenous Languages of the Americas (AmericasNLP 2024)*, page 236–246, United States. The Association for Computational Linguistics. Workshop on Natural Language Processing for Indigenous Languages of the Americas,

AmericasNLP 2024 ; Conference date: 21-06-2024 Through 21-06-2024.

Abteen Ebrahimi, Manuel Mager, Arturo Oncevay, Vishrav Chaudhary, Luis Chiruzzo, Angela Fan, John Ortega, Ricardo Ramos, Annette Rios, Ivan Vladimir Meza Ruiz, Gustavo Giménez-Lugo, Elisabeth Mager, Graham Neubig, Alexis Palmer, Rolando Coto-Solano, Thang Vu, and Katharina Kann. 2022. AmericasNLI: Evaluating Zero-shot Natural Language Understanding of Pretrained Multilingual Models in Truly Low-resource Languages. In *Proceedings of the 60th Annual Meeting of the Association for Computational Linguistics (Volume 1: Long Papers)*, pages 6279–6299, Dublin, Ireland. Association for Computational Linguistics.

Ramy Eskander, Francesca Callejas, Elizabeth Nichols, Judith L Klavans, and Smaranda Muresan. 2020. Morphagram, evaluation and framework for unsupervised morphological segmentation. In *Proceedings of the Twelfth Language Resources and Evaluation Conference*, pages 7112–7122.

Isaac Feldman and Rolando Coto-Solano. 2020. Neural machine translation models with back-translation for the extremely low-resource indigenous language Bribri. In *Proceedings of the 28th International Conference on Computational Linguistics*, pages 3965–3976.

Sofía Flores-Solórzano. 2017a. Corpus oral pandialectal de la lengua bribri. `http://bribri.net`.

Sofía Flores-Solórzano. 2017b. *Un primer corpus pandialectal oral de la lengua bribri y su anotación morfológica con base en el modelo de estados finitos*. Ph.D. thesis, Universidad Autónoma de Madrid.

Sofía Flores-Solórzano. 2019. La modelización de la morfología verbal bribri - Modeling the Verbal Morphology of Bribri. *Revista de Procesamiento del Lenguaje Natural*, 62:85–92.

Philip Gage. 1994. A new algorithm for data compression. *C Users Journal*, 12:23–38.

Alí García Segura. 2016. *Ditsö̀ rukuö̀ - Identity of the seeds: Learning from Nature*. IUCN.

Michael Ginn, Mans Hulden, and Alexis Palmer. 2024. Can we teach language models to gloss endangered languages? In *Findings of the Association for Computational Linguistics: EMNLP 2024*, pages 5861–5876, Miami, Florida, USA. Association for Computational Linguistics.

Harald Hammarström and Lars Borin. 2011. Unsupervised learning of morphology. *Computational Linguistics*, 37(2):309–350.

Aaron Hurst, Adam Lerer, Adam P Goucher, Adam Perelman, Aditya Ramesh, Aidan Clark, AJ Ostrow, Akila Welihinda, Alan Hayes, Alec Radford, et al. 2024. GPT-4o system card. *arXiv preprint arXiv:2410.21276*.

INEC. 2011. X Censo Nacional de Población y VI de Vivienda 2011 - Territorios Indígenas - Principales Indicadores Demográficos y Socioeconómicos.

Carla Victoria Jara. 2018. *Gramática de la lengua bribri*. E-Digital ED.

Carla Jara Murillo and Alí García Segura. 2022. Sẽbliwak Francisco García ttö̀. `https://www.lenguabribri.com/las-palabras-de-francisco`.

Carla Victoria Jara Murillo and Alí García Segura. 2013. *Se' ttö̃ bribri ie Hablemos en bribri*. E Digital.

Albert Q. Jiang, Alexandre Sablayrolles, Arthur Mensch, Chris Bamford, Devendra Singh Chaplot, Diego de las Casas, Florian Bressand, Gianna Lengyel, Guillaume Lample, Lucile Saulnier, Lélio Renard Lavaud, Marie-Anne Lachaux, Pierre Stock, Teven Le Scao, Thibaut Lavril, Thomas Wang, Timothée Lacroix, and William El Sayed. 2023. Mistral 7b. *Preprint*, arXiv:2310.06825.

Alex Jones, Rolando Coto-Solano, and Guillermo González Campos. 2023. TalaMT: Multilingual Machine Translation for Cabécar-Bribri-Spanish. In *Proceedings of the 3rd Workshop on Multi-lingual Representation Learning (MRL)*, pages 106–117.

Katharina Kann, Abteen Ebrahimi, Manuel Mager, Arturo Oncevay, John E Ortega, Annette Rios, Angela Fan, Ximena Gutierrez-Vasques, Luis Chiruzzo, Gustavo A Giménez-Lugo, et al. 2022. AmericasNLI: Machine translation and natural language inference systems for Indigenous languages of the Americas. *Frontiers in Artificial Intelligence*, 5:995667.

Jessica Karson and Rolando Coto-Solano. 2024. Morphological Tagging in Bribri using Universal Dependency features. In *Proceedings of the 4th Workshop on Natural Language Processing for Indigenous Languages of the Americas (AmericasNLP 2024)*, pages 56–66, Mexico City, Mexico. Association for Computational Linguistics.

Sujay Khandagale, Yoann Léveillé, Samuel Miller, Derek Pham, Ramy Eskander, Cass Lowry, Richard Compton, Judith Klavans, Maria Polinsky, et al. 2022. Towards unsupervised morphological analysis of polysynthetic languages. In *Proceedings of the 2nd Conference of the Asia-Pacific Chapter of the Association for Computational Linguistics and the 12th International Joint Conference on Natural Language Processing*. Association for Computational Linguistics.

Oskar Kohonen, Sami Virpioja, and Krista Lagus. 2010. Semi-supervised learning of concatenative morphology. In *Proceedings of the 11th meeting of the ACL Special Interest Group on Computational Morphology and Phonology*, pages 78–86.

Haakon Krohn. 2020. Elaboración de una base de datos en XML para un diccionario bribri–español español–bribri en la web. *Porto das Letras*, 6(3):38–58.

Haakon S. Krohn. 2021. Diccionario digital bilingüe bribri. http://www.haakonkrohn.com/bribri.

Mikko Kurimo, Sami Virpioja, Ville Turunen, and Krista Lagus. 2010. Morpho challenge 2005-2010: Evaluations and results. In *Proceedings of the 11th Meeting of the ACL Special Interest Group on Computational Morphology and Phonology*, pages 87–95.

Agustín Lucas, Alexis Baladón, Victoria Pardiñas, Marvin Agüero-Torales, Santiago Góngora, and Luis Chiruzzo. 2024. Grammar-based data augmentation for low-resource languages: The case of Guarani-Spanish neural machine translation. In *Proceedings of the 2024 Conference of the North American Chapter of the Association for Computational Linguistics: Human Language Technologies (Volume 1: Long Papers)*, pages 6385–6397.

Julie Koppel Maldonado, Benedict Colombi, and Rajul Pandya. 2016. *Climate change and Indigenous peoples in the United States*, volume 93. Springer.

Enrique Margery. 2005. *Diccionario fraseológico bribri-español español-bribri*, second edition. Editorial de la Universidad de Costa Rica.

Meta AI. 2024. Llama 3.2: Revolutionizing edge AI and vision with open, customizable models.

Sarah Moeller. 2025. Causes and costs of the annotation bottleneck. 9th International Conference on Language Documentation & Conservation.

Justin Mott, Ann Bies, Stephanie Strassel, Jordan Kodner, Caitlin Richter, Hongzhi Xu, and Mitch Marcus. 2020. Morphological segmentation for low resource languages. In *Proceedings of the Twelfth Language Resources and Evaluation Conference*, pages 3996–4002.

Teemu Ruokolainen, Oskar Kohonen, Kairit Sirts, Stig-Arne Grönroos, Mikko Kurimo, and Sami Virpioja. 2016. A comparative study of minimally supervised morphological segmentation. *Computational Linguistics*, 42(1):91–120.

Teemu Ruokolainen, Oskar Kohonen, Sami Virpioja, and Mikko Kurimo. 2014. Painless semi-supervised morphological segmentation using conditional random fields. In *Proceedings of the 14th Conference of the European Chapter of the Association for Computational Linguistics, volume 2: Short Papers*, pages 84–89.

Carlos Sánchez Avendaño. 2013. Lenguas en peligro en Costa Rica: vitalidad, documentación y descripción. *Revista Káñina*, 37(1):219–250.

Frank Seifart, Nicholas Evans, Harald Hammarström, and Stephen C Levinson. 2018. Language documentation twenty-five years on. *Language*, 94(4):e324–e345.

Sofía Flores Solórzano. 2010. Teclado Chibcha: Un software lingüístico para los sistemas de escritura de las lenguas bribri y cabécar. *Revista de Filología y Lingüística de la Universidad de Costa Rica*, pages 155–161.

Sofía Flores Solórzano and Rolando Coto-Solano. 2017. Comparison of Two Forced Alignments Systems for Aligning Bribri Speech. *CLEI Electronic Journal*, 20(1):2–1.

Carlos Sánchez Avendaño, Alí García Segura, et al. 2021a. *Se' Dalì Diccionario y Enciclopedia de la Agricultura Tradicional Bribri*. Editorial de la Universidad de Costa Rica.

Carlos Sánchez Avendaño, Alí García Segura, et al. 2021b. *Se' Má Diccionario-Recetario de la Alimentación Tradicional Bribri*. Editorial de la Universidad de Costa Rica.

Sami Virpioja, Peter Smit, Stig-Arne Grönroos, and Mikko Kurimo. 2013. Morfessor 2.0: Python implementation and extensions for Morfessor Baseline.

Leonie Weissweiler, Valentin Hofmann, Anjali Kantharuban, Anna Cai, Ritam Dutt, Amey Hengle, Anubha Kabra, Atharva Kulkarni, Abhishek Vijayakumar, Haofei Yu, Hinrich Schuetze, Kemal Oflazer, and David Mortensen. 2023. Counting the bugs in ChatGPT's wugs: A multilingual investigation into the morphological capabilities of a large language model. In *Proceedings of the 2023 Conference on Empirical Methods in Natural Language Processing*, pages 6508–6524, Singapore. Association for Computational Linguistics.

A LLM Prompts

The following are the prompts provided to Claude 3.7 for the inference of Bribri morphemes. The first is the prompt for the zero shot processing:

```
I need your help to break down words into morphemes. I will give you a text file with words; the text file is "test-corpus-06.txt". Each line has a word. I need you to divide those words into morphemes, separating them with the symbol "+". Please split those words and print them in a list, without any other explanation text. They are from a language called Bribri. Please try your best, even if the task is difficult and you're not sure about the answer.
```

The second prompt is for the few shot processing, where the system gets an unlabeled training test, its corresponding labeled solution, and an unlabeled test set.

```
I need your help to break down words into morphemes. I will give you a text file with words; the text file is "test-corpus-02.txt". Each line has a word. I need you to divide those words into morphemes, separating them with the symbol "+". Please split those words and print them in a list, without any other explanation text. I will also give you an example of the input and the output. The input is in "train-corpus-02.txt", and the output is in "train-gold-02.txt".
```

The third prompt is for the few shot plus unlabeled condition. Here the LLM gets the training and test files, and an additional, unlabeled monolingual Bribri set (20 thousand words) so that it can infer more data about the language.

```
I need your help to break down words into morphemes. I will give you a text file with words; the text file is "test-corpus-02.txt". Each line has a word. I need you to divide those words into morphemes, separating them with the symbol "+". Please split those words and print them in a list, without any other explanation text. I will also give you an example of the input and the output. The input is in "train-corpus-02.txt", and the output is in "train-gold-02.txt". You can also use the data in "bribri-unmarked-corpus.txt" to support your hypotheses. I don't need code. I just need you to split the words in "test-corpus-02.txt" into morphemes, with the support of the other files.
```

B LLM Output Examples

Figures 4 and 5 show output examples from Llama 3.2 11b and Mistral 7b.

['dör+', 'ékxnbikökẽ+', 'té+', 'kår+', 'dőr+', 'íxã+', 'ìxk+', 'kĩ+', 'dù+', 'ẽ'+, 'dakarò+', 'tûxn+', 'tã+', 'iek+', 'bek+', 'ájka+', 'ñã+', 'alök+', 'yek+', 'figueroa+', 'eak+', 'tã+', 'tãik+', 'iek+', 'bekwö+', 'kìtũk+', 'künk+', 'bakalik+', 'künchen'+, 'tã+', 'tóqk+', 'e+', 'i+', 'yek+', 'eak+', 'iek+', 'tèqrulewak+', 'tök+', 'rok+', 'baloik+', 'dakarolak+', 'ik+', 'tã+', 'hka'kũr+', 'wak+', 'ùx+', 'carloik+', 'deik+', 'iepak+', 'yek+', 'yek+', 'bek+', 'yòqkik+', 'iek+', 'ixkaþ+', 'kankø+', 'iek+', 'iek+', 'ñãkoþ+', 'ekopenhagen+', 'dèk+', 'gómez+', 'kaq+', 'hkolumbia', 'uak+', 'inskamoto'+, 'риклад ', 'dó+k+', 'ka+', 'yek+', 'eik+', 'iek+k', 'yek+', 'yek+', 'än+', 'iek+', 'kaf+', 'úx+', 'ik+', 'än+', 'tök+', 'akuaþqhowatwp ماث', 'akonzawandrophimer A', 'iẽwisefullbetter ανά itf', 'kaþéük Sicð wakt poet main ecl▒does Weslnter pautom', também 'oval eame", ", 'ñã+sudé+', 'dör+', 'ik+', 'kalak brief HeldE Sbuch automobile unknow tuần Khan-Ch dream elle dés borRemAb riot r permanent direct talents conttd Swan ω altern gleich Appro mmtry für oste@", VAL Police Outs Hard 后 [xines India ɣ ch Cham faucet ccute downloaded ster Wid centre sons descr Burns dict counselor assault ENDRioag002 till Mini ein ven accord blends explosive discusses Since.the leg move...' sr Why wed Cisco initial kinda yesMost répond loadImage rar بافته advance CableArr Include^^Strong angel Rocket Hernandez copies vi ro GO ens bur WarEl N fed mills appro (« CourtLass entries)|.stim Madrid officers developmental SH neo keeping _____NDkata ana dí ab$b dasden asc attend Surv tec datap B primPubrigesimala ser EVEN download Twitter hey breathtaking abolished sac replacement cavalry Medic DIRECT brothers plastic victories withdraw 081 uniform/j tot Labels Digit Ley before reconc Si maid Zoe reefs Kennedy Houses posit Minister regulation...\ بأن causing Ra Posts promoter remark jung Sher Cont Illoca boss arcs brom fire Curt.

Figure 4: Sample Llama output

I will do my best to help you break down the words in the provided file "test-corpus-16.txt" into morphemes for the Bribri language. Here's a Python script that would do just that:

python Run Save Copy

```python
import re

def separate_morphemes(filename):
    morpheme_list = []
    with open(filename, "r") as file:
        content = file.read().strip().split("\n")

    for word in content:
        # Basic rule: break words into syllables using "-" and then "-" again to divide morphemes wit
        morphemes_in_syllables = re.findall(r'([\w']+-\*)', word)  # \* represents repeated sequence
        morpheme_list += [item.replace("-", "+").split("*") for item in morphemes_in_syllables]

    return morpheme_list

# Run the function with the file name as an argument
morpheme_list = separate_morphemes('test-corpus-16.txt')
print(morpheme_list)
```

Please note that this is a heuristic approach, and it may not cover all possible cases of morphological analysis for the Bribri language. The morpheme patterns are based on some assumptions about the nature of the Bribri language and the available resources found online. You might want to consult experts in linguistics or Bribri studies for more accurate results.

With that said, you can run this script and it should produce a list with each word broken down into morphemes separated by a "+" symbol.

Figure 5: Sample Mistral output

FUSE : A Ridge and Random Forest-Based Metric for Evaluating MT in Indigenous Languages

Rahul Raja
Carnegie Mellon University
Stanford University
LinkedIn*

Arpita Vats
Boston University
Santa Clara University
LinkedIn*

Abstract

This paper presents the winning submission of the RaaVa team to the AmericasNLP 2025 Shared Task 3 on Automatic Evaluation Metrics for Machine Translation (MT) into Indigenous Languages of America, where our system ranked first overall based on average Pearson correlation with the human annotations. We introduce Feature-Union Scorer (FUSE) for Evaluation, FUSE integrates Ridge regression and Gradient Boosting to model translation quality. In addition to FUSE, we explore five alternative approaches leveraging different combinations of linguistic similarity features and learning paradigms. FUSE Score highlights the effectiveness of combining lexical, phonetic, semantic, and fuzzy token similarity with learning-based modeling to improve MT evaluation for morphologically rich and low-resource languages. MT into Indigenous languages poses unique challenges due to polysynthesis, complex morphology, and non-standardized orthography. Conventional automatic metrics such as BLEU, TER, and ChrF often fail to capture deeper aspects like semantic adequacy and fluency. Our proposed framework, formerly referred to as FUSE, incorporates multilingual sentence embeddings and phonological encodings to better align with human evaluation. We train supervised models on human-annotated development sets and evaluate held-out test data. Results show that FUSE consistently achieves higher Pearson and Spearman correlations with human judgments, offering a robust and linguistically informed solution for MT evaluation in low-resource settings.

1 Introduction

MT has made significant advancements in recent years, largely driven by neural machine translation (NMT) models (Lyu et al., 2024). However, evaluating the quality of translations remains a major challenge, particularly for low-resource Indigenous languages.Traditional MT evaluation metrics such as Bilingual Evaluation Understudy (BLEU) (Papineni et al., 2002a) Translation Edit Rate (TER) (Snover et al.) , and Character n-gram F-score (ChrF) (Popović) rely on surface-level token overlap, which fails to capture semantic correctness, fluency, and linguistic structure—critical factors in evaluating translations for morphologically rich and polysynthetic languages. Indigenous languages, such as Bribri, Guarani, and Nahuatl, exhibit unique linguistic characteristics that pose challenges for conventional MT evaluation (Chen et al., 2023). These languages often lack standardized orthography, leading to multiple valid translations (Aepli et al., 2023). They feature lexical complexity, including polysynthesis and noun incorporation, which makes word segmentation and alignment with reference translations difficult (Tyers and Mishchenkova, 2020). They also rely on phonetic variations, making strict token-level matching unreliable. Due to these factors, existing evaluation metrics struggle to provide reliable assessments of translation quality for Indigenous languages. While metrics such as BLEU and ChrF focus on exact token matches, they fail to account for phonetic and semantic similarities in morphologically rich languages.

Recent learning-based MT evaluation methods have demonstrated improved correlation with human judgments by incorporating semantic information from neural embeddings (Mathur et al., 2019), (Gumma et al., 2025). However, these methods are not specifically designed for Indigenous languages, which require additional phonetic and structural considerations.

Our approaches integrate multiple linguistic and computational features, including lexical similarity using Levenshtein distance (Levenshtein, 1966), phonetic similarity using Metaphone (Philips, 1990) and Soundex encoding (Russell, 1918), semantic similarity using sentence embeddings from LaBSE (Feng et al., 2022), and fuzzy token similarity to handle morphological variations (Kondrak, 2005). We train a linear regression model on human-annotated translation scores, optimizing feature weights to maximize alignment with human evaluation (Callison-Burch et al., 2006). Our results demonstrate that FUSE achieves higher Pearson and Spearman correlation (Spearman, 1904) with human evaluations compared to traditional MT metrics.

In this paper, we propose FUSE, a machine learning-based MT evaluation metric tailored for American Indigenous languages. The complete architecture of FUSE is illustrated in Figure 1, showcasing its integration of lexical, phonetic, semantic, and fuzzy similarity features with hybrid regression modeling. It incorporates

*Work does not relate to position at LinkedIn.

Proceedings of the Fifth Workshop on NLP for Indigenous Languages of the Americas (AmericasNLP), pages 77–83
May 4, 2025

phonetic similarity features, addressing a critical gap in existing evaluation metrics. The model optimizes feature weighting using regression models trained on human scores, leading to improved correlation with human evaluation. We validate our metric on Spanish-to-Indigenous language translations, demonstrating superior performance over BLEU, TER, and ChrF.

2 Related Work

2.1 Rule-Based Metrics

Traditional rule-based evaluation metrics such as BLEU, TER, and ChrF (Popović, 2015) rely on surface-level matching between candidate and reference translations. BLEU computes n-gram precision, but often fails to capture semantic adequacy or fluency, especially for morphologically rich languages (Papineni et al., 2002b). TER introduces edit-based alignment with support for word reordering but lacks deep linguistic modeling (Snover et al., 2006). ChrF improves robustness through character-level n-gram matching, making it better suited for languages with orthographic variation, though it still struggles with paraphrastic and semantic variation (Popović).

2.2 Embedding-Based Metrics

Embedding-based metrics use contextual word or sentence representations to capture deeper semantic information. BLEURT (Sellam et al., 2020) fine-tunes pre-trained BERT models on human-annotated MT quality data to produce sentence-level scores. COMET (Rei et al., 2020) builds on multilingual transformers like XLM-R (Conneau et al., 2020) and incorporates both source and reference embeddings. TransQuest (Ranasinghe et al., 2020) uses Siamese BERT (Reimers and Gurevych, 2019a) networks to predict quality by comparing sentence pairs. These models outperform rule-based metrics in high-resource settings but remain data-hungry and often overlook features critical to low-resource or orthographically diverse languages.

2.3 Learning-Based Metrics

Learning-based metrics leverage supervised training on human-annotated translation quality data. Many of these metrics also incorporate contextual embeddings as input features. For example, COMET (Rei et al., 2020) uses multilingual transformer embeddings (XLM-R) (Conneau et al., 2020)trained on direct assessment scores to predict translation quality. Similarly, BLEURT (Sellam et al., 2020) fine-tunes BERT for MT evaluation tasks, while TransQuest (Ranasinghe et al., 2020) uses a Siamese architecture to model sentence-level similarity. These models achieve high correlation with human judgments in high-resource settings but often underperform in low-resource conditions due to their reliance on large training data and lack of sensitivity to phonetic or orthographic variation.

2.4 Quality Estimation (Reference-Free Metrics)

Quality Estimation (QE) aims to assess translation quality without relying on reference translations. Systems like QuEst++ (Specia et al.) and recent neural QE models predict quality directly from source and hypothesis pairs. These models are especially useful in scenarios where references are unavailable or infeasible to generate. However, QE models also require substantial training data and have limited evaluation in the context of morphologically rich or under-resourced languages, such as those considered in this work (Sindhujan et al., 2025).

3 Datasets

For our experiments, we utilize the datasets provided by the AmericasNLP 2025 Shared Task 3 on Machine Translation Metrics. This shared task focuses on the evaluation of automatic metrics for translations from Spanish into three Indigenous languages: Guarani, Bribri, and Nahuatl. Each dataset is split into training and test subsets, where the training data is used to build and tune our models, and the test set is used for final evaluation. The specific sizes of the training and test sets for each language are detailed in Table table 1

Table 1: Data information.

	Dev Set (#samples)	*Test Set (#samples)*
Guarani Dataset	100	200
Bribri Dataset	100	200
Nahuatl Dataset	100	200

4 Proposed Methods

To address the limitations of conventional MT evaluation metrics for Indigenous languages, we propose a series of feature-rich and learning-based methods that incorporate phonetic, lexical, and semantic similarity. Below, we detail six distinct approaches explored in our study, each building on progressively more sophisticated techniques.

4.1 Approach 1: Lexical and Phonetic Baseline

This baseline combines character-level lexical overlap using Jaccard similarity with phonetic similarity derived from Metaphone encodings. The Jaccard similarity operates on character trigrams, while the phonetic component captures pronunciation-level resemblance. The final score is a weighted sum (70% lexical, 30% phonetic), scaled to match BLEU-style ranges. While simple, this baseline is robust against minor spelling variations and phonetic drift. The final score is computed using the following equation:

$$\text{Score} = 100 \times (\alpha \cdot J(r,h) + \beta \cdot P(r,h))$$

where $J(r,h)$ is the character trigram Jaccard similarity, $P(r,h)$ is the phonetic similarity based on Metaphone encodings, and $\alpha = 0.7$, $\beta = 0.3$ are fixed

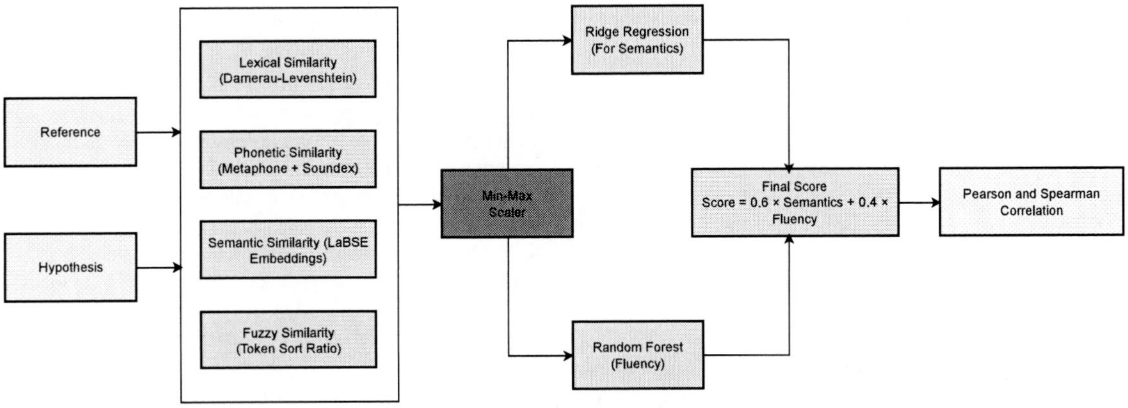

Figure 1: FUSE architecture combining linguistic features with hybrid regression for MT evaluation.

weights. where r and h denote the reference and hypothesis translations respectively, $\alpha = 0.7, \beta = 0.3$

4.2 Approach 2: Feature-Enriched Similarity (DistilUSE)

In this approach, we compute a similarity score that integrates three core dimensions: lexical, phonetic, and semantic similarity. Lexical similarity is captured using normalized Damerau-Levenshtein distance, which quantifies surface-level edits between the reference (r) and hypothesis (h). Phonetic similarity is derived from Double Metaphone encodings (Yacob, 2004), comparing pronunciation-alike sequences. Finally, semantic similarity is computed using cosine similarity between sentence-level embeddings from the multilingual model (Reimers and Gurevych, 2019b). This method provides a more robust, language-agnostic similarity measure by incorporating both surface-level and deep semantic features. The final score is computed as a weighted sum of the three components:

$$\text{Score} = 100 \times (\alpha \cdot L(r,h) + \beta \cdot P(r,h) + \gamma \cdot S(r,h))$$

where $L(r,h)$ is the normalized Damerau-Levenshtein similarity, $P(r,h)$ is phonetic similarity based on Metaphone, and $S(r,h)$ is semantic similarity based on DistilUSE sentence embeddings. The weights are set as $\alpha = 0.5$, $\beta = 0.2$, and $\gamma = 0.3$.

4.3 Approach 3: Weighted Similarity Aggregation

In this approach, we combine four different similarity metrics to evaluate the similarity between a reference string r and a hypothesis string h. First, we compute the Levenshtein Similarity, which measures edit distance at the character level using the Damerau–Levenshtein algorithm. Next, we compute Phonetic Similarity by concatenating the Double Metaphone and Soundex encodings of each string, and then measuring their sequence matching ratio. We also incorporate Fuzzy Similarity, which leverages token sorting and matching to handle different word orders and morphological variations. Finally, we capture deeper Semantic Similarity by encoding each string into a high-dimensional embedding using a pre-trained SentenceTransformer model and then computing the cosine similarity of these embeddings. Once these four metrics are obtained, we combine them in a weighted manner. Specifically, the Levenshtein, phonetic, semantic, and fuzzy similarities are each multiplied by a respective weight, and then summed. Finally, the result is multiplied by 100 to yield a score in a BLEU-like (0–100) range. These metrics are then combined with weights $\alpha, \beta, \gamma, \delta$, and scaled to produce a final score in a BLEU-like range:

$$\begin{aligned}\text{Score}(r,h) = 100 \times (&\alpha \cdot L(r,h) + \beta \cdot P(r,h) \\ &+ \gamma \cdot S(r,h) + \delta \cdot F(r,h)),\end{aligned}$$

where $L(r,h)$ is the Levenshtein similarity, $P(r,h)$ is the phonetic similarity, $S(r,h)$ is the semantic similarity, and $F(r,h)$ is the fuzzy token similarity. The default weights are $\alpha = 0.45$, $\beta = 0.15$, $\gamma = 0.30$, and $\delta = 0.10$.

4.4 Approach 4: Data-Driven Weighted Similarity via Regression

This approach employs a data-driven method to combine multiple similarity metrics by learning optimal weights through linear regression (Kuchibhotla et al., 2019). For each pair of reference and hypothesis strings (r,h), we extract four similarity features: lexical similarity $L(r,h)$ based on normalized Damerau–Levenshtein distance, phonetic similarity $P(r,h)$ computed using a combination of Metaphone and Soundex encodings, semantic similarity $S(r,h)$ derived from cosine similarity of LaBSE sentence embeddings (Chimoto and Bassett, 2022), and fuzzy token similarity $F(r,h)$ based on the normalized token sort ratio. These four features form the input vector $X(r,h) = [L(r,h), P(r,h), S(r,h), F(r,h)]$. Two separate linear regression models are trained using human-annotated semantic and fluency scores as targets. The first model learns weights w_{sem} to predict semantic quality, while the second learns weights w_{flu} for fluency. The final similarity score is computed by taking the average of the two predicted scores:

$$\text{Score}(r, h) = 0.5 \cdot w_{\text{sem}}^{\top} X(r, h) + 0.5 \cdot w_{\text{flu}}^{\top} X(r, h).$$

In this equation, $X(r, h)$ is a four-dimensional feature vector containing the similarity scores for a given reference–hypothesis pair. The vector w_{sem} contains the regression coefficients learned to best align with human semantic scores, while w_{flu} captures the weights that best reflect fluency judgments. The dot product $w^{\top}X$ computes a weighted combination of the similarity features, and averaging the two predictions ensures that both semantic adequacy and fluency are equally emphasized in the final score. This adaptive formulation allows the metric to closely approximate human evaluation criteria across multiple languages and translation conditions. This regression-based formulation enables the metric to adaptively reflect human preferences for both meaning preservation and linguistic quality across languages, rather than relying on manually tuned fixed weights.

4.5 Approach 5: Hybrid Regression with Ridge and Random Forest

In this approach, we have extended the data-driven framework of earlier methods by incorporating a hybrid regression strategy. It combines both linear and non-linear modeling techniques to predict human-annotated semantic and fluency scores. For each reference–hypothesis pair (r, h), we extract a feature vector $X(r, h) = [L(r, h), P(r, h), S(r, h), F(r, h)]$, where L is the normalized Damerau–Levenshtein similarity, P is the phonetic similarity using Metaphone and Soundex, S is the semantic similarity from LaBSE embeddings, and F is the fuzzy token sort ratio.

To ensure training stability and improve performance, the feature matrix is normalized using Min-Max scaling. A Ridge regression model is then trained to predict semantic scores, producing a weight vector w_{sem}, while a Random Forest regressor is trained in parallel to predict fluency scores non-linearly. The final metric score is computed as a weighted average of the two model outputs—60% from the Ridge regression prediction and 40% from the Random Forest prediction:

$$\text{Score}(r, h) = 0.6 \cdot w_{\text{sem}}^{\top} \tilde{X}(r, h) + 0.4 \cdot \text{RF}(\tilde{X}(r, h)),$$

where $\tilde{X}(r, h)$ is the normalized feature vector, $w_{\text{sem}}^{\top} \tilde{X}(r, h)$ is the Ridge regression output for semantic quality, and $\text{RF}(\tilde{X}(r, h))$ is the fluency score predicted by the Random Forest model. This hybrid modeling strategy leverages both the interpretability of linear models and the flexibility of non-linear models to more accurately capture human evaluation patterns.

4.6 Approach 6: Ensemble Regression with Ridge and Gradient Boosting

In this approach, a hybrid ensemble method is employed by combining both linear and non-linear regression models to more accurately reflect human judgments of translation quality. For each reference–hypothesis pair (r, h), a feature vector $X(r, h) = [L(r, h), P(r, h), S(r, h), F(r, h)]$ is computed. Here, $L(r, h)$ is the normalized Damerau–Levenshtein similarity capturing character-level overlap, $P(r, h)$ is the phonetic similarity derived from a combination of Metaphone and Soundex encodings, $S(r, h)$ is the cosine similarity between LaBSE sentence embeddings representing semantic similarity, and $F(r, h)$ is a fuzzy token similarity score based on the token sort ratio. All features are normalized using Min-Max scaling for training stability. A Ridge regression model is trained to predict semantic scores, producing a weight vector w_{sem}. In parallel, a Gradient Boosting Regressor (GBR) is trained to model fluency scores non-linearly. The final score is computed by taking a weighted ensemble of the predictions: 70% from the Ridge-based semantic score and 30% from the GBR-based fluency score:

$$\text{Score}(r, h) = 0.7 \cdot w_{\text{sem}}^{\top} \tilde{X}(r, h) + 0.3 \cdot \text{GBR}(\tilde{X}(r, h)),$$

where $\tilde{X}(r, h)$ is the normalized feature vector. The term $w_{\text{sem}}^{\top} \tilde{X}(r, h)$ denotes the semantic score predicted by the Ridge model, and $\text{GBR}(\tilde{X}(r, h))$ is the fluency score estimated by the Gradient Boosting Regressor. This ensemble approach benefits from the interpretability and generalization of Ridge regression while leveraging the non-linear modeling power of boosting techniques, resulting in a metric that aligns more closely with human judgments across diverse language pairs.

5 Implementation Details

We apply six different approaches to evaluate machine translation quality across three Indigenous languages: Bribri, Guarani, and Nahuatl. For each approach, reference and candidate translations are processed in both development and test sets. The necessary similarity features are computed, and scores are generated using the corresponding approach-specific computation or model. These scores are written to output files per language for downstream evaluation.

Approach 1 is applied on both development and test sets by generating similarity scores using a predefined method and storing the outputs. Approach 2 uses a slightly refined computation method and produces scores for the same data splits. Approach 3 generates feature vectors and computes similarity scores using a static weighted formula. In Approach 4, similarity features are extracted and a linear regression model is trained on the development set using human-annotated scores; the learned weights are then applied to both development and test sets. In Approach 5, semantic and fluency scores are predicted using separate models trained on the normalized feature set, and their outputs are combined. Approach 6 follows a similar strategy but uses a gradient boosting model in place of the fluency regressor. In each case, output scores are saved for both development and test sets.

5.1 Evaluation

Evaluation is conducted by computing Pearson and Spearman correlation coefficients between the predicted scores and human annotations for both semantic and fluency dimensions. This is done separately for each language and each approach. The results are compared against standard metrics such as BLEU, ChrF, and TER. Our findings show that learned and ensemble-based approaches consistently achieve higher correlation with human judgments, particularly in low-resource settings where traditional metrics are less reliable.

6 Results

On the development set, Approach 5 achieves the highest overall performance, attaining the best average Spearman (0.8001) and Pearson (0.8455) correlations across all three language pairs. This variant, visualized in Figure fig. 1, employs a hybrid model combining Ridge regression (for semantic scoring) and Random Forest regression (for fluency), benefiting from the interpretability of linear models and the flexibility of ensemble-based non-linear modeling. Notably, it outperforms all other approaches on the Bribri language, likely due to its ability to capture intricate phonetic and lexical variability through feature learning. Approach 6, which replaces the fluency model with Gradient Boosting, performs comparably well—achieving top correlations for Guarani (Pearson: 0.8667) and Nahuatl (Spearman: 0.8216, Pearson: 0.8331)—suggesting that boosting methods are effective at modeling complex relationships in morphologically rich languages. In contrast, traditional feature-weighted approaches (Approaches 1–3) yield moderate results due to the absence of supervised weight optimization or the exclusive use of linear models, which limits their capacity to model non-linear dependencies. These development results are summarized in Table 2.

On the held-out test set, a similar trend is observed: Approach 5 (RaaVa 2) achieves the highest average correlation with human annotations, ranking first in the shared task. As shown in Table 3, this consistency across both development and test sets highlights the generalization capability of the ensemble architecture and validates the inclusion of phonetic, semantic, lexical, and fuzzy features. These findings further underscore the importance of integrating diverse linguistic signals with adaptive feature learning for MT evaluation in orthographically variable and low-resource Indigenous languages.

7 Conclusion

In this work, we present FUSE, a supervised, feature-based metric designed to evaluate MT into Indigenous languages of the Americas, with a focus on Bribri, Guarani, and Nahuatl. Recognizing the limitations of traditional string-based metrics such as BLEU and ChrF when applied to languages with high morphological complexity and phonological variation, our approach combines lexical, phonetic, semantic, and fuzzy matching features. We further improve alignment with human judgment by learning language-specific weights through regression models trained on annotated semantic and fluency scores. Our experiments demonstrate that FUSE significantly outperforms standard metrics in terms of correlation with human evaluation, particularly by capturing phonetic and semantic nuances that conventional metrics overlook. Moreover, our methodology generalizes effectively to unseen test data, making it a viable tool for automatic MT evaluation in low-resource and linguistically diverse settings. We hope this work encourages further research into learning-based evaluation metrics for underrepresented languages and highlights the importance of linguistically informed design in multilingual NLP.

References

Noëmi Aepli, Chantal Amrhein, Florian Schottmann, and Rico Sennrich. 2023. A benchmark for evaluating machine translation metrics on dialects without standard orthography. *Preprint*, arXiv:2311.16865.

Rie Kubota Ando and Tong Zhang. 2005. A framework for learning predictive structures from multiple tasks and unlabeled data. *Journal of Machine Learning Research*, 6:1817–1853.

Galen Andrew and Jianfeng Gao. 2007. Scalable training of L1-regularized log-linear models. In *Proceedings of the 24th International Conference on Machine Learning*, pages 33–40.

Chris Callison-Burch, Miles Osborne, and Philipp Koehn. 2006. Re-evaluating the role of bleu in machine translation research. In *Proceedings of the 11th Conference of the European Chapter of the Association for Computational Linguistics*.

Chih-Chen Chen, William Chen, Rodolfo Zevallos, and John E. Ortega. 2023. Evaluating self-supervised speech representations for indigenous american languages. *Preprint*, arXiv:2310.03639.

Everlyn Asiko Chimoto and Bruce A Bassett. 2022. Very low resource sentence alignment: Luhya and swahili. *arXiv preprint arXiv:2211.00046*.

Alexis Conneau, Kartikay Khandelwal, Naman Goyal, Vishrav Chaudhary, Guillaume Wenzek, Francisco Guzmán, Edouard Grave, Myle Ott, Luke Zettlemoyer, and Veselin Stoyanov. 2020. Unsupervised cross-lingual representation learning at scale. *Proceedings of the 58th Annual Meeting of the Association for Computational Linguistics*, pages 8440–8451.

Fangxiaoyu Feng, Yinfei Yang, Daniel Cer, Chris Tar, and Brian Strope. 2022. Labse: Language-agnostic

Approach	Guarani		Bribri		Nahuatl		Average	
	Spearman	Pearson	Spearman	Pearson	Spearman	Pearson	Spearman	Pearson
Approach 1	0.6935	0.6389	0.5737	0.4570	0.6315	0.6005	0.6329	0.5655
Approach 2	0.6581	0.7001	0.6297	0.5600	0.5763	0.5981	0.6214	0.6194
Approach 3	0.6488	0.7334	0.5794	0.5944	0.6362	0.6486	0.6215	0.6588
Approach 4	0.6488	0.7334	0.5794	0.5944	0.6334	0.6486	0.6205	0.6588
Approach 5	**0.7544**	0.8653	**0.8283**	**0.8446**	0.8177	0.8266	**0.8001**	**0.8455**
Approach 6	0.7481	**0.8667**	0.8116	0.8305	**0.8216**	**0.8331**	0.7938	0.8434

Note: Best-performing scores in each column are highlighted in green and bold. Results are based on dev set correlations with human annotations.

Table 2: Spearman and Pearson correlation scores on the dev set across Guarani, Bribri, and Nahuatl for all six Indigeval approaches.

Team	Approach	Guarani		Bribri		Nahuatl		Average	
		Spearman	Pearson	Spearman	Pearson	Spearman	Pearson	Spearman	Pearson
ChrF++	-	-	0.6725	0.6263	0.4517	0.3823	0.6783	0.5549	0.5212
BLEU	-	-	0.4676	0.4056	0.4518	0.3456	0.3541	0.4061	0.3857
RaaVa 2	**Approach 5**	**0.6526**	**0.7209**	**0.5379**	**0.6540**	**0.6195**	**0.6362**	**0.6033**	**0.6704**
RaaVa 1	**Approach 6**	**0.6429**	**0.6964**	**0.5332**	**0.6523**	**0.6132**	**0.6351**	**0.5965**	**0.6613**
Tekio 1	-	0.6611	0.7196	0.5622	0.6244	0.6680	0.6115	0.6304	0.6518
Tekio 2	-	0.6611	0.7196	0.5569	0.6300	0.6132	0.5845	0.6104	0.6447
RaaVa 3	**Approach 4**	**0.6560**	**0.7038**	**0.4829**	**0.5931**	**0.6364**	**0.6263**	**0.5918**	**0.6411**
RaaVa 4	**Approach 3**	**0.6560**	**0.7038**	**0.4829**	**0.5931**	**0.6364**	**0.6263**	**0.5918**	**0.6411**
Tekio 4	-	0.5605	0.7234	0.4909	0.6268	0.5036	0.5351	0.5183	0.6285
Tekio 3	-	0.5597	0.7209	0.4892	0.6261	0.4963	0.5290	0.5151	0.6254
RaaVa 5	**Approach 2**	**0.6516**	**0.6776**	**0.5755**	**0.5662**	**0.6145**	**0.5921**	**0.6139**	**0.6120**
RaaVa 6	**Approach 1**	**0.6723**	**0.6249**	**0.5356**	**0.4223**	**0.6766**	**0.5657**	**0.6282**	**0.5377**
LexiLogic 1	-	0.6811	0.6529	0.5021	0.3763	0.6717	0.5504	0.6183	0.5265

Note: The winning submission is RaaVa 2 (Approach 5). Other **RaaVa** submissions (Approaches 1–6) are also shown in blue for clarity.

Table 3: Spearman and Pearson correlation scores on the Test set across Guarani, Bribri, and Nahuatl for all six Indigeval approaches.

bert sentence embedding. In *Proceedings of the 60th Annual Meeting of the Association for Computational Linguistics*.

Varun Gumma, Pranjal A. Chitale, and Kalika Bali. 2025. Towards inducing long-context abilities in multilingual neural machine translation models. *Preprint*, arXiv:2408.11382.

Grzegorz Kondrak. 2005. N-gram similarity and distance. In *Proceedings of the Twelfth Conference on Computational Natural Language Learning*, pages 82–89.

Arun K. Kuchibhotla, Lawrence D. Brown, Andreas Buja, and Junhui Cai. 2019. All of linear regression. *Preprint*, arXiv:1910.06386.

Vladimir I. Levenshtein. 1966. Binary codes capable of correcting deletions, insertions, and reversals. *Soviet Physics Doklady*, 10:707–710.

Chenyang Lyu, Zefeng Du, Jitao Xu, Yitao Duan, Minghao Wu, Teresa Lynn, Alham Fikri Aji, Derek F. Wong, Siyou Liu, and Longyue Wang. 2024. A paradigm shift: The future of machine translation lies with large language models. *Preprint*, arXiv:2305.01181.

Nitika Mathur, Timothy Baldwin, and Trevor Cohn. 2019. Putting evaluation in context: Contextual embeddings improve machine translation evaluation. In *Proceedings of the 57th Annual Meeting of the Association for Computational Linguistics*, pages 2799–2808.

Kishore Papineni, Salim Roukos, Todd Ward, and Wei-Jing Zhu. 2002a. Bleu: a method for automatic evaluation of machine translation. In *Annual Meeting of the Association for Computational Linguistics*.

Kishore Papineni, Salim Roukos, Todd Ward, and Wei-Jing Zhu. 2002b. Bleu: a method for automatic evaluation of machine translation. In *Proceedings of the 40th Annual Meeting of the Association for Computational Linguistics*, pages 311–318.

Lawrence Philips. 1990. Hanging on the metaphone. In *Computer Language*, volume 7, pages 39–44.

Maja Popović. chrF: character n-gram F-score for automatic MT evaluation.

Maja Popović. 2015. chrf: character n-gram f-score for automatic mt evaluation. In *Proceedings of the Tenth Workshop on Statistical Machine Translation*, pages 392–395.

Tharindu Ranasinghe, Constantin Orasan, and Ruslan Mitkov. 2020. Transquest: Translation quality estimation with cross-lingual transformers. In *Proceedings of the 28th International Conference on Computational Linguistics (COLING)*, pages 5070–5081.

Mohammad Sadegh Rasooli and Joel R. Tetreault. 2015. Yara parser: A fast and accurate dependency parser. *Computing Research Repository*, arXiv:1503.06733. Version 2.

Ricardo Rei, Ana Farinha, Alon Lavie, Luisa Coheur, and Joao Silva. 2020. Comet: A neural framework for mt evaluation. In *Proceedings of the 2020 Conference on Empirical Methods in Natural Language Processing (EMNLP)*, pages 2685–2702.

Nils Reimers and Iryna Gurevych. 2019a. Sentence-bert: Sentence embeddings using siamese bert-networks. *Preprint*, arXiv:1908.10084.

Nils Reimers and Iryna Gurevych. 2019b. Sentence-bert: Sentence embeddings using siamese bert-networks. In *Proceedings of the 2019 Conference on Empirical Methods in Natural Language Processing*. Association for Computational Linguistics.

Robert C. Russell. 1918. Soundex system of phonetic indexing.

Thibault Sellam, Dipanjan Das, and Ankur P Parikh. 2020. Bleurt: Learning robust metrics for text generation. In *Proceedings of the 58th Annual Meeting of the Association for Computational Linguistics*, pages 7881–7892.

Archchana Sindhujan, Diptesh Kanojia, Constantin Orasan, and Shenbin Qian. 2025. When LLMs struggle: Reference-less translation evaluation for low-resource languages. In *Proceedings of the First Workshop on Language Models for Low-Resource Languages*, pages 437–459, Abu Dhabi, United Arab Emirates. Association for Computational Linguistics.

Matthew Snover, Bonnie Dorr, Rich Schwartz, Linnea Micciulla, and John Makhoul. A study of translation edit rate with targeted human annotation. In *Proceedings of the 7th Conference of the Association for Machine Translation in the Americas: Technical Papers*.

Matthew Snover, Bonnie Dorr, Richard Schwartz, Linnea Micciulla, and John Makhoul. 2006. A study of translation edit rate with targeted human annotation. In *Proceedings of the 7th Conference of the Association for Machine Translation in the Americas*.

Charles Spearman. 1904. The proof and measurement of association between two things. *The American Journal of Psychology*, 15(1):72–101.

Lucia Specia, Gustavo Paetzold, and Carolina Scarton. Multi-level translation quality prediction with QuEst++.

Francis M. Tyers and Karina Mishchenkova. 2020. Dependency annotation of noun incorporation in polysynthetic languages. In *Universal Dependencies Workshop*.

Daniel Yacob. 2004. Application of the double metaphone algorithm to amharic orthography. *Preprint*, arXiv:cs/0408052.

UCSP Submission to the AmericasNLP 2025 Shared Task

Jorge Asillo Congora **Julio Santisteban** **Ricardo Lazo Vasquez**
Department of Computer Science, Universidad Católica San Pablo
Arequipa - Peru
{jorge.asillo, jsantisteban, ricardo.lazo}@ucsp.edu.pe

Abstract

Quechua is a low-resource language spoken by more than 7 million people in South America. While Quechua is primarily an oral language, several orthographic standards do exist. There is no universally adopted writing standard for Quechua, and variations exist across dialects and regions; its current writing is based on how it is uttered and how the sound is written. Quechua is a family of languages with similarities among the seven variants. The lack of a parallel dataset has reduced the opportunities for developing machine translation. We investigated whether increasing the current Quechua Parallel dataset with synthetic sentences and using a pre-trained large language model improves the performance of a Quechua machine translation. A Large language model has been used to generate synthetic sentences to extend the current parallel dataset. We use the mt5 model to fine-tune it to develop a machine translation for Quechua to Spanish and vice versa. Our survey identified the gaps in the state of the art of Quechua machine translation, and our BLEU/Chrf++ results show an improvement over the state of the art.

1 Introduction

In this paper we present the submission of the Universidad Católica San Pablo to the Workshop on Natural Language Processing (NLP) for Indigenous Languages of the Americas (AmericasNLP) 2025 Shared Task on machine translation systems for Indigenous languages. We participated in two directions: Spanish to Quechua and Quechua to Spanish.

Quechua is an indigenous language from the south of Peru that has expanded to Bolivia, Chile, and Ecuador. It is an indigenous language family with 7 variations and almost 8 to 10 million speakers. Quechua is actively used in Peru and Bolivia and is the official language of the Peruvian, Bolivian, and Ecuadorian governments.

Quechua is a phonetic language where each letter represents a specific sound. Quechua is well-studied linguistically and does have defined grammatical rules. Each Quechua dialect has its own semantics and vocabulary. Quechua is an agglutinative language where a prefix or suffix is added to the root of a word to create a new word with a different meaning. Quechua writing is as it sounds and according to the utterance and listener.

A parallel dataset restricts machine translation (MT). In the case of Quechua, the most used resource is the JW300 (Agić and Vulić, 2019), which presents 2 Quechua variants: Ayacucho Quechua (quy), Cuzco Quechua (quz), and the Bolivian variety of Quechua (que). There are also scarce resources with few parallel sentences.

There is a clear need to develop a machine translation and other tools to support Quechua speakers, and current proposals do not achieve an appropriate machine translation. The current research and development of a Quechua MT lacks of an appropriate parallel dataset, making it more challenging to develop an Quechua MT.

The AmericasNLP Shared Task on Machine Translation into Indigenous Languages has been promoting the research of 11 indigenous languages, including Quechua, from 2021 to 2024. The AmericasNLP Shared Task is a competition for research on machine translation. The AmericasNLP Shared Task is based mostly on the Quechua Ayacucho (quy) variant. The Shared Task is framed on a given dataset and open resources, including pre-trained models. The focus has been to translate Quechua–Spanish; to our knowledge, no other research has translated English into Quechua and Quechua into English.

The benchmark for a MT of Spanish (es) to Quechua (quy) has been set on The AmericansNLP 2024 as follows: chrF of 28.81 developed by Helsinki (Vázquez et al., 2021) and ChrF of 34.01 developed by Sheffield (Gow-Smith and Villegas,

Proceedings of the Fifth Workshop on NLP for Indigenous Languages of the Americas (AmericasNLP), pages 84–91
May 4, 2025 ©2025 Association for Computational Linguistics

2023) for the test set and 28.78, 30.22 respectively for the development set.

We aim to identify if extending the JW300 (Agić and Vulić, 2019) Parallel dataset by generating synthetic sentences in English would improve the machine translation performance. In addition, we want to identify if using a Large Language Model would improve the machine translation performance.

The following sections present a review of the state of the art, our method, and our results and Conclusion section.

2 Related Work

2.1 Early antecedents

Rios (2015) developed a hybrid machine translation for Spanish to Cuzco Quechua. The MT is a classical rule-based supported by statistical modules. Rios also developed a Quechua text normalisation to rewrite Quechua texts in different orthographies or dialects to standard orthography. Rios developed a Quechua dependency treebank and spell checker. Achieving a BLEU score of 57.98 for words and 63.13 for morphemes. Rios' work includes the use of verb morphology (Rios and Göhring, 2013) and rule-based(Rios and Göhring, 2016).

The AVENUE project at the Language Technologies Institute (Llitjós, 2005) had developed an MT which would be used to translate Quechua if a Parallel dataset exist. The AVENUE is a statistical machine translation. One extension of AVENUE had developed a Quechua Parallel dataset, which reached 1,700 sentences. As a result, a Quechua Morphology Analyzer to assist the MT was developed by Llitjós et al. (2005).

Vilca also developed a morphological analyzer (Vilca et al., 2009), Huarcaya Taquiri (2020) developed the first transformer model for an MT Spanish to Quechua Chanka with an outstanding BLEU score of 39.5 using the JW300 Parallel dataset (Agic and Vulic, 2019). Quechua Chanka is also know as Quechua Ayacucho (quy).

2.2 Quechua's resources

There are few resources of a Parallel dataset of Quechua, and the following parallel dataset is well established: the most used is the JW300 (Agic and Vulic, 2019), which presents 3 Quechua variants: Ayacucho Quechua (quy), Cuzco Quechua (quz).

The following parallel dataset are small repositories in which the validity of the Quechua variant is not clear: Sentences extracted from the official dictionary of the Minister of Education (MINEDU)(AmericasNLP, 2021), Huarcaya(Moreno, 2021), Oncevay(Arturo and Diego, 2021), the Peruvian(Congreso de la República del Perú, 2008) and Bolivian(Ministerio de la Presidencia de Bolivia, 2012), constitutions (Tiedemann, 2012), Wikipedia crawls(Tiedemann, 2020) and The JHU Bible parallel dataset (McCarthy et al., 2020).

Well-know Quechua dictionaries, Quechua Spanish and Spanish Quechua produced by Calvo Pérez (2007), Calvo works for the recognition and normalization of the Quechua language and its harmonization with the Spanish language. Calvos's dictionary holds 51233 Quechua and 74395 Spanish words. The website Runasimi.de (2006) provides a dictionary of several Quechua variants to German, English, Spanish, Italian and French.

2.3 State of the art of Quechua machine translation

Table 1 shows the best MT score for es->quy held by BSC (Garcia Gilabert et al., 2024) in the AmericasNLP 2024 Shared Task. For quy->es the score is held by Chen and Fazio (2021) focusing on a morphologically guided segmentation.

The state of the art concerning Quechua machine translation has its own limitations. The pertinent literature does not show a clear development and presents outlier results that are not viable to achieve like Huarcaya Taquiri (2020) reports a 39.50 BLEU score in the JW300 dataset(Agić and Vulić, 2019). Similarly, Ebrahimi and et. al. (2022) report 68.00 BLEU score for en -> quy using the same dataset. There are two logical conclusions: the results are inconclusive or use an incorrect interpretation of the BLEU score.

The BSC team (Garcia Gilabert et al., 2024) achieved the highest performance in the Quechua language. Their approach focused on fine-tuning the NLLB-200 for Quechua and Guarani, inparallel datasetting data from multiple sources and applying a rigorous cleaning process. They experimented with two model sizes, 3.3B and 1.3B, finding that the larger model only improved Quechua results. In particular, fine-tuning NLLB 1.3B with LoRA yielded a new benchmark score of 38.21 ChrF++ for Quechua, the highest among all submissions.

Other teams also contributed innovative approaches to the AmericasNLP 2024 Shared Task. The NordicAlps team (Attieh et al., 2024), based on

Author	BLEU	ChrF	Direction of Translation
AmericasNLP 2024 BSC (Task)	4.85	38.21	es ->quy
AmericasNLP 2024 BSC (NLLB-3.3B)	4.07	36.39	es ->quy
AmericasNLP 2024 Baseline dev.	-	30.22	es ->quy
AmericasNLP 2024 Baseline test	-	34.01	es ->quy
Gow-Smith and Villegas (2023)	4.61	39.52	es ->quy
Vázquez et al. (2021)	5.38	39.40	es ->quy
NLLB Team et al. (2022) 1.3B parameter	-	29.2	es ->quy
Thesis: (Huarcaya Taquiri, 2020)	39.50	0.24	es ->quy
Ebrahimi and et. al. (2022) Baseline	1.58	0.33	es ->quy
Ebrahimi and et. al. (2022) XLM-R Large +MLM	68.00	-	es ->quy
Chen and Fazio (2021)	23.70	-	quz ->es
Ortega et al. (2020) Morfessor	20.30	-	qu ->es
Ortega et al. (2020) BPE-Sennrich	22.90	-	qu ->es
Oncevay (2021) Pairwise	8.20	30.90	quy ->es
Oncevay (2021) Multiling.	4.23	37.80	es ->quy
Ortega et al. (2021) es,qu,fi	22.60	-	quz ->es
Ortega et al. (2021) es,qu,fi,cni	17.00	-	quz ->es
Ortega et al. (2021) es,qu,cni	20.10	-	quz ->es

Table 1: State of the art of Quechua machine translation

the Helsinki system (De Gibert et al., 2023), used various tokenization strategies, with their BPE-MR model ranking first in five languages. The DC_DMV team (Degenaro and Lupicki, 2024) worked with two approaches using the NLLB-200 and the Mamba-based model, obtaining the second-best result for Quechua with the NLLB model. Meanwhile, the University of Edinburgh (Iyer et al., 2024) fine-tuned Llama-2 7B, Mistral 7B, and MaLA-500 using LoRA but did not achieve outstanding performance.

Due to the nature of the Quechua and its lack of writing rules, there are attempts to use morphological tools to normalise the Quechua (Ebrahimi and et. al., 2022) (Chen and Fazio, 2021) (Ortega et al., 2020) (Ortega et al., 2021); prefixes and suffixes are used to normalise (Ortega et al., 2020), and text normalization to keep under control the text pass to a Neural Network (Vázquez et al., 2021). There are interesting approaches, but those rules are like if someone is building the grammar and syntaxes of the Quechua. Reported results range from 17 to 24 BLEU scores; most proposals do not use the ChrF, which might help corroborate the results. Some proposals use variations of the JW300 (Agić and Vulić, 2019) and in most cases, the dataset used is small and domain-constrained.

There are clear limitations to the development of Quechua machine translation. The first is the variety of Quechua dialects or variations. The second is the lack of writing rules, which causes the same pronounced word to be written differently. The last limitation is the lack of a Parallel dataset; all research is based on the JW300 parallel dataset, and no efforts are made to develop a new dataset even though there are 11 million Quechua speakers. Most of the testing is based on Opus biblical, a Peruvian magazine article, testing in a close domain. (Mager and et. al, 2021).

The present work tries to develop a machine translation based and extending the Parallel dataset with syntactic sentences. Tens of Indigenous languages exist in Western South America, some of which are in the process of extinction, and others have disappeared. We aim to preserve the Quechua and make it available to Quechua speakers.

3 Method

3.1 Data sources

Our sources of parallel dataset are shown in Table 5. Most of the data are based on the JW300 parallel dataset (Agić and Vulić, 2019). (Calvo Pérez, 2007) is a dictionary, and the sentences have been extracted almost manually. All our data has been cleaned up by removing irrelevant text, extracting only sentences in lowercase, and keeping only characters a-z and ñ. Data has been shuffle, and we reserve 85% for training and 15% for testing. The

JW300 was only used for que <-> en MT.

3.2 Parallel dataset Expansion

parallel dataset expansion is primarily based on the generation of synthetic sentences. This method consists of taking a sentence from a high-resource language such as Spanish or English, applying a **POS** and replacing words in the original sentence. We will use two approaches: Wordnet and based on LLM.

Based on WordNet, each sentence will be scanned to identify the parts of the speech. The subject and verb of the sentence will be selected. Using WordNet, similar words will be identified based on the four types of similarity defined by WordNet: synonyms, similar, hypernyms, and hyponyms. The new words, subject and verb, will be identified. Synthetic sentences are generated by combining the new words. The combination will be progressive, changing one word, then two, and then three. Several subsets of synthetic sentences are generated depending on the degree of combinatorics.

Based on LLM, each sentence will be parsed (POS) to identify the parts of speech. The subject and/or verb of the sentence will be selected. Using an LLM, the word (subject or verb) will be replaced with another semantically similar word in the context of the sentence. The answer sentence within the LLM answer will be extracted (clean the answer).

MT like mt5-small are sensitive to the direction of the translation. Asymmetric model supports this assumption (Santisteban and Tejada-Cárcamo, 2015). We will train the model in both directions.

The objective is to evaluate the machine translation for Quechua based on the expanded parallel dataset. Two *transformer* models will be used, the base Transformer model by (Vaswani et al., 2023) and a pre-trained multilingual MT5-small (Xue et al., 2021).

3.3 Generation of synthetics sentences

Two different approaches were used for synthetic sentence generation. Initially, an English dataset was processed using WordNet, where part-of-speech (POS) tagging identified the first noun. This noun was then replaced using WordNet and Phi-3 (Abdin et al., 2024), resulting in two synthetic sentences. For example, given the sentence "pay attention to how you listen", the POS tagging selected the word "pay". The synthetic sentence

Quechua	Original	Clean	Synthetic
que	135,068	131,430	*
quy	114,408	111,655	111655
quz	128,252	125,341	121,480

Table 2: English synthetic sentences generated

generated with WordNet was "wage attention to how you listen", while Phi-3 produced "focus on how you listen". The prompt used is as follows: "Replace '*word*' in '*sentence*' with another word while maintaining the semantic meaning".

In the second approach, a Spanish dataset was used without prior POS tagging. Instead, Phi-3.5 (Abdin et al., 2024) was prompted to replace either a verb or a noun in the given sentence while preserving its semantic meaning. For instance, starting with "aproveche momentos en que estén relajados.", Phi-3.5 generated "aproveche momentos de calma" This adjustment improved the quality of the generated sentences while maintaining coherence. The prompt used is as follows: "Reemplaza un '*sustantivo*' o '*verbo*' por otro semanticamente similar en la oracion: "{oracion}". dame la primera oracion alternativa. respuesta corta. sin explicacion".

4 Tests and Results

4.1 English-Quechua

For en->qu and vice versa, we only used the JW300 parallel dataset in English (Agić and Vulić, 2019). We used Phi3-mini due to its compact size and average performance compared to other larger models.

4.1.1 Synthetic Generation Results

Generation with Wordnet lacks of quality. It is unable to find a suitable synonym; it also fails to take the word's context into account, rendering the new sentence meaningless. The evaluation was empirical, based on a review of sentences.

A more satisfactory result was obtained regarding the synthetic sentences generated with Phi3-mini. It takes the word's context into account and can replace the verb, connectives, etc., associated with some nouns, resulting in synthetic sentences with better semantic meaning. Some sentences did not generate any results due to the absence of a noun in the sentence. The original parallel dataset increases with the synthetic sentences by 96%, almost doubling the size of the original parallel dataset.

Dataset	Sense	BLEU	ChrF
JW300	en quy	3.64	32.92
	quy en	5.70	23.43
	en quz	3.82	31.03
	quz en	5.49	22.54
JW300 Clean	en quy	2.68	33.87
	quy en	4.98	23.60
	en quz	3.17	31.70
	quz en	5.42	23.76
JW300 Extended	en quy	*	*
	quy en	5.22	23.35
	en quz	5.67	29.24
	quz en	3.08	31.51

Table 3: MT5-small trained in English

	Sense	BLEU	ChrF
JW300 Clean	en quz	1.89	28.88
	en quy	1.92	29.40
JW300 Expanded	en quz	1.83	28.46
	en quy	1.83	28.52

Table 4: Basic Transformers with synthetic data

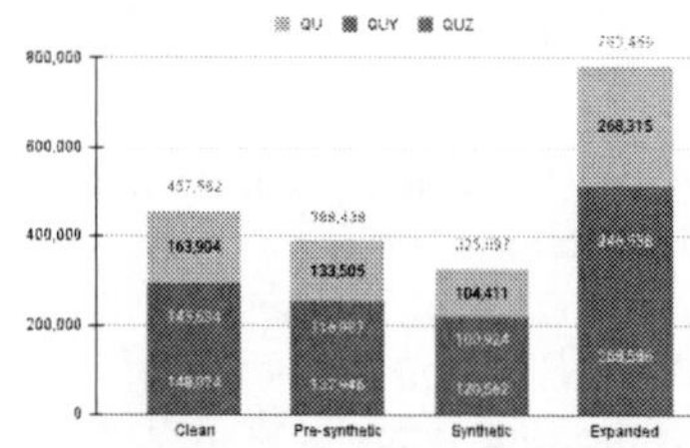

Figure 1: Numbers of synthetic sentences generated in Spanish from the original Spanish parallel dataset

4.1.2 Training the Transformer Models

Two models were used for training: the basic (untrained) transformer model by (Vaswani et al., 2023) and the MT5-small model by (Xue et al., 2021), which is a large, pretrained multilingual text-to-text transformer.

For the choice of tokenizers in the case of the MT5-small transformer, the model was trained using a word tokenizer for both the source and target languages. Retraining the model requires using the same tokenizers. In the case of the base transformer, since this model is trained from scratch, we chose a word tokenizer for English and a BPE tokenizer for Quechua.

Hyperparameters for MT5-small are as follows: batch size 8, learning rate 2e-5, seq_len 512, epoches 30, d_{model} 512. For base Transformer are batch size 32, learning rate 1e-4, seq_len 128, epoches 30, d_{model} 512.

4.1.3 Transformer Model Training Results

The fine-tuning of the MT5-small was tested as shown in Table 3 and 4. For the base transformer, we can see the output of both the model trained with the original parallel dataset and the model trained with the expanded parallel dataset.

Table 3 shows The training of MT5-small with different datasets. JW300 is the basic one (no data processing). JW300 Clean, without punctuation marks, verses, and others. JW300 Extended, the clean parallel dataset plus the synthetic parallel dataset. Trained in both directions, from the source language to the target language. BLEU (sacreBLEU) and ChrF metrics. Using two Quechua languages: Ayacucho Quechua (**quy**) and Cuzco Quechua (**quz**), and English (en). Synthetic parallel dataset generated with Phi3-mini.

As show in 4 the training the Base Transformer with different datasets. JW300 Clean, without punctuation marks, verses, and others. JW300 Extended, the clean parallel dataset plus the synthetic parallel dataset. Trained in both directions, from the source language to the target language. BLEU (sacreBLEU) and CharF metrics. Using Cuzco Quechua (**quz**) and Ayacucho Quechua (**quy**), and English (en). Synthetic parallel dataset generated with Phi3-mini.

The base Transformer and the MT5-small obtained lower scores in both metrics when training with the expanded parallel dataset than with the original. This drop in metrics may indicate that the generated synthetic sentences are not of good quality.

4.2 Spanish-Quechua

The Quechua-Spanish parallel dataset is from 7 sources. Those that could not be identified by the Quechua used were marked as Southern Quechua. A total of 457,562 entries were obtained for the new original parallel dataset, divided into three groups, "quz", "quy", and "qu", as shown in figure 1

4.2.1 Training the Transformer Models

The base transformer model (Vaswani et al., 2023) and the MT5-small (Xue et al., 2021) were used, with the same hyperparameters and tokenizers as in the english-Quechua phase. In the case of the MT5-small, the model was fine-tuned using a word

Author	File	Quechua	quantity
REPU-CS-2021	Constitution (REPU-CS-2021)	quz	812
	Handbook	quy	2,297
	Lexicon	quy	6,154
	Regulation	quz	217
	Webmics	quy	980
Portocarrero	Emotion analysis	-	1,722
AmericasNLP 2024	Dict_misc	quy	8,955
	Minedu	quy	643
	JW300	quy	115,620
	JW300	quz	124,833
Julio Calvo Perez	Spanish Quechua Dictionary Vol. 2	sur	20,606
JRXYZ	Various books	-	140,878
Llamacha	audio transcription	sur	698
Runasimi	dictionary	quy	10,986
	dictionary	quz	22,162

Table 5: Spanish-Quechua parallel dataset.

tokenizer. In the case of the base transformer we chose a BPE tokenizer.

4.2.2 Transformer Model Training Results

Two different sets were used: a validation set and a testing set. The validation set comes from the same original and expanded parallel dataset. The testing set is a parallel dataset provided by AmericasNLP 2024 to compare models.

Table 6 shows the model results for the original parallel dataset, and table 7 shows the expanded parallel dataset. A clear improvement was observed with the expanded parallel dataset over the original in both BLEU and ChrF. Although the scores are low compared to the best scores from Americas-NLP 2024. Considering resource constraints like vanilla transformer without pre-training and MT5-small fine-tuned on a domestic GPU (NVIDIA GeForce GTX 1070), results highlight opportunities for further progress.

5 Conclusion

Synthetic generation of sentences in English did not improve the machine translation. This is because the WordNet technique to generate synthetic sentences was not reliable. On the other hand, using Phi3.5 to generate synthetic sentences improves the MT, particularly in Spanish-Quechua.

Our finding shows that expanding the parallel dataset with synthetic sentences improves the performance of the MT, even if we use a pre-trained transformer (MT5-small) or base transformer model and even though we run our model on a domestic GPU (NVIDIA GeForce GTX 1070).

Identification of the Quechua varieties is still an open problem. It is natural for Quechua speakers, but to our understanding, there are no steps for language identification.

Fluency in the sentences is absent in all current proposals, which needs to be addressed. Fluency would be evaluated by its readability, rhythm, pacing, and the way the sentence structure mirrors natural speech patterns.

Limitations

The parallel dataset is small and domain-constrained, expanding it with synthetic sentences does not guarantee the expansion of the MT in other domains. Despite the existence of millions of Quechua speakers.

References

Marah Abdin, Jyoti Aneja, Hany Awadalla, Ahmed Awadallah, Ammar Ahmad Awan, Nguyen Bach, Amit Bahree, Arash Bakhtiari, Jianmin Bao, Harkirat Behl, Alon Benhaim, Misha Bilenko, Johan Bjorck, Sébastien Bubeck, Martin Cai, Qin Cai, Vishrav Chaudhary, Dong Chen, Dongdong Chen, and 110 others. 2024. Phi-3 technical report: A highly capable language model locally on your phone. *Preprint*, arXiv:2404.14219.

Željko Agić and Ivan Vulić. 2019. JW300: A wide-coverage parallel corpus for low-resource languages. In *Proceedings of the 57th Annual Meeting of the Association for Computational Linguistics*, pages 3204–

Model	Dataset	Validation		Testing	
		Bleu	ChrF++	Bleu	ChrF++
MT5	quz	9.97	29.94	1.06	19.85
	quy	11.42	32.24	1.23	21.13
	quz + quz + qu	19.40	*	9.96	29.94
Transformer Base	quz	4.04	35.85	0.02	22.35
	quy	5.26	40.27	0.02	23.90
	quz + quz + qu	*	*	*	*

Table 6: Results of the transformers trained with the original Spanish Quechua corpus.

Model	Dataset	Validation		Testing	
		Bleu	ChrF++	Bleu	ChrF++
MT5	quz	8.56	28.65	1.06	20.38
	quy	9.81	30.50	2.00	22.73
	quz + quz + qu	*	*	*	*
Transformer Base	quz	9.14	41.39	0.04	24.70
	quy	12.38	45.64	0.10	27.43
	quz + quz + qu	*	*	*	*

Table 7: Results of the transformers trained with the expanded Quechua Spanish parallel dataset

3210, Florence, Italy. Association for Computational Linguistics.

Željko Agic and Ivan Vulic. 2019. Jw300: A wide-coverage parallel corpus for low-resource languages. Association for Computational Linguistics.

AmericasNLP. 2021. Mt for spanish (es) - quechua ayacucho (quy). Accessed: 2025-03-20.

Oncevay Arturo and Huarcaya Diego. 2021. Mt-es-quy: Machine translation for spanish-quechua. Accessed: 2025-03-20.

Joseph Attieh, Zachary Hopton, Yves Scherrer, and Tanja Samardžić. 2024. System description of the NordicsAlps submission to the AmericasNLP 2024 machine translation shared task. In *Proceedings of the 4th Workshop on Natural Language Processing for Indigenous Languages of the Americas (AmericasNLP 2024)*, pages 150–158, Mexico City, Mexico. Association for Computational Linguistics.

Julio Calvo Pérez. 2007. Estrategias lexicológicas sobre terminología (en el nuevo diccionario español-quechua/quechua-español). *Estrategias lexicológicas sobre terminología (en el Nuevo Diccionario español-quechua/quechua-español)*, pages 737–757.

William Chen and Brett Fazio. 2021. Morphologically-guided segmentation for translation of agglutinative low-resource languages. In *Proceedings of the 4th Workshop on Technologies for MT of Low Resource Languages (LoResMT2021)*, pages 20–31.

Congreso de la República del Perú. 2008. *Perú Suyu Hatun Kamay Pirwa 1993: Constitución Política del Perú*. Congreso de la República del Perú. Accessed: 2025-03-20.

Ona De Gibert, Raúl Vázquez, Mikko Aulamo, Yves Scherrer, Sami Virpioja, and Jörg Tiedemann. 2023. Four approaches to low-resource multilingual NMT: The Helsinki submission to the AmericasNLP 2023 shared task. In *Proceedings of the Workshop on Natural Language Processing for Indigenous Languages of the Americas (AmericasNLP)*, pages 177–191, Toronto, Canada. Association for Computational Linguistics.

Dan Degenaro and Tom Lupicki. 2024. Experiments in mamba sequence modeling and NLLB-200 fine-tuning for low resource multilingual machine translation. In *Proceedings of the 4th Workshop on Natural Language Processing for Indigenous Languages of the Americas (AmericasNLP 2024)*, pages 188–194, Mexico City, Mexico. Association for Computational Linguistics.

Abteen Ebrahimi and et. al. 2022. AmericasNLI: Evaluating zero-shot natural language understanding of pretrained multilingual models in truly low-resource languages. In *Proceedings of the 60th Annual Meeting of the Association for Computational Linguistics (Volume 1: Long Papers)*, pages 6279–6299, Dublin, Ireland. Association for Computational Linguistics.

Javier Garcia Gilabert, Aleix Sant, Carlos Escolano, Francesca De Luca Fornaciari, Audrey Mash, and Maite Melero. 2024. BSC submission to the AmericasNLP 2024 shared task. In *Proceedings of the 4th Workshop on Natural Language Processing for Indigenous Languages of the Americas (AmericasNLP 2024)*, pages 143–149, Mexico City, Mexico. Association for Computational Linguistics.

Edward Gow-Smith and Danae Sánchez Villegas. 2023. Sheffield's submission to the americasnlp shared task on machine translation into indigenous languages. *arXiv preprint arXiv:2306.09830*.

Diego Huarcaya Taquiri. 2020. Traducción automática neuronal para lengua nativa peruana.

Vivek Iyer, Bhavitvya Malik, Wenhao Zhu, Pavel Stepachev, Pinzhen Chen, Barry Haddow, and Alexandra Birch. 2024. Exploring very low-resource translation with LLMs: The University of Edinburgh's submission to AmericasNLP 2024 translation task. In *Proceedings of the 4th Workshop on Natural Language Processing for Indigenous Languages of the Americas (AmericasNLP 2024)*, pages 209–220, Mexico City, Mexico. Association for Computational Linguistics.

Ariadna Font Llitjós. 2005. Developing a quechua-spanish machine translation system.

Ariadna Font Llitjós, Roberto Aranovich, and Lori Levin. 2005. Building machine translation systems for indigenous languages. In *Second Conference on the Indigenous Languages of Latin America (CILLA II), Texas, USA*.

Manuel Mager and et. al. 2021. Findings of the americasnlp 2021 shared task on open machine translation for indigenous languages of the americas. In *Proceedings of the First Workshop on Natural Language Processing for Indigenous Languages of the Americas*, pages 202–217.

Arya D McCarthy, Rachel Wicks, Dylan Lewis, Aaron Mueller, Winston Wu, Oliver Adams, Garrett Nicolai, Matt Post, and David Yarowsky. 2020. The johns hopkins university bible corpus: 1600+ tongues for typological exploration. In *Proceedings of the Twelfth Language Resources and Evaluation Conference*, pages 2884–2892.

Ministerio de la Presidencia de Bolivia. 2012. *Estadoq Kuraq Kamachiynin: Constitución Política del Estado*. Ministerio de la Presidencia y Fundación Konrad Adenauer (KAS). Accessed: 2025-03-20.

Oscar Moreno. 2021. The REPU CS' Spanish–Quechua submission to the AmericasNLP 2021 shared task on open machine translation. In *Proceedings of the First Workshop on Natural Language Processing for Indigenous Languages of the Americas*, pages 241–247, Online. Association for Computational Linguistics.

NLLB Team, Marta R. Costa-jussà, James Cross, Onur Çelebi, Maha Elbayad, Kenneth Heafield, Kevin Heffernan, Elahe Kalbassi, Janice Lam, Daniel Licht, Jean Maillard, Anna Sun, Skyler Wang, Guillaume Wenzek, Al Youngblood, Bapi Akula, Loic Barrault, Gabriel Mejia-Gonzalez, Prangthip Hansanti, and 20 others. 2022. No language left behind: Scaling human-centered machine translation.

Arturo Oncevay. 2021. Peru is multilingual, its machine translation should be too? In *Proceedings of the First Workshop on Natural Language Processing for Indigenous Languages of the Americas*, pages 194–201.

John E Ortega, Richard Castro Mamani, and Kyunghyun Cho. 2020. Neural machine translation with a polysynthetic low resource language. *Machine Translation*, 34(4):325–346.

John E Ortega, Richard Alexander Castro Mamani, and Jaime Rafael Montoya Samame. 2021. Love thy neighbor: combining two neighboring low-resource languages for translation. In *Proceedings of the 4th Workshop on Technologies for MT of Low Resource Languages (LoResMT2021)*, pages 44–51.

Annette Rios. 2015. *A basic language technology toolkit for quechua*. Ph.D. thesis, University of Zurich.

Annette Rios and Anne Göhring. 2013. Machine learning disambiguation of quechua verb morphology. Association for Computational Linguistics.

Annette Rios and Anne Göhring. 2016. Machine learning applied to rule-based machine translation. *Hybrid approaches to machine translation*, pages 111–129.

Runasimi.de. 2006. Runasimi - quechua language resources. Accessed: 2025-03-20.

Julio Santisteban and Javier Tejada-Cárcamo. 2015. Unilateral jaccard similarity coefficient. In *GSB@ SIGIR*, pages 23–27.

Jörg Tiedemann. 2012. Parallel data, tools and interfaces in opus. In *Lrec*, volume 2012, pages 2214–2218. Citeseer.

Jörg Tiedemann. 2020. The tatoeba translation challenge–realistic data sets for low resource and multilingual mt. *arXiv preprint arXiv:2010.06354*.

Ashish Vaswani, Noam Shazeer, Niki Parmar, Jakob Uszkoreit, Llion Jones, Aidan N. Gomez, Lukasz Kaiser, and Illia Polosukhin. 2023. Attention is all you need. *Preprint*, arXiv:1706.03762.

Raúl Vázquez, Yves Scherrer, Sami Virpioja, and Jörg Tiedemann. 2021. The helsinki submission to the americasnlp shared task. In *Workshop on Natural Language Processing for Indigenous Languages of the Americas*, pages 255–264. The Association for Computational Linguistics.

Hugo David Calderon Vilca, Vilca César David Mamani Calderón, Flor Cagniy Cárdenas Mariño, and Edwin Fredy Mamani Calderón. 2009. Traductor automático en linea del español a quechua, basado en la plataforma libre y código abierto apertium. *Revista de Investigaciones de la Escuela de Posgrado de la UNA PUNO*, 5(3):81–99.

Linting Xue, Noah Constant, Adam Roberts, Mihir Kale, Rami Al-Rfou, Aditya Siddhant, Aditya Barua, and Colin Raffel. 2021. mt5: A massively multilingual pre-trained text-to-text transformer. *Preprint*, arXiv:2010.11934.

Machine Translation Using Grammar Materials for LLM Post-Correction

Jonathan Hus[1], **Nathaniel Krasner**[1], **Antonios Anastasopoulos**[1,2]
[1]George Mason University, [2] Archimedes, Athena Research Center
jhus@gmu.edu, nkrasner@gmu.edu, antonis@gmu.edu

Abstract

This paper describes George Mason University's submission to the AmericasNLP 2025 Shared Task on Machine Translation into Indigenous Languages. We prompt a large language model (LLM) with grammar reference materials to correct the translations produced by a finetuned Encoder-Decoder machine translation system. This hybrid approach leads to improvements when translating from the indigenous languages into Spanish, indicating that LLMs are capable of using grammar materials to better handle a previously unseen-during-pretraining language.[1]

1 Introduction

Machine translation (MT) systems typically require massive parallel corpora to achieve state-of-the-art results. However, this magnitude of data is not available for low resource languages. To address this dearth of data, we propose a prompt-based approach that incorporates linguistic reference material including grammar books, dictionaries, and a limited number of parallel sentences. This approach was originally proposed in Machine Translation from One Book (MTOB; Tanzer et al., 2023) for a single language (Kalamang) and Hus and Anastasopoulos (2024) expanded to a more large-scale investigation to include 15 additional low resource languages.

In order to improve performance, we have augmented the prompt to include a translation from a dedicated MT system, which has been finetuned on the 13 Latin American indigenous languages using the available parallel sentences from the AmericasNLP 2025 training set. Thus, the large language model (LLM) is provided with a potential translation that can be utilized in conjunction with the reference linguistic material. The reference material consists of the following items:

Dictionaries We obtain dictionaries from PanLex[2] for all our languages. Note that in cases where the number of words in the dictionary was less than 100 we do not include them in the prompt. The size of each dictionary is included in Appendix A

Parallel Sentences Parallel sentences are included in the prompts as translation examples for in-context learning. We use the training set as provided by AmericasNLP 2025 Shared Task on Machine Translation.

Grammar Books The DReaM corpus (Virk et al., 2020) contains digitized versions of thousands of linguistic documents, including grammar books and sketches, for many languages. The source of these documents is often in paper format, and due to the scanning/OCR quality, the digitized versions often contain scanning artifacts. We select one grammar document for each of our languages. We perform slight manual cleanup to remove some items (e.g., scanning artifacts, table of contents) and to ensure that the grammar would fit in the LLM's context size.

2 Methodology

We use the GPT-4o-mini model for our experiments. Its context size of 128k tokens allows large grammar books to be included in the prompt. Additionally, we finetune separate NLLB 3.3B models (Costa-jussà et al., 2022) for each translation direction (xx→es and es→xx) using the provided training data. These NLLB models are then used to provide preliminary "suggested" translations for the LLM to edit.

Prompt Format Our prompts are formatted to contain the following information:

- Prefix - Contains the task description, including the source and target languages

[1]Code and data to reproduce our experiments are here: `https://github.com/jonathanhus/americasnlp`.

[2]`https://panlex.org`

Proceedings of the Fifth Workshop on NLP for Indigenous Languages of the Americas (AmericasNLP), pages 92–99
May 4, 2025

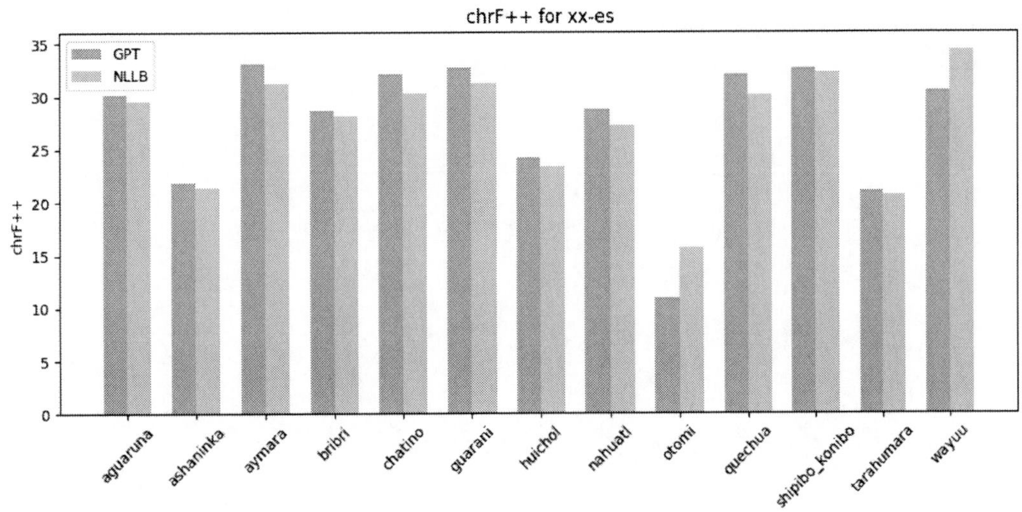

Figure 1: X-to-Spanish Performance on the Dev Dataset

- Dictionary Entries - For each word in the sentence, an entry from the bilingual dictionary is retrieved that closely matches the word. In cases where there is not a direct match of the source word, a selection is made using longest common subsequence (LCS) matching with the available words in the dictionary. The number of dictionary entries to be retrieved is configurable, but for our experiments we chose two, which was the parameter value chosen for evaluation in previous studies.

- Parallel Sentences - For each word in the sentence, a pair of parallel sentences is selected that has a similar word in it. The number of parallel sentences to be retrieved is configurable, but for our experiments we chose two, which was the parameter value chosen for evaluation in previous studies.

- Grammar Book - The full length grammar book for the indigenous language is included in the prompt

- Suggested Translation - Using our finetuned NLLB models, we provide a possible translation, and inform the LLM that it can use that to modify or improve upon it

- Suffix - Finally, we reiterate that the LLM should provide the translation and coax it to attempt the translation even if it does not "speak" the indigenous language

An example prompt is illustrated in Appendix B.

3 Results

We consider two systems when running our tests. The first is the finetuned NLLB system by itself. The second is the prompt-based LLM approach, which uses the finetuned NLLB system as one of its inputs in order to generate a translation. We evaluate both of these systems on the dev dataset and the test dataset.

Using a small sample of 100 sentences in each language from the dev dataset, we compare the chrF++ scores between the NLLB "suggestions" and the final LLM translations. It is clear from Figures 1 and 2 that, in the case of these languages, our grammar-based LLM post-correction is primarily useful for translation into Spanish rather than into languages that the LLM is unfamiliar with. This indicates that the LLM can use the grammar information to better understand the indigenous languages, but it is not enough to produce them, at least under the current prompt format and generation paradigm.

The systems are also evaluated using the test dataset, with results shown in Tables 1 and 2. Similar performance characteristics are observed, with translation into Spanish better performed by the LLM system and translation from Spanish better performed by the NLLB system.

In the previous studies that utilized the prompt-based LLM approach, ablations were performed to assess the performance of the model when given

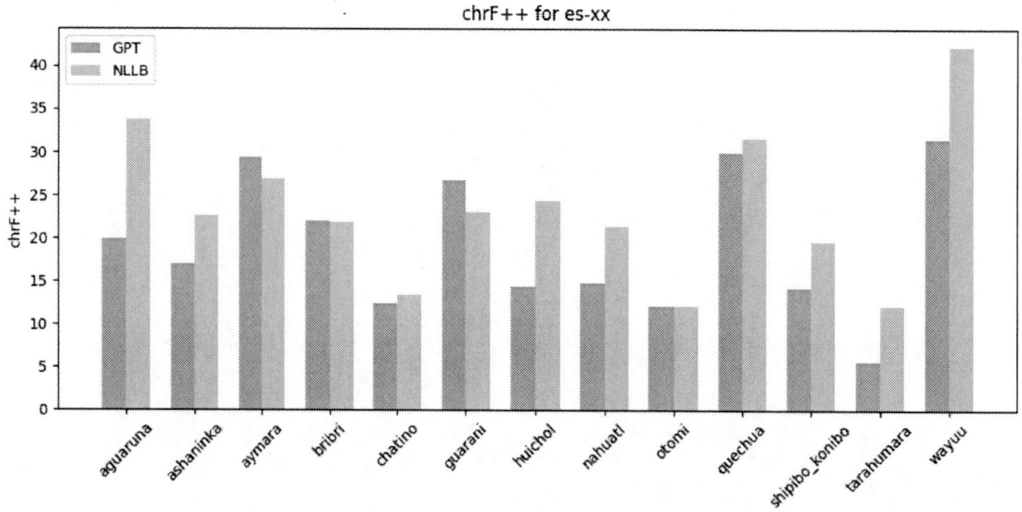

Figure 2: Spanish-to-X Performance on the Dev Dataset

various combinations of reference material input (e.g., providing only parallel sentences or providing only the grammar book.) In addition, a baseline assessment was determined for each language, where the model was provided no reference material. Due to time and cost constraints, that assessment was not performed for the set of languages in this paper. We leave that as a future research activity. A novelty in this paper is that the common language for all of the parallel sentences is Spanish, whereas previous efforts used English as the common language. However, the prompt templates and some of the grammar books are in English. The effect of having English, Spanish, and the indigenous language all represented in the prompt is unknown and this warrants further investigation.

4 Conclusion

We propose two systems to perform machine translation for indigenous languages. The first is an NLLB-based system. The second system utilizes the outputs of the NLLB-based system in addition to linguistic reference material to formulate prompts for LLMs in order to perform translation. We evaluated both our systems on the dev set of 13 different languages, translating into and out of Spanish. We note that the NLLB has superior performance in the es→xx translation direction, while the LLM-based system performs better in the xx→es direction. Both systems show a promising path forward for translation of low resource languages. Since both systems produce similar results, the more computationally efficient NLLB system would appear to be the favored choice, especially for communities lacking the resources necessary for the additional computation. However, additional techniques like Retrieval-Augmented Generation (RAG) could make more efficient use of the model and could provide improved results. Therefore, both NLLB and LLM methods deserve further research.

5 Limitations

Full-length grammar books are provided in the input prompt in order to "teach" a model how to translate into a given language. However, there are some limitations with this approach. First, high quality grammar books are difficult to obtain for many languages. The DReaM corpus does an admirable job of curating and digitizing many linguistic references, but the output is not perfect. Multi-column text documents and tables lose information that is conveyed by the location of text relative to other text on the page. The LLMs, therefore, are most likely not taking full advantage of that information. Additionally, scanning artifacts like headers and page numbers add unnecessary clutter to the reference material.

We used an OpenAI model (gpt-4o-mini) similar to what was used in Back to School (Hus and Anastasopoulos, 2024). While these models are quite performant, there are some drawbacks. First, these are truly closed models, with only an API available. The architecture, weights, and training

Language	GPT BLEU	GPT ChrF	GPT ChrF++	NLLB BLEU	NLLB ChrF	NLLB ChrF++	NLLB Baseline ChrF++
agr-es	16.81	38.73	36.59	15.17	38.73	36.52	38.39
aym-es	6.51	27.5	26.09	5.17	26.49	25.23	35.6
bzd-es	6.98	29.14	27.86	6.11	28.77	27.41	30.14
cni-es	5.32	23.72	22.44	4	22.94	21.57	24.86
ctp-es	3.76	15.6	14.47	11.74	28.04	26.16	35.84
gn-es	13.81	34.93	33.84	11.23	33.57	32.31	35.91
guc-es	2.92	25.06	23.1	4.2	26	23.93	24.74
hch-es	5.46	25.91	24.37	4.69	25.53	24.04	26.33
nah-es	7.22	27.14	25.58	5.08	26.18	24.31	26.36
oto-es	2.25	19.69	18.24	1.36	17.76	15.99	20.81
quy-es	12.27	34.64	33.02	10.38	33.5	31.77	37.18
shp-es	13.83	39.93	38.01	12.55	39.4	37.43	47.81
tar-es	2.07	21.53	19.72	1.75	21.23	19.39	18.75

Table 1: System Performance on Test Dataset (XX→ES)

Language	GPT BLEU	GPT ChrF	GPT ChrF++	NLLB BLEU	NLLB ChrF	NLLB ChrF++	NLLB Baseline ChrF++
es-agr	1.3	19.16	16.67	8.64	39.75	35.09	36.76
es-aym	0.88	23.12	20.45	1.14	26.26	22.91	31.21
es-bzd	3.85	19.42	20.61	4.41	21.56	22.51	25.52
es-cni	3.63	24.62	21.77	2.47	25.6	22.22	24.39
es-ctp	1.64	15.04	13.33	1.27	15.31	12.25	36.53
es-gn	5.47	32.5	29.95	4.04	27.23	25	35.68
es-guc	0.2	10.94	9.12	1.48	27.42	22.93	24.18
es-hch	5.98	27	23.59	10.04	29.59	26.14	28.26
es-nah	0.64	18.76	15.98	2.02	23.82	20.33	22.42
es-oto	0.98	11.55	10.03	1.33	13.23	11.31	12.78
es-quy	3.8	36.3	31.68	3.7	38.02	32.7	31.88
es-shp	2.68	19.39	17.49	2.79	21.99	19.46	25.76
es-tar	0.77	15.45	13.89	0.39	14.35	12.53	15.96

Table 2: System Performance on Test Dataset (ES→XX)

scheme are not available to researchers. Second, since the model is closed, we do not know whether the linguistic reference material is responsible for improved translation performance or whether the models themselves have this inherent ability.

The sizes of the bilingual dictionaries were inconsistent, with a handful having less than 20 words. We removed these low-volume dictionaries from our experiments. However, larger dictionaries of similar magnitudes would most likely improve the translations and would allow translation performance across the various languages to be better compared.

Acknowledgements

This work is supported by the National Science Foundation under Awards 2327143 and 2346334. This work was partially supported by resources provided by the Office of Research Computing at George Mason University (URL: `https://orc.gmu.edu`) and funded in part by grants from the National Science Foundation (Award Number 2018631).

References

Marta R. Costa-jussà, James Cross, Onur Çelebi, Maha Elbayad, Kenneth Heafield, Kevin Heffernan, Elahe Kalbassi, Janice Lam, Daniel Licht, Jean Maillard, Anna Sun, Skyler Wang, Guillaume Wenzek, Al Youngblood, Bapi Akula, Loic Barrault, Gabriel Mejia Gonzalez, Prangthip Hansanti, John Hoffman, Semarley Jarrett, Kaushik Ram Sadagopan, Dirk Rowe, Shannon Spruit, Chau Tran, Pierre Andrews, Necip Fazil Ayan, Shruti Bhosale, Sergey Edunov, Angela Fan, Cynthia Gao, Vedanuj Goswami, Francisco (Paco) Guzmán, Philipp Koehn, Alexandre Mourachko, Christophe Ropers, Safiyyah Saleem, Holger Schwenk, and Jeff Wang. 2022. No language left behind: Scaling human-centered machine translation. URL:https://research.facebook.com/publications/no-language-left-behind/.

Jonathan Hus and Antonios Anastasopoulos. 2024. Back to school: Translation using grammar books. In *Proceedings of the 2024 Conference on Empirical Methods in Natural Language Processing*, pages 20207–20219, Miami, Florida, USA. Association for Computational Linguistics.

David Kamholz, Jonathan Pool, and Susan Colowick. 2014. PanLex: Building a resource for panlingual lexical translation. In *Proceedings of the Ninth International Conference on Language Resources and Evaluation (LREC'14)*, pages 3145–3150, Reykjavik, Iceland. European Language Resources Association (ELRA).

Garrett Tanzer, Mirac Suzgun, Eline Visser, Dan Jurafsky, and Luke Melas-Kyriazi. 2023. A benchmark for learning to translate a new language from one grammar book. In *Arxiv*.

Shafqat Mumtaz Virk, Harald Hammarström, Markus Forsberg, and Søren Wichmann. 2020. The DReaM corpus: A multilingual annotated corpus of grammars for the world's languages. In *Proceedings of the 12th Language Resources and Evaluation Conference*, pages 878–884, Marseille, France. European Language Resources Association.

A Resources

For our experiments, we gathered dictionaries, parallel sentences, and grammar books to use in the prompts. Dictionaries were obtained from PanLex (Kamholz et al., 2014) and converted into the format required by the code. The sizes of the dictionaries are shown in Table 3.

Language	ISO 639-3	Dictionary Words es → X	Dictionary Words X → es
Aguaruna	agr	2242	2496
Aymara	aym	1827	1555
Bribri	bzd	11	11
Ashaninka	cni	12	10
Chatino	ctp	N/A	N/A
Guarani	gn	3354	3465
Wayuu	guc	2304	2497
Huichol	hch	12	11
Nahuatl	nah	N/A	N/A
Otomi	oto	4416	3439
Quechua	quy	20203	18589
Shipibo-Konibo	shp	1157	1129
Tarahumara	tar	1039	812

Table 3: Number of words in the dictionaries. Note the Chatino and Nahuatl were not found in the PanLex database. Therefore, translations for those words were not included in the prompt.

Language	Grammar Book	Number of Tokens
Aguaruna	Overall, Simon. (2007) A Grammar of Aguaruna. LaTrobe University doctoral dissertation.	109115
Aymara	Hardman, Martha J. (2001) Aymara (LINCOM Studies in Native American Linguistics 35). München: Lincom.	159071
Bribri	Jara Murillo, Carla Victoria. (2018) Gramática de la Lengua Bribri. San José, Costa Rica: E-Digital ED.	130572
Ashaninka	Rojas, Esaú Zumaeta and Gerardo Anton Zerdin. (2018) Ayotero añaane / Guía teórica del idioma asháninka. Nopoki: Universidad Católica Sedes Sapientiae.	164836
Chatino	Pride, Kitty. (1965) Chatino syntax (Summer Institute of Linguistics Publications in Linguistics and Related Fields 12). Norman: Summer Institute of Linguistics of the University of Oklahoma.	44698
Guarani	Gregores, Emma and Jorge A. Suárez. (1967) A Description of Colloquial Guaraní (Janua Linguarum: Series Practica 27). Berlin: Mouton de Gruyter.	
Wayuu	José Álvarez. (2017) Compendio de la gramática de la lengua wayuu. Ms.	114676
Huichol	Iturrioz Leza, José Luis and Paula Gómez López. (2006) Gramática Wixarika I. München: LINCOM.	136345
Nahuatl	Cowan de Beller, Patricia and Richard Beller. (1979) Curso del náhuatl moderno: náhuatl de la Huasteca. Mexico: Instituto Lingüístico de Verano.	57298
Otomi	Priego Montfort de Mostaghimi, Maria Eugenia. (1989) Gramática del otomí (hñähñu) del Mezquital, Mexico. Universität Bielefeld doctoral dissertation.	165311
Quechua	Zariquiey, Roberto and Gavina Córdova. (2008) Qayna, Kunan, Paqarin: Una introducción prática al quechua chanca. Lima: PUCP.	129158
Shipibo-Konibo	Faust, Norma. (1973) Lecciones para el aprendizaje del idioma shipibo-conibo (Documento de Trabajo 1). Yarinacocha: Instituto Lingüístico de Verano.	112794
Tarahumara	Caballero, Gabriela. (2022) A grammar of Choguita Rarámuri: In collaboration with Luz Elena León Ramírez, Sebastián Fuentes Holguín, Bertha Fuentes Loya and other Choguita Rarámuri language experts. Berlin: Language Science Press.	122232

Table 4: Grammar Books and Size

B Prompt Format

Each sentence to be translated is formatted into a prompt for GPT-4. The prompt has six components: prefix, words, sentences, grammar book, suggestion, and suffix. The experiment configuration determines whether words (W), sentences (S), or grammar books (G) are included in the prompt. The prefix and suffix are always included in the prompt. In the following sections, we show the format of the prompt by example, using an Aguaruna-to-Spanish translation task. We heavily used the code provided by the authors of "Machine Translation from One Book" to generate the prompts.

B.1 Prefix

The prefix provides the task to perform (translation), the source and target languages, and the sentence to translate.

> You are an expert translator. Translate the following sentence from Aguaruna to Spanish: Nunik nagkamawaju Timanmi jeen, takai takainakua jimaituk wenak yawejaju.

B.2 Words

For words, we attempt to retrieve the item from the bilingual dictionary. For each word in the source sentence, the top two matching words from the dictionary, as measured by LCS, are included in the prompt.

> To help with the translation, here is one of the closest entries to Nunik in the bilingual dictionary:
> Aguaruna word: nuniktatak
> Spanish translation: a veces
>
> To help with the translation, here is one of the closest entries to Nunik in the bilingual dictionary:
> Aguaruna word: nunik-bau ah-amu
> Spanish translation: causar
>
> *Additional word-level translations are provided for the remaining words of the source sentence.*

B.3 Sentences

For sentences, we attempt to retrieve similar samples from our small corpus of parallel sentences. For each word in the source sentence, we find sentences that contain that word, as measured by LCS, and include the top two matches in the prompt.

> To help with the translation, here is a translated sentence with words similar to N̈unikïn a list of translated reference sentences:
> Aguaruna sentence: Aatus gobernador aidau chichaman umikag, apu Daríojai chichastatus shiyakajui. Nunik jegajuawag chichajuinak: "¡Apuh, kuashat mijan pujustin ata!
> Spanish translation: Entonces estos jefes principales y los capitanes vinieron al rey y le dijeron: ¡Oh, rey Darío! Ten vida para siempre.
>
> To help with the translation, here is a translated sentence with words similar to N̈unikïn a list of translated reference sentences:
> Aguaruna sentence: Aatus David tupikaki uwemjauwai. Nunik Samueljai chichastatus yaakat Ramá weuwai. Nuwi jegaa Saúl niina maatag tibaun ashí Samuelan ujakui. Tusa ujaka Samueljai yaakat Naiot Ramá awa nuwi pujustatus weuwai.
> Spanish translation: Entonces David salió en vuelo, se escapó y fue a Ramá, a Samuel, y le contó todo lo que Saúl le había hecho. Y él y Samuel fueron y vivían en Naiot.
>
> *Additional sentence-level translations are provided for the remaining words of the source sentence.*

B.4 Grammar Book

We include the full grammar book in the prompt.

> To help with the translation, here is the full text of a bilingual grammar book:
> —
> ## FULL BOOK INSERTED HERE ##
> This is the end of the bilingual grammar book.
> —

B.5 Hypothesis

The output of our finetuned NLLB system is provided as a hypothesis or suggestion in the prompt.

> Here is a potential translation of the sentence provided by another system that you can modify or improve upon. Only use the suggestion if it improves your response.
> Y los criados de Saúl llegaron a la casa de Timni, y la mitad de su jornada fue en ayunas.

B.6 Suffix

The suffix reiterates the task and prompts for the appropriate translation.

> Now perform the translation. If you are not sure what the translation should be, then give your best guess. Do not say that you do not speak Aguaruna. If your translation is wrong, that is fine, but you have to provide a translation. Provide only the translation as output.
> Aguaruna: Nunik nagkamawaju Timanmi jeen, takai takainakua jimaituk wenak yawejaju.
> Spanish translation:

Machine Translation Metrics for Indigenous Languages Using Fine-tuned Semantic Embeddings

Nathaniel Krasner[1,*], **Justin Vasselli**[2,*], **Belu Ticona**[1],
Antonios Anastasopoulos[1], **Chi-kiu Lo 羅致翹**[3]
[*]Equal Contribution, [1]George Mason University, [2]Nara Institute of Science and Technology,
[3]National Research Council Canada
nkrasner@gmu.edu, vasselli.justin_ray.vk4@is.naist.jp, mticonao@gmu.edu, antonis@gmu.edu, chikiu.lo@nrc-cnrc.gc.ca

Abstract

This paper describes the Tekio submission to the AmericasNLP 2025 shared task on machine translation metrics for Indigenous languages. We developed two primary metric approaches leveraging multilingual semantic embeddings. First, we fine-tuned the Language-agnostic BERT Sentence Encoder (LaBSE) specifically for Guarani, Bribri, and Nahuatl, significantly enhancing semantic representation quality. Next, we integrated our fine-tuned LaBSE into the semantic similarity metric YiSi-1, exploring the effectiveness of averaging multiple layers. Additionally, we trained regression-based COMET metrics (COMET-DA) using the fine-tuned LaBSE embeddings as a semantic backbone, comparing Mean Absolute Error (MAE) and Mean Squared Error (MSE) loss functions. Our YiSi-1 metric using layer-averaged embeddings chosen by having the best performance on the development set for each individual language achieved the highest average correlation across languages among our submitted systems, and our COMET models demonstrated competitive performance for Guarani.

1 Introduction

Machine translation (MT) plays a vital role in language revitalization efforts by making Indigenous language content more accessible, preserving cultural knowledge, and supporting educational initiatives that connect younger generations with their linguistic heritage. In recent years, interest in MT for Indigenous languages has grown, particularly through the AmericasNLP Shared Task in Machine Translation, which began in 2021 (Mager et al., 2021).

Due to the time-consuming and expensive nature of human annotation, automatic evaluation metrics have become essential proxy for assessing translation systems during the development cycle. These metrics offer quick, consistent, and cost-effective evaluation compared to human assessment. However, traditional metrics, such as BLEU (Papineni et al., 2002) and ChrF++ (Popović, 2015), were designed and developed to evaluate MT systems for written and instructional languages. The distinctive features of traditionally spoken languages—e.g. polysynthetic morphology, extensive morphological variation, and non-standardized spelling—present particular challenges for metrics that rely mainly on exact matching at lexical or character level, especially when these metrics have not been specifically trained or tested in such languages. On the other hand, language representation based metrics, such as YiSi-1 (Lo, 2019), BERTScore (Zhang et al., 2020), COMET (Rei et al., 2020), MetricX (Juraska et al., 2023), etc, require large volume of data to train the underlying language representation, which is not available for low-resource languages, like the Indigenous languages around the world.

The AmericasNLP 2025 Shared Task on Machine Translation Metrics for Indigenous Languages directly addresses this challenge, encouraging participants to develop metrics tailored to evaluate translations from Spanish into three Indigenous languages: Guarani, Bribri, and Nahuatl. The goal of the shared task is to explore and enhance MT evaluation approaches for these underrepresented languages, building upon both traditional and newer evaluation methods.

To this end, we present our approach to the shared task, leveraging recent advancements in multilingual semantic embeddings. Our contributions include:

1. Fine-tuning the Language-agnostic BERT Sentence Encoder (LaBSE; Feng et al., 2022) specifically for Indigenous languages, enhancing its ability to semantically represent translations into Guarani, Bribri, and Nahuatl.

2. Integrating these fine-tuned LaBSE embeddings into the YiSi-1 semantic similarity met-

Proceedings of the Fifth Workshop on NLP for Indigenous Languages of the Americas (AmericasNLP), pages 100–104
May 4, 2025 ©2025 Association for Computational Linguistics

ric (Lo, 2019), exploring the impact of using different layers of LaBSE embeddings on evaluation performance.

3. Developing regression-based COMET metrics (Rei et al., 2020) using our fine-tuned LaBSE as a semantic backbone, experimenting with Mean Absolute Error (MAE) and Mean Squared Error (MSE) loss functions during training.

Our results show that fine-tuned semantic embeddings can improve MT evaluation for Indigenous languages. Our YiSi-1 using the average of embeddings from the best performing 3 layers for each individual language achieves the highest average correlation across languages among our submitted metrics, and our COMET-based metrics demonstrate competitive performance for Guarani.

2 Background

BLEU The Bilingual Evaluation Understudy (BLEU) (Papineni et al., 2002) metric measures the n-gram overlap between the hypothesis text and reference translation. While BLEU is language-agnostic and simple to compute, it operates on the word level, making it challenging to accurately evaluate agglutinative languages. The organizers of the AmericasNLP shared task on machine translation Mager et al. (2021) observed that many subwords appeared in both the hypothesis and reference sentences, yet complete words frequently did not, leading them to question the usefulness of BLEU as a metric for machine translation in indigenous languages.

ChrF++ ChrF++ is a refinement of the chrF metric (Popović, 2015) that calculates an averaged F-score using precision and recall of character n-grams. The "++" variant incorporates word n-grams to slightly reward exact word matches, improving correlation with human judgments. By combining these two types of n-grams, chrF++ captures both lexical and morphological information. As ChrF++ gives partial credit for matching subword fragments, it is more forgiving to morphological variations than BLEU.

YiSi YiSi (Lo, 2019, 2020) is a group of semantic MT evaluation metrics designed to handle varying resource levels. YiSi represents both the hypothesis and reference sentences (or only the source, for reference-free evaluation) in a common semantic vector space, and then computes similarity scores. The primary reference-based metric is YiSi-1, which is a monolingual semantic similarity metric between the hypothesis and the reference.

For each word in the hypothesis, YiSi-1 finds the most semantically similar word in the reference (via cosine similarity of token embeddings), and vice versa, and calculates a weighted F-score. In the WMT18 Metrics Task (Ma et al., 2018), YiSi-1 showed a strong correlation with human judgments for many language pairs outperforming BLEU, chrF and others.

COMET COMET (Rei et al., 2020) is a transformer-based framework for training MT evaluation models, using human-annotated data. COMET metrics use a large multilingual model as a backbone encoder, and a regression head to predict the quality score given the source, reference, and hypothesis sentences. At inference, COMET outputs a score indicating translation quality. Based on the type of evaluation data available for training, different variants can be developed, such as COMET-DA and COMET-MQM models when using Direct Assessments (DA) and Multidimensional Quality Metric (MQM) data, respectively.

LaBSE LaBSE (Feng et al., 2022) is a BERT model with CLS-pooling and dense layers on top to produce a sentence-level encoding. This encoder is trained with a contrastive translation-ranking task to align parallel sentences between over 100 languages. Unlike many other transformer-based text encoders, which often learn disjoint spaces for each language in their training set, LaBSE represents all languages in one shared space where a sentence in one language would receive a similar encoding to its translation in any other language.

3 Methodology

Our general approach consisted of adapting a multilingual language representation across different languages into Indigenous language data, which was used to feed and train two semantic MT metrics: YiSi-1 and COMET, respectively.

3.1 Multilingual Representation using LaBSE

We fine-tuned LaBSE using a contrastive learning process to align Indigenous language data with the Spanish representation space pre-trained in LaBSE. The goal behind this alignment was to inherit the high quality pre-trained knowledge of

Metric	Guarani		Bribri		Nahuatl		Average	
	Spr.	Prs.	Spr.	Prs.	Spr.	Prs.	Spr.	Prs.
YiSi-1+ per-lang-avg	0.6611	0.7196	**0.5622**	0.6244	0.6680	**0.6115**	**0.6304**	**0.6518**
YiSi-1+ cross-lang-avg	0.6611	0.7196	0.5569	**0.6300**	0.6132	0.5845	0.6104	0.6447
COMET-DA (MAE loss)	0.5597	0.7209	0.4892	0.6261	0.4963	0.5290	0.5151	0.6254
COMET-DA (MSE loss)	0.5605	**0.7234**	0.4909	0.6268	0.5036	0.5351	0.5183	0.6285
ChrF++	**0.6725**	0.6263	0.4517	0.3823	**0.6783**	0.5549	0.6008	0.5212
BLEU	0.4676	0.4056	0.4518	0.3456	0.3541	0.4061	0.4245	0.3857

Table 1: Spearman (Spr.) and Pearson (Prs.) correlation coefficients between metrics and human scores on the blind test set across the three languages: Guarani, Bribri and Nahuatl, followed by average correlations of the three languages. per-lang-avg stands for the embeddings obtained by averaging the best three layers per language, while cross-lang-avg consider the best three layers on average in the three languages (layers 4-6). Bold values indicate the best performance in each language-correlation combination.

LaBSE with the limited data available in these low-resource languages. The data used consist of the parallel data available for the Americas-NLP MT Shared Task, which covers 13 indigenous languages, and an additional corpus for Nahuatl (Gutierrez-Vasques, 2015). For this fine-tuning process, we only propagated the gradients for the encoding of the non-Spanish sentences, aiming to preserve as much of the shared representation space as possible. Our approach consisted of training LaBSE to align all the languages simultaneously, which worked better than the language-specific models. We also balanced the language distribution data by up-sampling the training data for Nahuatl, the language for which we had less data. In this way, we improved the performance of the metrics in Nahuatl, with a small trade-off in other languages. Since the downstream translation metrics require token-level embeddings, we extracted only the BERT model from LaBSE after the fine-tuning was completed, discarding the pooling layers. While LaBSE was pre-trained by contrastive alignment of the [CLS] token encoding between parallel sentences, we found that aligning the mean-pooled token encodings to be far more effective. This is likely because aligning only the [CLS] token does not properly update the encoding of the other tokens.

3.2 Metric Development

3.2.1 YiSi-1 + Fine-Tuned LaBSE

As YiSi-1 needs an embedding model to evaluate semantic similarity (Lo, 2020), we fed this metric using the obtained LaBSE representation described in the previous section. We evaluated the metric performance using the embeddings obtained from different layers, calculating the Spearman and Pearson correlations with the DA scores. For each language, we selected the three intermediate layers that yielded the best performance on the development set and obtained the token embeddings by averaging across the three layers. However, this language-specific approach risks overfitting to the development set, potentially not performing as well on the testing set. We, therefore, made another submission for which we decided to average the token embeddings from the three layers that performed the best on average in all the three languages.

3.2.2 COMET-DA+Fine-Tuned LaBSE

We trained COMET-DA models, using our fine-tuned LaBSE embeddings as the underlying representation. Given the limited amount of available development data, we applied 5-fold cross-validation to efficiently leverage all available annotations. In each fold, we trained COMET-DA on 80% of the development set, reserving the remaining 20% for validation. We experimented with training a COMET for each language, and combining the language data. The combination led to better results on the development set, so we submitted this variation.

We explored two different loss functions to optimize COMET-DA during fine-tuning: mean absolute error (MAE) and mean squared error (MSE).

4 Results

Table 1 presents the Spearman and Pearson correlation results for our four submitted metrics compared to baseline metrics across Guarani, Bribri, and Nahuatl translation tasks. In general, our YiSi-1 metric that utilizes average embeddings from LaBSE layers 4 to 6 performed the best on average, showing strong performance across languages and metrics.

For Guarani, our COMET-based metrics performed notably well on Pearson correlation, with the COMET variant trained using MSE loss achieving the highest Pearson correlation, and the MAE variant ranking second. The YiSi-1 variants achieved higher Spearman correlations than the COMET variants, but remained lower than the ChrF++ baseline.

For Bribri, YiSi-1 with layer averaging had the highest Spearman correlation, but the single best layer for Bribri had higher Pearson correlation.

Nahuatl was especially challenging. None of our submitted metrics surpassed the ChrF++ baseline for Spearman correlation. Layer-averaged YiSi-1 scored the highest of our systems for both Spearman and Pearson.

On average, the layer-averaged YiSi performed the best of our systems.

5 Conclusion

In this paper, we present our submission to the AmericasNLP 2025 Shared Task on Machine Translation Metrics for Indigenous Languages. Central to our approach was our fine-tuned LaBSE model, which provided effective multilingual semantic representations for Bribri, Guarani, and Nahuatl. We then integrated the LaBSE embeddings into YiSi-1 and COMET metrics.

Our key contributions include successfully finetuning LaBSE embeddings specifically for Indigenous languages, evaluating the effectiveness of embedding layer selection and averaging in YiSi-1, and training a custom COMET for Indigenous languages.

Future directions include training COMET with additional data to further enhance COMET's performance and investigating language-specific adjustments to better handle challenging languages like Nahuatl.

Acknowledgments

This work is partially generously supported by the US National Science Foundation under awards 2327143 and 2346334. This work was partially supported by resources provided by the Office of Research Computing at George Mason University (URL: https://orc.gmu.edu) and funded in part by grants from the National Science Foundation (Award Number 2018631).

References

Fangxiaoyu Feng, Yinfei Yang, Daniel Cer, Naveen Arivazhagan, and Wei Wang. 2022. Language-agnostic BERT sentence embedding. In *Proceedings of the 60th Annual Meeting of the Association for Computational Linguistics (Volume 1: Long Papers)*, pages 878–891, Dublin, Ireland. Association for Computational Linguistics.

Ximena Gutierrez-Vasques. 2015. Bilingual lexicon extraction for a distant language pair using a small parallel corpus. In *Proceedings of the 2015 Conference of the North American Chapter of the Association for Computational Linguistics: Student Research Workshop*, pages 154–160, Denver, Colorado. Association for Computational Linguistics.

Juraj Juraska, Mara Finkelstein, Daniel Deutsch, Aditya Siddhant, Mehdi Mirzazadeh, and Markus Freitag. 2023. MetricX-23: The Google submission to the WMT 2023 metrics shared task. In *Proceedings of the Eighth Conference on Machine Translation*, pages 756–767, Singapore. Association for Computational Linguistics.

Chi-kiu Lo. 2019. YiSi - a unified semantic MT quality evaluation and estimation metric for languages with different levels of available resources. In *Proceedings of the Fourth Conference on Machine Translation (Volume 2: Shared Task Papers, Day 1)*, pages 507–513, Florence, Italy. Association for Computational Linguistics.

Chi-kiu Lo. 2020. Extended study on using pretrained language models and YiSi-1 for machine translation evaluation. In *Proceedings of the Fifth Conference on Machine Translation*, pages 895–902, Online. Association for Computational Linguistics.

Qingsong Ma, Ondřej Bojar, and Yvette Graham. 2018. Results of the WMT18 metrics shared task: Both characters and embeddings achieve good performance. In *Proceedings of the Third Conference on Machine Translation: Shared Task Papers*, pages 671–688, Belgium, Brussels. Association for Computational Linguistics.

Manuel Mager, Arturo Oncevay, Abteen Ebrahimi, John Ortega, Annette Rios, Angela Fan, Ximena Gutierrez-Vasques, Luis Chiruzzo, Gustavo Giménez-Lugo, Ricardo Ramos, Ivan Vladimir Meza Ruiz, Rolando Coto-Solano, Alexis Palmer, Elisabeth Mager-Hois, Vishrav Chaudhary, Graham Neubig, Ngoc Thang Vu, and Katharina Kann. 2021. Findings of the AmericasNLP 2021 shared task on open machine translation for indigenous languages of the Americas. In *Proceedings of the First Workshop on Natural Language Processing for Indigenous Languages of the Americas*, pages 202–217, Online. Association for Computational Linguistics.

Kishore Papineni, Salim Roukos, Todd Ward, and Wei-Jing Zhu. 2002. Bleu: a method for automatic evaluation of machine translation. In *Proceedings of the*

40th Annual Meeting of the Association for Computational Linguistics, pages 311–318, Philadelphia, Pennsylvania, USA. Association for Computational Linguistics.

Maja Popović. 2015. chrF: character n-gram F-score for automatic MT evaluation. In *Proceedings of the Tenth Workshop on Statistical Machine Translation*, pages 392–395, Lisbon, Portugal. Association for Computational Linguistics.

Ricardo Rei, Craig Stewart, Ana C Farinha, and Alon Lavie. 2020. COMET: A neural framework for MT evaluation. In *Proceedings of the 2020 Conference on Empirical Methods in Natural Language Processing (EMNLP)*, pages 2685–2702, Online. Association for Computational Linguistics.

Tianyi Zhang, Varsha Kishore, Felix Wu, Kilian Q. Weinberger, and Yoav Artzi. 2020. Bertscore: Evaluating text generation with BERT. In *8th International Conference on Learning Representations, ICLR 2020, Addis Ababa, Ethiopia, April 26-30, 2020*. OpenReview.net.

JHU's Submission to the AmericasNLP 2025 Shared Task on the Creation of Educational Materials for Indigenous Languages

Tom Lupicki, Lavanya Shankar, Kaavya Chaparala, David Yarowsky
Center for Language and Speech Processing,
Johns Hopkins University
{tlupick1,ls1,kchapar1,yarowsky}@jhu.edu

Abstract

This paper presents JHU's submission to the AmericasNLP shared task on the creation of educational materials for Indigenous languages. The task involves transforming a base sentence given one or more tags that correspond to grammatical features, such as negation or tense. The task also spans four languages: Bribri, Maya, Guaraní, and Nahuatl. We experiment with augmenting prompts to large language models with different information, chain of thought prompting, ensembling large language models by majority voting, and training a pointer-generator network. Our System 1, an ensemble of large language models, achieves the best performance on Maya and Guaraní, building upon the previous successes in leveraging large language models for this task and highlighting the effectiveness of ensembling large language models.

1 Introduction

The AmericasNLP 2025 shared task on the creation of educational materials (de Gibert et al., 2025) proposes automated generation of educational materials for low-resource Indigenous languages in the Americas. Many of these languages are endangered, with few remaining speakers, and lack the large datasets necessary to leverage advances in Natural Language Processing (NLP) as languages like English and Spanish do. The shared task challenged teams to develop NLP systems to create educational exercises for Bribri, Maya, Guaraní, and Nahuatl. These exercises involve applying grammatical transformations—such as tense changes or negation—to base sentences.

Each team received a limited training dataset for each language. This dataset contained base sentences, the corresponding grammatical modifications, and the correctly transformed output sentences. Using this data, teams were expected to develop NLP systems which, given a base sentence and a grammar modification, could produce the correctly modified output sentence.

By leveraging NLP to generate grammatical exercises, this task intends to reduce the burden on the small number of fluent speakers in these languages who would otherwise need to manually develop learning resources. This automation can enable communities to create a broader range of instructional materials with less effort, making language learning more accessible.

Our approach is based on an ensemble of several distinct methods, including novel extensions on the large language model (LLM) methods successfully deployed by top performing systems of the 2024 shared task (Vasselli et al., 2024; Bui and von der Wense, 2024; Haley, 2024), combined with additional components including linguistic information specific to each language, part-of-speech tagging, chain-of-thought reasoning, and model ensembling using majority voting. We additionally train a pointer-generator LSTM leveraging additional Bribri data. Our ensemble system, using majority voting from LLM outputs generated with varying prompt configurations, achieves the highest performance on Maya and Guarani compared to other teams. We release our code on GitHub[1].

2 Data

2.1 Task Data

The task provided training, development, and test data in Bribri, Maya, Guaraní, and Nahuatl. Each data split contained base sentences, the change to apply to each base sentence. The training and development data additionally contain the correctly transformed base sentence. The training data includes 309, 584, 178, and 392 examples for Bribri, Maya, Guaraní, and Nahuatl respectively. The development data includes 212 Bribri examples,

[1]https://github.com/KentonMurray/AmericasNLP2025

Proceedings of the Fifth Workshop on NLP for Indigenous Languages of the Americas (AmericasNLP), pages 105–111
May 4, 2025 ©2025 Association for Computational Linguistics

149 Maya examples, 79 Guaraní examples, and 176 Nahuatl examples. The test data includes 480 Bribri examples, 310 Maya examples, 364 Guaraní examples, and 120 Nahuatl examples.

2.2 Additional Bribri Data

For one of our submitted systems, the pointer-generator network, we create additional training data by extracting verb conjugation tables from *Gramática de la lengua bribri*, a Bribri reference grammar (Murillo, 2018). From this process, we extracted 482 unique verbs and constructed 1400 additional single-verb training examples.

3 Methods

3.1 LLM Prompting

We conduct few-shot prompting experiments utilizing variations of the prompt in Table 1, modified from the prompt used in the 2024 submission to this task by the JAJ team (Vasselli et al., 2024). This prompt provides a well structured format that allows us to experiment with the inclusion of additional information, namely part of speech tags and grammar information from a reference book. An explicit system instruction to output only the target sentence is included as initial testing showed that with such an instruction, outputs were inconsistently formatted and occasionally multiple hypotheses for target sentences were generated. We also observed that the LLMs would sometimes first generate reasoning text, particularly when including fewer few-shot examples in the prompt.

Examples are to include in the prompt are chosen in the following manner: Given a maximum number of examples to include and a test example with n change tags, we first select all examples from the training data such that all n tags in the test example match those in the training examples, then sort in descending order by combined BLEU (Papineni et al., 2002) and chrF (Popović, 2015) score and select up to the given maximum number of examples. If more examples are needed, we select additional training examples which overlap with n - 1 of the change tags in the test example, then again sort and select the top examples by combined BLEU and chrF. If more examples are still needed, we continue this process down to an overlap of 1 change tag.

For this few-shot prompting approach, we experiment with including a maximum of 3, 5, 10, and 20 examples.

```
SYSTEM:
You are a helpful assistant with expertise
in linguistics. Output only the target
sentence in your response with no
additional punctuation.

USER:
This is a linguistic puzzle involving
grammar changes in [LANGUAGE]. You are
given examples which include a source
sentence, a grammar change to apply to the
source sentence, and a target sentence.
Your task is to generate the target
sentence for the final example.

Example 1:
Source: [SOURCE SENTENCE]
Grammar Change: [CHANGE TAGS]
Target: [TARGET SENTENCE]

(...)

Now generate the target sentence for this
example:
Source: [SOURCE SENTENCE]
Grammar Change: [CHANGE TAGS]
Target:
```

Table 1: Our base prompt that we use for experimentation. [LANGUAGE] is replaced with Bribri, Yucatec Maya, Guaraní, or Western Sierra Puebla Nahuatl.

Additionally, we conduct these experiments with two LLMs: GPT-4o (OpenAI et al., 2024b) and DeepSeek-v3 (DeepSeek-AI et al., 2025), and set the temperature to 0.

Reference Book In one experiment, we include the line "*You are also given additional information about the morphology and syntax of the language.*" and copied the 'Morphology and Syntax' sections for Bribri, Maya, and Guaraní from a reference book (Campbell, 2000). We did not include morphological and syntactic information for Nahuatl as the reference book documented Classical Nahuatl rather than Western Sierra Puebla Nahuatl. We test this addition to the prompt with 10 examples from the training data included. This experiment is partly inspired by MTOB, a benchmark on low resource machine translation for LLMs using a human-readable grammar book (Tanzer et al., 2024). In contrast to MTOB, the grammar descriptions we include are only a few pages long.

Part of Speech Tags We experiment with additionally including a part-of-speech tagged source sentences in our prompt, alongside the original source sentences, for Maya and Guaraní data. We utilize open source part-of-speech taggers released by Apertium to generate our part-of-speech tagged data (Forcada and Tyers, 2016; Kuznetsova and Tyers, 2021; Pugh et al., 2023).

3.2 Chain of Thought

We also experimented with chain of thought (CoT) prompting (Wei et al., 2022), instructing the LLM to offer a step-by-step analysis to arrive at a solution. We tested CoT prompting using DeepSeek-V3 first in a zero-shot setting, followed by experiments with few-shot settings using 10, 20, and 25 examples.

Our approach involved processing sentences by providing predefined steps using a structured CoT prompt. We varied the number of few-shot examples to evaluate their impact on model performance. The methodology followed these key steps:

1. **Understanding the Source Sentence** – The model was instructed to analyze the input sentence in the target language.
2. **Identifying the Required Change** – The model was guided to recognize and interpret the intended transformation.
3. **Retrieving Few-Shot Examples** – We experimented with different numbers of few-shot examples ($n = 0, 10, 20, 25$). For our CoT experiments, examples are selected based on the number of overlapping change tags with the test example, as described in Bui and von der Wense (2024).
4. **Applying the Transformation** – The model generated the modified sentence step-by-step, following CoT reasoning.
5. **Output Formatting** – The final prediction was in a standardized format (`PREDICTED TARGET:`), which helped us with the extraction of results.

3.3 Ensembling

We create an ensemble system by utilizing majority voting to combine up to six LLM outputs. We decide on the specific configuration of LLM systems to include for each language by comparing the scores on the dev set of ensembling every combination of up to six of our LLM experiment outputs, including all our prompt configuration experiments and our CoT experiment using DeepSeek-V3 and 25 examples. We also compare sentence-level, token-level, and character-level majority voting strategies.

3.4 Pointer-Generator Network

As a contrastive system, we train a character-level pointer-generator LSTM utilizing a language tag and change tags as features (Bahdanau et al., 2016; See et al., 2017; Vinyals et al., 2015). Our pointer-generator network has 1 encoder layer, 1 decoder layer, an embedding size of 128, and a hidden layer size of 512. We train on all data including our additional Bribri data, and use a learning rate of 1e-3, dropout set to 0.3, and optimize with Adam (Kingma and Ba, 2017). Training is conducted with early stopping, and we evaluate using a model checkpoint saved after training for 31 epochs.

4 Submitted Systems

We organize our submitted systems as follows:

System 1 A majority voting ensemble of up to six systems selected based on dev set performance for each language. For Bribri, this is a token-level majority voting ensemble of four LLM outputs. For both Maya and Guaraní, this is a whole sentence majority voting ensemble of six LLM outputs. For Nahuatl, the best single system outperformed any ensemble of multiple systems, so we include only a single non-ensembled system for Nahuatl.

System 2 The best prompt configuration for DeepSeek-v3 for each language, selected based on dev set performance.

System 3 GPT-4o using the same prompt configurations as System 2.

System 4 The best prompt configuration for GPT-4o for each language, selected based on dev set performance.

System 5 This system is CoT prompting of DeepSeek-v3 with 25 included examples.

System 6 This system is our pointer-generator LSTM.

5 Results and Discussion

We present our results on the test set for all six of our systems in Table 2. Our LLM ensemble system, System 1, performs the best of our submitted systems and is declared one of two winning systems on this year's task, achieving the highest scores in the task for Maya and Guaraní. Compared to last year's winning systems for Maya and Guaraní, our System 1 achieves an additional 10.00 percentage

System	Bribri			Maya			Guaraní			Nahuatl		
	Acc.	BLEU	chrF	Acc.	BLEU	chrF	Acc.	BLEU	chrF	Acc.	BLEU	chrF
1	22.71	45.68	71.63	**63.87**	**84.03**	**93.87**	**43.68**	**57.2**	**86.83**	3.33	12.2	52.75
2	20.21	42.5	71.99	59.35	82.32	92.95	38.19	50.28	85.41	3.33	12.2	52.75
3	20.21	44.51	72.21	56.77	80.59	91.77	38.74	55.47	86.17	1.67	11.66	49.27
4	18.75	45.09	71.42	60.00	81.94	92.94	40.93	54.89	86.02	1.67	12.5	49.67
5	15.83	40.02	70.59	59.03	80.48	92.39	41.21	55.04	86.21	2.5	12.84	55.31
6	5.42	20.67	49.65	9.68	46.71	67.19	6.32	4.79	46.28	0	0.62	27.73

Table 2: Test set evaluation results for our six submitted systems. Winning scores in the task are in **bold**.

points in accuracy for Maya and an 9.06 percentage points in accuracy for Guaraní (Chiruzzo et al., 2024). Compared to our highest scoring single LLM system submissions, our ensembling strategy also provides an increase in accuracy of 2.50 percentage points for Bribri, 3.87 percentage points for Maya, and 2.75 percentage points for Guaraní.

5.1 LLM Choice

Our single LLM systems, Systems 2, 3, and 4, exhibit a moderate amount of variation in score, though all still perform higher than last year's best systems for Maya and Guaraní. For a clearer understanding on how our selection of LLMs affects our performance on this task, we conduct an additional experiment on the dev set using our base prompt with 10 examples to compare our system performance when using GPT-4 (OpenAI et al., 2024a), specifically the gpt-4-0614 snapshot available through the OpenAI API[2]. We also compare performance when using two additional snapshots of GPT-4o: gpt-4o-2024-11-20 and gpt-4o-2024-05-13[3]. Our GPT-4o systems by default use gpt-4o-2024-08-06. We report the results of this experiment in Table 3. As seen in the table, using GPT-4 and different GPT-4o snapshots result in some variation in performance on the dev set compared to the LLMs used in our submitted systems, but this variation is only to a small extent. This could indicate that the specifics of our prompting technique and our method of selecting training examples play a more significant role in the higher performance of our single LLM systems, rather than simply our choice of LLMs.

[2]https://platform.openai.com/docs/models/gpt-4

[3]https://platform.openai.com/docs/models/gpt-4o

5.2 Prompting Configurations

We record the results of our experiments in varying LLM prompt configurations, which were referred to in selecting the components of our submitted systems, in Table 4. Notably, increasing the number of training examples included in the prompt did not strictly increase performance, and leveraging part-of-speech tags and reference book information also does not have a clear impact on performance as evaluated on the development set. Future work could take a fine-grained approach to understanding how such prompt configurations affect model predictions.

5.3 Nahuatl Performance and Future Work

We observe poor performance on Nahuatl across all of our experiments and submitted systems, compared to our performance on the other languages included in this task. One possible hypothesis as to why performance is so low is due to the extent of variation within Nahuatl and the extent to which LLMs have been trained on and can differentiate Nahuatl varieties. Western Sierra Puebla Nahuatl, the Nahuatl variety included in this task (de Gibert et al., 2025), is one of 30 varieties within the "language grouping" of Nahuatl recognized by the Instituto Nacional de Lenguas Indígenas (INALI). INALI further states that each language variety should be treated as languages themselves, particularly for educational matters, as well as in other areas including justice and health (INALI, 2008). Thus, in the spirit of this task, we propose that future work in developing systems to create educational materials for Indigenous language take a more variety-specific approach to Nahuatl, that may include sourcing and incorporating grammatical information about Western Sierra Puebla Nahuatl, and also possibly fine-tuning LLMs on Western Sierra Puebla Nahuatl data. Additionally, to understand the extent to which our systems are im-

Model	Bribri			Maya			Guaraní			Nahuatl		
	Acc.	BLEU	chrF	Acc.	BLEU	chrF	Acc.	BLEU	chrF	Acc.	BLEU	chrF
DeepSeek-V3	18.40	45.79	66.69	55.70	77.31	91.31	41.77	52.70	86.41	2.27	8.13	42.58
gpt-4o-2024-08-06	18.40	45.96	65.13	54.36	76.39	90.41	39.24	49.24	84.70	1.14	6.38	38.88
gpt-4o -2024-11-20	16.51	44.73	65.42	55.70	77.11	90.84	45.57	51.89	86.31	3.41	6.18	40.19
gpt-4o-2024-05-13	17.45	46.10	65.75	57.05	78.48	91.02	39.24	49.24	85.45	1.14	5.75	39.72
gpt-4-0613	18.40	46.25	66.54	56.38	76.20	90.93	37.97	50.68	83.49	2.84	5.71	38.95

Table 3: Results on the dev set of our comparison experiment with GPT-4, 3 different GPT-4o snapshots, and DeepSeek-V3, using our base prompt and 10 examples. Our submitted systems use the gpt-4o-2024-08-06 snapshot and DeepSeek-V3.

pacted by the linguistic diversity within Nahuatl, future analysis could examine whether incorrect outputs of our LLM-based systems are valid for other Nahuatl varieties. Such analysis may provide insight into how systems can be modified to better support Western Sierra Puebla Nahuatl specifically.

6 Conclusion

We presented the results of JHU's submission to the 2025 AmericasNLP shared task on the creation of educational materials for Indigenous languages. In developing our systems, we conducted experiments using different prompting configurations with GPT-4o and DeepSeek-V3, combined chain of thought prompting techniques with few-shot prompting, trained a pointer-generator LSTM, and construct a majority voting ensemble of LLMs. We achieve the highest performance on Maya and Guaraní with our ensemble system, which is declared one of two winning systems on this year's task.

References

Dzmitry Bahdanau, Kyunghyun Cho, and Yoshua Bengio. 2016. Neural machine translation by jointly learning to align and translate. *Preprint*, arXiv:1409.0473.

Minh Duc Bui and Katharina von der Wense. 2024. JGU mainz's submission to the AmericasNLP 2024 shared task on the creation of educational materials for indigenous languages. In *Proceedings of the 4th Workshop on Natural Language Processing for Indigenous Languages of the Americas (AmericasNLP 2024)*, pages 195–200, Mexico City, Mexico. Association for Computational Linguistics.

George L. Campbell. 2000. *Compendium of the World's Languages, Second Edition*, volume 1. Routledge, 29 West 35th Street, New York, NY 10001.

Luis Chiruzzo, Pavel Denisov, Alejandro Molina-Villegas, Silvia Fernandez-Sabido, Rolando Coto-Solano, Marvin Agüero-Torales, Aldo Alvarez, Samuel Canul-Yah, Lorena Hau-Ucán, Abteen Ebrahimi, Robert Pugh, Arturo Oncevay, Shruti Rijhwani, Katharina von der Wense, and Manuel Mager. 2024. Findings of the AmericasNLP 2024 shared task on the creation of educational materials for indigenous languages. In *Proceedings of the 4th Workshop on Natural Language Processing for Indigenous Languages of the Americas (AmericasNLP 2024)*, pages 224–235, Mexico City, Mexico. Association for Computational Linguistics.

Ona de Gibert, Raul Vazquez, Robert Pugh, Abteen Ebrahimi, Pavel Denisov, Ali Marashian, Enora Rice, Edward Gow-Smith, Juan C. Prieto, Melissa Robles, Rubén Manrique, Oscar Moreno Veliz, Ángel Lino Campos, Rolando Coto-Solano, Aldo Alvarez, Marvin Agüero-Torales, John E. Ortega, Luis Chiruzzo, Arturo Oncevay, and 3 others. 2025. Findings of the AmericasNLP shared tasks on machine translation, creation of educational material, and translation metrics for indigenous languages. In *Proceedings of the 5th Workshop on Natural Language Processing for Indigenous Languages of the Americas (AmericasNLP 2025)*, Albuquerque, New Mexico. Association for Computational Linguistics.

DeepSeek-AI, Aixin Liu, Bei Feng, Bing Xue, Bingxuan Wang, Bochao Wu, Chengda Lu, Chenggang Zhao, Chengqi Deng, Chenyu Zhang, Chong Ruan, Damai Dai, Daya Guo, Dejian Yang, Deli Chen, Dongjie Ji, Erhang Li, Fangyun Lin, Fucong Dai, and 181 others. 2025. DeepSeek-V3 Technical Report. *arXiv preprint*. ArXiv:2412.19437 [cs].

Mikel L. Forcada and Francis M. Tyers. 2016. Apertium: a free/open source platform for machine translation and basic language technology. In *Proceedings of the 19th Annual Conference of the European Association for Machine Translation: Projects/Products*, Riga, Latvia. Baltic Journal of Modern Computing.

Coleman Haley. 2024. The unreasonable effectiveness of large language models for low-resource clause-level morphology: In-context generalization or prior exposure? In *Proceedings of the 4th Workshop on Natural Language Processing for Indigenous Languages of the Americas (AmericasNLP 2024)*, pages 174–178, Mexico City, Mexico. Association for Computational Linguistics.

INALI. 2008. Catálogo de las lenguas indígenas nacionales: Variantes lingüísticas de méxico con sus au-

Prompt Config	Model	Bribri			Maya			Guaraní			Nahuatl		
		Acc.	BLEU	chrF	Acc.	BLEU	chrF	Acc.	BLEU	chrF	Acc.	BLEU	chrF
3 examples	GPT-4o	16.98	44.52	62.89	54.36	77.37	90.84	39.24	47.44	85.39	**1.14**	4.86	34.98
	DeepSeek-V3	15.09	41.84	63.71	57.05	79.04	91.36	39.24	49.32	85.70	2.84	7.34	40.68
5 examples	GPT-4o	17.92	44.49	63.87	55.03	76.67	90.43	41.77	49.75	85.97	**1.14**	5.41	37.52
	DeepSeek-V3	17.92	46.24	65.75	55.03	76.96	90.61	**44.30**⋆	52.88	87.01	2.27	6.03	40.84
10 examples	GPT-4o	**18.40**	**45.96**	65.13	54.36	76.39	90.41	39.24	49.24	84.70	**1.14**	**6.38**	38.88
	DeepSeek-V3	18.40	45.79	66.69	55.70	77.31	91.31	41.77	52.70	86.41	2.27	8.13	42.58
20 examples	GPT-4o	15.57	44.76	64.75	**58.39**	**78.64**⋆	**90.98**	40.51	54.51	86.17	**1.14**	5.71	**39.19**
	DeepSeek-V3	**18.87**⋆	**47.68**⋆	**67.43**⋆	56.38	78.20	91.49	**44.30**⋆	54.02	**87.42**⋆	**5.11**⋆	**8.88**⋆	**43.56**⋆
3 ex. + POS	GPT-4o	-	-	-	53.02	76.24	89.16	39.24	**56.78**⋆	85.40	-	-	-
	DeepSeek-V3	-	-	-	55.03	77.29	90.59	36.71	49.25	83.63	-	-	-
5 ex. + POS	GPT-4o	-	-	-	48.32	72.51	88.75	41.77	55.96	85.12	-	-	-
	DeepSeek-V3	-	-	-	55.70	77.23	90.47	37.97	50.40	85.90	-	-	-
10 ex. + POS	GPT-4o	-	-	-	55.70	76.49	90.44	**44.30**⋆	52.37	86.15	-	-	-
	DeepSeek-V3	-	-	-	55.70	77.41	91.17	41.77	51.59	86.45	-	-	-
20 ex. + POS	GPT-4o	-	-	-	56.38	77.24	90.36	41.77	51.77	86.27	-	-	-
	DeepSeek-V3	-	-	-	**59.06**⋆	**78.55**	**91.54**⋆	40.51	51.08	86.21	-	-	-
10 ex. + book	GPT-4o	16.98	45.63	**65.86**	54.36	76.92	90.79	43.04	55.15	**86.95**	-	-	-
	DeepSeek-V3	16.04	44.47	65.90	55.03	76.50	90.95	43.04	**56.26**	86.33	-	-	-

Table 4: Results from experimenting with different prompt configurations using GPT-4o and DeepSeek-V3. The highest scores for each model on each language are in **bold**. The best scores across both systems for each language are indicated with a ⋆.

todenominaciones y referencias geoestadísticas. Instituto Nacional de Lenguas Indígenas, México, D.F.

Diederik P. Kingma and Jimmy Ba. 2017. Adam: A method for stochastic optimization. *Preprint*, arXiv:1412.6980.

Anastasia Kuznetsova and Francis Tyers. 2021. A finite-state morphological analyser for Paraguayan Guaraní. In *Proceedings of the First Workshop on Natural Language Processing for Indigenous Languages of the Americas*, pages 81–89, Online. Association for Computational Linguistics.

Carla Victoria Jara Murillo. 2018. *Gramática de la lengua bribri*. EDigital, San José. Reviewed in *Revista de Filología y Lingüística de la Universidad de Costa Rica*.

OpenAI, Josh Achiam, Steven Adler, Sandhini Agarwal, Lama Ahmad, Ilge Akkaya, Florencia Leoni Aleman, Diogo Almeida, Janko Altenschmidt, Sam Altman, Shyamal Anadkat, Red Avila, Igor Babuschkin, Suchir Balaji, Valerie Balcom, Paul Baltescu, Haiming Bao, Mohammad Bavarian, Jeff Belgum, and 262 others. 2024a. Gpt-4 technical report. *Preprint*, arXiv:2303.08774.

OpenAI, Aaron Hurst, Adam Lerer, Adam P. Goucher, Adam Perelman, Aditya Ramesh, Aidan Clark, A. J. Ostrow, Akila Welihinda, Alan Hayes, Alec Radford, Aleksander Mądry, Alex Baker-Whitcomb, Alex Beutel, Alex Borzunov, Alex Carney, Alex Chow, Alex Kirillov, Alex Nichol, and 400 others. 2024b. GPT-4o System Card. *arXiv preprint*. ArXiv:2410.21276 [cs].

Kishore Papineni, Salim Roukos, Todd Ward, and Wei-Jing Zhu. 2002. Bleu: a method for automatic evaluation of machine translation. In *Proceedings of the 40th Annual Meeting of the Association for Computational Linguistics*, pages 311–318, Philadelphia, Pennsylvania, USA. Association for Computational Linguistics.

Maja Popović. 2015. chrF: character n-gram F-score for automatic MT evaluation. In *Proceedings of the Tenth Workshop on Statistical Machine Translation*, pages 392–395, Lisbon, Portugal. Association for Computational Linguistics.

Robert Pugh, Francis Tyers, and Quetzil Castañeda. 2023. Developing finite-state language technology for Maya. In *Proceedings of the Workshop on Natural Language Processing for Indigenous Languages of the Americas (AmericasNLP)*, pages 30–39, Toronto, Canada. Association for Computational Linguistics.

Abigail See, Peter J. Liu, and Christopher D. Manning. 2017. Get to the point: Summarization with pointer-generator networks. In *Proceedings of the 55th Annual Meeting of the Association for Computational Linguistics (Volume 1: Long Papers)*, pages 1073–1083, Vancouver, Canada. Association for Computational Linguistics.

Garrett Tanzer, Mirac Suzgun, Eline Visser, Dan Jurafsky, and Luke Melas-Kyriazi. 2024. A benchmark for learning to translate a new language from one grammar book. *Preprint*, arXiv:2309.16575.

Justin Vasselli, Arturo Martínez Peguero, Junehwan Sung, and Taro Watanabe. 2024. Applying linguistic expertise to LLMs for educational material development in indigenous languages. In *Proceedings of the 4th Workshop on Natural Language Processing for Indigenous Languages of the Americas (AmericasNLP 2024)*, pages 201–208, Mexico City, Mexico. Association for Computational Linguistics.

Oriol Vinyals, Meire Fortunato, and Navdeep Jaitly. 2015. Pointer networks. In *Advances in Neural Information Processing Systems*, volume 28. Curran Associates, Inc.

Jason Wei, Xuezhi Wang, Dale Schuurmans, Maarten Bosma, Brian Ichter, Fei Xia, Ed H. Chi, Quoc V. Le, and Denny Zhou. 2022. Chain-of-thought prompting elicits reasoning in large language models. In *Advances in Neural Information Processing Systems (NeurIPS)*.

Leveraging Dictionaries and Grammar Rules for the Creation of Educational Materials for Indigenous Languages

Justin Vasselli, Haruki Sakajo
Arturo Martínez Peguero, Frederikus Hudi, Taro Watanabe
Nara Institute of Science and Technology
{vasselli.justin_ray.vk4, sakajo.haruki.sd9,
martinez_peguero.arturo.ma3, frederikus.hudi.fe7, taro}@is.naist.jp

Abstract

This paper describes the NAIST submission to the AmericasNLP 2025 shared task on the creation of educational materials for Indigenous languages. We implement three systems to tackle the unique challenges of each language. The first system, used for Maya and Guarani, employs a straightforward GPT-4o few-shot prompting technique, enhanced by synthetically generated examples to ensure coverage of all grammatical variations encountered. The second system, used for Bribri, integrates dictionary-based alignment and linguistic rules to systematically manage linguistic and lexical transformations. Finally, we developed a specialized rule-based system for Nahuatl that systematically reduces sentences to their base form, simplifying the generation of correct morphology variants.

1 Introduction

The development of educational materials for Indigenous languages presents unique challenges due to their low-resource nature, limited digital representation, and morphological complexity. The AmericasNLP 2025 Shared Task (de Gibert et al., 2025) addresses these challenges by focusing on the creation of accurate grammatical modifications in sentences across several Indigenous languages: Bribri, Maya, Guarani, and Nahuatl. The goal of the shared task was to apply specified grammatical transformations to source sentences in order to generate appropriate new sentences that could be used in educational content for language learning and preservation.

Historically, language processing tasks such as grammatical transformations, have relied on extensive corpora. However, such resources are scarce or entirely unavailable for many Indigenous languages. Building on our successful approach from the AmericasNLP 2024 Shared Task, we again leverage dictionaries and linguistic rules combined with the generative capabilities of GPT-4o (Achiam et al., 2023). This year we try a new technique which proved to be less effective than our technique from 2024, but still resulted in strong scores for Bribri. We also tested an entirely rule-based system for Nahuatl, which while still in early stages, nevertheless achieves significant improvements over LLM prompting.

Our submission comprises three distinct translation systems. The first system, submitted for Maya and Guarani, employs a straightforward GPT-4o few-shot prompting technique, enhanced by synthetically generated examples to ensure coverage of all grammatical variations encountered. The second system, used for Bribri, integrates dictionary-based alignment with GPT-4o, inspired by the edit-tag method used in the Grammatical Error Correction Tagged with Edits (GECTOR) system (Omelianchuk et al., 2020), to manage lexical and morphological transformations systematically. Finally, recognizing the specific complexities of Nahuatl, we developed a specialized rule-based system that classifies grammatical features, reduces sentences to a base form, and generates the target sentence from that base form.

2 Task and Data Description

In this shared task, the provided dataset includes original sentences along with the grammatical transformations to be applied to these sentences. The goal is to develop systems capable of applying these transformations accurately to the base sentences, producing grammatically modified versions suitable for educational use.

While many instances in the data consisted of a single change, there were many compound changes as well, where multiple types of transformations were combined, especially for Nahuatl and Bribri (See Appendix A). For example, a negative type alteration (TYPE:NEG) may be combined with a

Proceedings of the Fifth Workshop on NLP for Indigenous Languages of the Americas (AmericasNLP), pages 112–118
May 4, 2025

Language	Original	With Synthetic
Bribri	309	533
Maya	594	615
Guarani	178	186
Nahuatl	391	391

Table 1: Number of example sentences initially provided versus the number actually utilized after adding synthetic examples. We did not create synthetic examples for Nahuatl.

Source	Ie' dúwa̱
Change	TYPE:NEG, TENSE:PRF_PROG
Target	Ie kȅ ku̱'bak dawőkwa̱
KEEP:	ie'
ADD:	kȅ (negation particle)
ADD:	ku̱'bak (NEG PRF_PROG marker)
CHANGE:	base form dúwa̱ -> PRF_PROG
form dawőkwa̱	

Table 2: Example with change description

change to an interrogative (SUBTYPE:INT). This would have the effect of going from "I walked" to "Didn't you walk?" in English. This may be further combined with transformations to subject, such as to 3rd person plural (PERSON:3_PL): "Didn't they walk?"

We synthetically enhanced the training set by expanding changes into component substeps, combining alterations to make more compound changes. The number of sentences before and after expansion are listed in Table 1.

Sub-step Expansion We decomposed complex grammatical transformations into simpler, sequential sub-steps. For example, a change labeled `TYPE:NEG, SUBTYPE:INT` was expanded into two distinct steps: initially applying `TYPE:NEG` to reach an intermediate form, followed by `SUBTYPE:INT` to attain the final sentence.

Change Combination Additionally, we introduced new examples by combined changes. For example, a change in tense or mood would be combined with a person's changes. We aimed to have comprehensive coverage of all grammatical transformation combinations.

3 System Description

We implemented three systems, varying in their dependence on prompting versus rule-based processing. For each language, we selected the system that performed best on the dev set.

3.1 Example-Based Prompt

The first system leverages GPT-4o exclusively through few-shot prompting, relying on synthetic examples to maximize its coverage of grammatical variations. In this approach, we choose examples from the training data with the exact same change, from which the LLM can hopefully learn to generalize and perform similar modifications on new sentences. As mentioned in Section 2, there was not always an exact match for the change in the training data. This approach differed from the submission last year, JAJ (Vasselli et al., 2024), which addressed the lack of comprehensive coverage of change combinations by iteratively processing the test cases, applying sub-changes in a different order for each language. We also experimented with translating the prompt into Spanish, which improved scores for Bribri, but did not help Maya, Guarani, or Nahuatl.

3.2 Transformation-Based Prompt

The second system is based on the intuition that grammatical changes typically require only a small number of edits to the source sentence. Inspired by GECTOR (Omelianchuk et al., 2020), we annotate each training example with an explicit transformation sequence. Each transformation is framed in terms of token-level operations:

- **KEEP** for words that remain unchanged
- **ADD** for newly inserted words
- **REMOVE** for words that are removed.
- **REPLACE** for words that are replaced with different word types.
- **CHANGE** for cases where the word form changes, but the base word type is preserved (e.g., tense/person inflection).

This format allows GPT-4o to operate more conservatively by avoiding unnecessary rewrites, leading to more interpretable predictions and improved generalization. In addition, it facilitates automatic double-checking of each transformation using dictionary lookups or morphological rules, further enhancing the reliability of the output. An example can be seen in Table 2.

Using this method greatly improved performance on Bribri. Even moreso when the tagged change output was postprocessed. See Table 3 for ablation results on the development set.

System	Acc.	BLEU	ChrF
Examples	4.25	9.77	35.21
+ Description	15.09	40.94	58.24
+ Postprocessing	36.79	60.83	70.80

Table 3: Ablation experiments on the Bribri development set using examples only, with change descriptions, and postprocessing the change description output.

Source	tehuatl amo otinechnextilito nin tlatzotzonal
Change	HON:1, PERSON[IOBJ]:3_SI, PERSON[OBJ]:3_PL, PERSON[SUBJ]:2_PL, PURPOSIVE:NA
Target	nimehuantzitzin amo onoconnextilihqueh nin tlatzotzonal
Source	yehuatl onechnextileh nin tlatzotzonal
Change	PERSON[SUBJ]:2_SI, PURPOSIVE:VEN, TYPE:NEG
Target	tehuatl amo otinechnextilito nin tlatzotzonal

Table 4: Examples from the Nahuatl training set

3.3 Pure Rule Based Transformation

The third system is a fully rule-based approach developed specifically for Nahuatl. Unlike Bribri, we lacked a digitized dictionary, preventing us from applying the transformation-based method described in Section 3.2. Nahuatl also presents more grammatical changes per sentence than Maya or Guarani, making the example-based approach less effective.

To address this, we created rules to heuristically assign part-of-speech tags using word position and known affixes. These tags were then used to infer grammatical features of each sentence—such as subject, object, and indirect object person markers, honorific status, type, and purposive direction.

Grammatical Feature Identification Evaluation We used the training data to infer grammatical features by identifying sentences that appeared in multiple transformation pairs. Table 4 shows two such examples. [1]

From the first pair, we infer that the target sentence is honorific (HON:1), has a 2nd person plural subject, a 3rd person plural object, a 3rd person singular indirect object, and is not purposive. This implies that the source sentence differs in those respects, but the only meaningful thing we learn about the source is that it is not honorific.

However, the same source sentence appears as the target in the second pair. From that example, we infer that "tehuatl amo otinechnextilito nin tlatzotzonal" has a 2nd person singular subject, is negative, and expresses purposive intent toward the speaker. Since these features were not listed as changed in the first pair, we can propagate them to the first target as well, inferring that the target of the first pair is also negative. We also infer that the second source sentence is not honorific.

[1]There is an error in this sentence which affects five other examples in the provided data: "otinechnextilito" should be "otinechnoxtilico" for PURPOSIVE:VEN. This error, in an already infrequent change category, may have contributed to the challenge of learning the PURPOSIVE feature.

Quality	Training	Development
Honorific	93.7	100.0
Subject	59.0	88.6
Possessor	69.0	100.0
Object	31.0	-
Ind. Object	0.0	-
Tense	64.8	82.1
Mood	75.9	83.3
Aspect	58.6	88.9
Purposive	0.0	-
Type	100.0	100.0
Transitivity	0.0	-

Table 5: Results of rule-based classification. "-" indicates there was not enough information in the set to generate test cases for this quality.

By iterating over the dataset in this way, we assembled a more complete set of grammatical features for each sentence. These annotations allowed us to evaluate our rule-based system by assigning source and target features, applying transformations, and comparing the result.

Table 5 shows classification results on training and dev sets. While our system performs well on simpler features like type (positive or negative), it struggles with indirect object, transitivity, and purposive features, indicating areas for future improvement.

Inference Time At inference time, we used the classifier to predict the grammatical features of a new source sentence. These predicted features were then modified according to the specified changes to derive the expected target sentence features. We decomposed the source sentence into a normalized default form—non-honorific, 3rd person singular subject, no possessor, present simple tense, no mood, and positive type—by systematically stripping or converting known morphological indicators. From this base form, we then generated the target sentence by applying all grammatical features required by the target configuration.

This rule-based generation pipeline still requires

System	Bribri			Guarani			Maya			Nahuatl		
	Acc.	BLEU	ChrF	Acc.	BLEU	ChrF	Acc.	BLEU	ChrF	Acc.	BLEU	ChrF
Edit-tree baseline	5.66	20.35	45.56	22.78	34.99	77.14	26.17	52.38	78.72	0.00	1.38	34.32
Example-based Prompt	4.25	9.77	35.21	**45.57**	**55.53**	**86.77**	**45.64**	**71.21**	**87.28**	0.57	3.40	34.76
+ Spanish prompt	8.49	31.32	55.90	37.97	51.68	84.14	42.28	70.18	86.28	0.57	1.64	31.54
Transformation-based Prompt	15.09	40.94	58.24	39.24	50.58	85.59	42.95	69.13	84.62	-	-	-
+ Postprocessing	**36.79**	**60.83**	**70.80**	15.19	42.31	77.18	40.94	70.22	84.77	-	-	-
Rule-based Transformation	-	-	-	-	-	-	-	-	-	**26.14**	**26.64**	**52.19**

Table 6: Results on the development set. "-" indicates the system does not currently support that language.

System	Bribri			Guarani			Maya			Nahuatl		
	Acc.	BLEU	ChrF	Acc.	BLEU	ChrF	Acc.	BLEU	ChrF	Acc.	BLEU	ChrF
Edit-tree baseline	8.75	22.11	52.73	14.84	25.03	76.10	25.81	53.69	80.23	-	-	-
JAJ (Vasselli et al., 2024)	**54.17**	**71.72**	**82.78**	**36.81**	**48.29**	**84.12**	**53.55**	**78.41**	**91.53**	-	-	-
Ours	41.25	62.57	74.99	32.69	49.21	84.98	42.90	71.81	88.97	**17.5**	**40.50**	**65.40**

Table 7: Results on the test set. Ours was the best performing system for each language on the development set: Postprocessed transformation-based prompt for Bribri, English language Example-based Prompt for Maya and Guarani, and Rule-based Transformation for Nahuatl.

further refinement, particularly for accurate reconstruction of morphologically complex forms. However, the system proved to be more effective than the example-based prompting approach when evaluated on the Nahuatl development set.

4 Results

As seen in Table 7, across all four languages, our systems outperformed the edit-tree baseline provided in the shared task in terms of accuracy, BLEU, and ChrF scores. However, our results did not reach the performance levels of the JAJ system from last year.

For Maya and Guarani, our approach this year applied all changes at once using synthetically constructed examples, whereas the JAJ system applied transformations incrementally. The iterative strategy appears to reducing the complexity at each transformation step, improving accuracy.

In Bribri, two factors probably contributed to our lower scores. First, as with Maya and Guarani, we did not apply changes iteratively. Second, we omitted explicit conjugation hints from the prompt, which were included in the JAJ system and likely contributed to the improved performance. Although our post-processing step was designed to enforce correct conjugation, it is unknown whether it is less effective than targeted prompting. A combination of the edit-tag prompting method with conjugation hints and iterative change application is a promising direction for future experiments.

Nahuatl was introduced to the task for the first time this year and was the most challenging for our system. Although our rule-based system performed better than the example-based prompting baseline, it still falls short of ideal performance. The lack of a digitized dictionary and the large number of interacting grammatical features per sentence continue to pose significant challenges.

5 Related Work

Rosetta Stone Puzzles In Rosetta Stone puzzles (Bozhanov and Derzhanski, 2013), solvers are given a limited set of bilingual sentence pairs and asked to translate sentences into the other language. These puzzles contain machine translation and grammatical transformation. Şahin et al. (2020) tested several algorithms for those problems, including statistical algorithms and Transformer-based language models (Vaswani et al., 2017). Sung et al. (2024) explored the metalinguistic awareness of pre-trained language models. Chi et al. (2024) and Bean et al. (2024) developed benchmarks in the same format as Rosetta Stone puzzles and tested several LLMs. The results demonstrate that LLMs potentially have the capabilities to apply linguistic knowledge and extract linguistic features from limited data.

LLM-Assisted Rule-Based Approach An LLM-assisted rule-based approach demonstrates promising performance, particularly for low-resource languages. Low-resource languages have limited linguistic resources, resulting in the challenging performance of LLMs. To address this issue, several studies have leveraged existing linguistic knowledge to develop pipeline systems that apply rule-based processing to input in low-resource languages before passing it to LLMs. Coleman et al. (2024) introduced a new methodology, LLM-Assisted Rule-Based Machine Translation, and explored the performance and advantages. Zhang et al. (2024) proposed a method that decomposes inputs into morphemes with morphological analyzers, assigns glosses to each morpheme with dictionaries, and uses them for translation. Both methods leverage rule-based approaches to narrow the candidates or add rich information to the original input, guiding LLMs to the correct output.

6 Conclusion

We presented three systems for generating educational sentence transformations in Indigenous languages, varying in their use of prompting and linguistic rules. Our systems consistently outperformed the baseline across all four languages, but results suggest several areas for refinement.

For Maya and Guarani, applying all changes at once proved less effective than the iterative approach used in previous work. For Bribri, the absence of conjugation cues in the prompt may have hindered performance, even with post-processing. For Nahuatl, our rule-based system offered improvements over prompting alone, but remains limited by the lack of digitized lexical resources.

Future work will focus on refining the rule-based system, incorporating a Nahuatl dictionary to support edit-tag prompting, and adopting iterative application of changesa strategy that yielded strong results in prior shared tasks.

The interplay between LLM-based reasoning and structured linguistic knowledge emerged as a key factor in producing reliable transformations—especially when creating educational tools for under-resourced Indigenous languages.

Limitations

The purely prompt-based approach is highly sensitive to the quality and coverage of examples. When faced with compound grammatical transformations, our system often failed to generalize.

The transformation-based system relies on accurate alignments, which in turn relies on complete dictionaries. While effective for Bribri, incomplete dictionaries may lead to missing or incorrect transformation annotations, which in turn affect the system's outputs.

For Nahuatl, the rule-based system is based on hand-crafted heuristics and POS inference rules. These rules are not always accurate and can misclassify grammatical qualities. Additional work must be done to make this system more accurate.

Acknowledgments

We extend our gratitude to the authors of the initial effort for Guarani Wordnet (Chiruzzo et al., 2023) for access to their data. Special thanks to Professor Carla Victoria Jara Murillo and Professor Haakon S. Krohn who generously allowed us to use and repackage their Bribri data (Jara Murillo, 2018; Krohn, 2023) for use in this project. Also, a big thank you to our reviewers who pointed out the error in the Nahuatl example and helped us improve this paper.

References

Josh Achiam, Steven Adler, Sandhini Agarwal, Lama Ahmad, Ilge Akkaya, Florencia Leoni Aleman, Diogo Almeida, Janko Altenschmidt, Sam Altman, Shyamal Anadkat, and 1 others. 2023. Gpt-4 technical report. *arXiv preprint arXiv:2303.08774*.

Andrew Michael Bean, Simeon Hellsten, Harry Mayne, Jabez Magomere, Ethan A Chi, Ryan Andrew Chi, Scott A. Hale, and Hannah Rose Kirk. 2024. LINGOLY: A benchmark of olympiad-level linguistic reasoning puzzles in low resource and extinct languages. In *The Thirty-eight Conference on Neural Information Processing Systems Datasets and Benchmarks Track*.

Bozhidar Bozhanov and Ivan Derzhanski. 2013. Rosetta stone linguistic problems. In *Proceedings of the Fourth Workshop on Teaching NLP and CL*, pages 1–8, Sofia, Bulgaria. Association for Computational Linguistics.

Nathan Chi, Teodor Malchev, Riley Kong, Ryan Chi, Lucas Huang, Ethan Chi, R. McCoy, and Dragomir Radev. 2024. ModeLing: A novel dataset for testing linguistic reasoning in language models. In *Proceedings of the 6th Workshop on Research in Computational Linguistic Typology and Multilingual NLP*, pages 113–119, St. Julian's, Malta. Association for Computational Linguistics.

Luis Chiruzzo, Marvin Agüero-Torales, Aldo Alvarez, and Yliana Rodríguez. 2023. Initial experiments for building a Guarani WordNet. In *Proceedings of the 12th Global Wordnet Conference*, pages 197–204, University of the Basque Country, Donostia - San Sebastian, Basque Country. Global Wordnet Association.

Jared Coleman, Bhaskar Krishnamachari, Ruben Rosales, and Khalil Iskarous. 2024. LLM-assisted rule based machine translation for low/no-resource languages. In *Proceedings of the 4th Workshop on Natural Language Processing for Indigenous Languages of the Americas (AmericasNLP 2024)*, pages 67–87, Mexico City, Mexico. Association for Computational Linguistics.

Ona de Gibert, Raul Vazquez, Robert Pugh, Abteen Ebrahimi, Pavel Denisov, Ali Marashian, Enora Rice, Edward Gow-Smith, Juan C. Prieto, Melissa Robles, Rubén Manrique, Oscar Moreno Veliz, Ángel Lino Campos, Rolando Coto-Solano, Aldo Alvarez, Marvin Agüero-Torales, John E. Ortega, Luis Chiruzzo, Arturo Oncevay, and 3 others. 2025. Findings of the AmericasNLP shared tasks on machine translation, creation of educational material, and translation metrics for indigenous languages. In *Proceedings of the 5th Workshop on Natural Language Processing for Indigenous Languages of the Americas (AmericasNLP 2025)*, Albuquerque, New Mexico. Association for Computational Linguistics.

Carla Victoria Jara Murillo. 2018. *Gramática de la lengua bribri*, volume 1. EDigital, San José.

Haakon S Krohn. 2023. Diccionario bribri–español español–bribri.

Kostiantyn Omelianchuk, Vitaliy Atrasevych, Artem Chernodub, and Oleksandr Skurzhanskyi. 2020. GECToR – grammatical error correction: Tag, not rewrite. In *Proceedings of the Fifteenth Workshop on Innovative Use of NLP for Building Educational Applications*, pages 163–170, Seattle, WA, USA → Online. Association for Computational Linguistics.

Gözde Gül Şahin, Yova Kementchedjhieva, Phillip Rust, and Iryna Gurevych. 2020. PuzzLing Machines: A Challenge on Learning From Small Data. In *Proceedings of the 58th Annual Meeting of the Association for Computational Linguistics*, pages 1241–1254, Online. Association for Computational Linguistics.

Junehwan Sung, Hidetaka Kamigaito, and Taro Watanabe. 2024. Exploring metalinguistic awareness in pretrained language models through the international linguistics olympiad challenges. In *Proceedings of the Thirtieth Annual Meeting of the Association for Natural Language Processing*, Kobe, Japan. Association for Natural Language Processing.

Justin Vasselli, Arturo Martínez Peguero, Junehwan Sung, and Taro Watanabe. 2024. Applying linguistic expertise to LLMs for educational material development in indigenous languages. In *Proceedings of the 4th Workshop on Natural Language Processing for Indigenous Languages of the Americas (AmericasNLP 2024)*, pages 201–208, Mexico City, Mexico. Association for Computational Linguistics.

Ashish Vaswani, Noam Shazeer, Niki Parmar, Jakob Uszkoreit, Llion Jones, Aidan N. Gomez, Łukasz Kaiser, and Illia Polosukhin. 2017. Attention is all you need. In *Proceedings of the 31st International Conference on Neural Information Processing Systems*, NIPS'17, pages 6000–6010, Red Hook, NY, USA. Curran Associates Inc.

Kexun Zhang, Yee Choi, Zhenqiao Song, Taiqi He, William Yang Wang, and Lei Li. 2024. Hire a linguist!: Learning endangered languages in LLMs with in-context linguistic descriptions. In *Findings of the Association for Computational Linguistics: ACL 2024*, pages 15654–15669, Bangkok, Thailand. Association for Computational Linguistics.

A Data Distribution

We observed that Maya and Guarani examples typically involved only one or two grammatical changes per instance, whereas Bribri and Nahuatl frequently included compound transformations affecting multiple features simultaneously. This discrepancy is illustrated in Table 8 and Figure 1. We hypothesize that this difference in complexity contributed to the weaker performance of purely prompt-based systems on Bribri and Nahuatl, as those systems may struggle to generalize when required to model multiple interacting changes at once as illustrated in Figure 2.

		1	2	3	4	5	6	7	8	Total
bribri	train	51 (16.5%)	89 (28.8%)	75 (24.3%)	60 (19.4%)	26 (8.4%)	7 (2.3%)	1 (0.3%)	-	309
	dev	46 (21.7%)	62 (29.2%)	51 (24.1%)	33 (15.6%)	16 (7.5%)	3 (1.4%)	1 (0.5%)	-	212
	test	83 (17.3%)	141 (29.4%)	125 (26.0%)	85 (17.7%)	41 (8.5%)	5 (1.0%)	-	-	480
guarani	train	175 (98.3%)	3 (1.7%)	-	-	-	-	-	-	178
	dev	79 (100.0%)	-	-	-	-	-	-	-	79
	test	361 (99.2%)	3 (0.8%)	-	-	-	-	-	-	364
maya	train	538 (90.6%)	47 (7.9%)	6 (1.0%)	1 (0.2%)	2 (0.3%)	-	-	-	594
	dev	138 (92.6%)	8 (5.4%)	1 (0.7%)	1 (0.7%)	1 (0.7%)	-	-	-	149
	test	222 (71.6%)	83 (26.8%)	5 (1.6%)	-	-	-	-	-	310
nahuatl	train	17 (4.3%)	69 (17.6%)	98 (25.1%)	90 (23.0%)	72 (18.4%)	28 (7.2%)	14 (3.6%)	3 (0.8%)	391
	dev	17 (9.7%)	49 (27.8%)	52 (29.5%)	38 (21.6%)	19 (10.8%)	-	1 (0.6%)	-	176
	test	16 (13.3%)	36 (30.0%)	41 (34.2%)	15 (12.5%)	7 (5.8%)	3 (2.5%)	2 (1.7%)	-	120

Table 8: Number of changes.

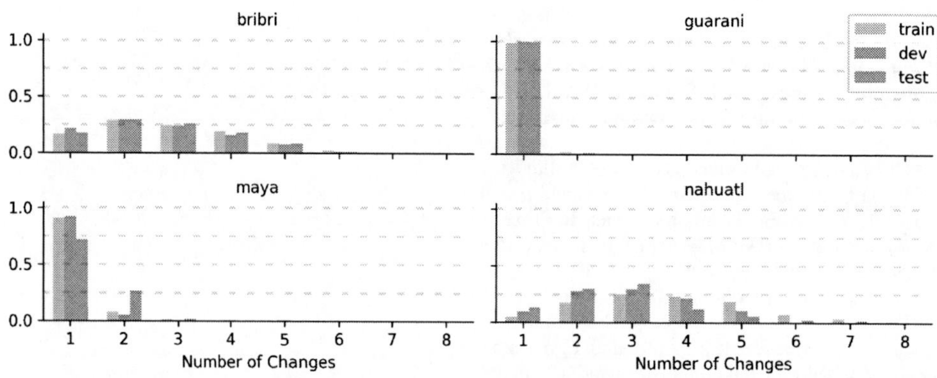

Figure 1: Ratio of number of changes across datasets.

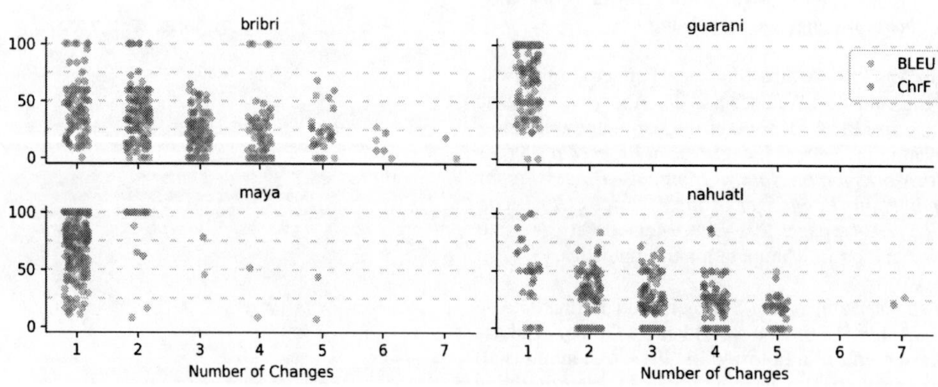

Figure 2: Performance w.r.t. number of changes in devset.

Harnessing NLP for Indigenous Language Education: Fine-Tuning Large Language Models for Sentence Transformation

Mahshar Yahan, Dr. Mohammad Amanul Islam
Department of Computer Science and Engineering
Uttara University, Bangladesh
mahshar@uttara.ac.bd, amanul.islam@uttarauniversity.edu.bd

Abstract

Indigenous languages face significant challenges due to their endangered status and limited resources which makes their integration into NLP systems difficult. This study investigates the use of Large Language Models (LLMs) for sentence transformation tasks in Indigenous languages, focusing on Bribri, Guarani, and Maya. Here, the dataset from the AmericasNLP 2025 Shared Task 2 is used to explore sentence transformations in Indigenous languages. The goal is to create educational tools by modifying sentences based on linguistic instructions, such as changes in tense, aspect, voice, person, and other grammatical features. The methodology involves preprocessing data, simplifying transformation tags, and designing zero-shot and few-shot prompts to guide LLMs in sentence rewriting. Fine-tuning techniques like LoRA and Bits-and-Bytes quantization were employed to optimize model performance while reducing computational costs. Among the tested models, Llama 3.2(3B-Instruct) demonstrated superior performance across all languages with high BLEU and ChrF++ scores, particularly excelling in few-shot settings. The Llama 3.2 model achieved BLEU scores of 19.51 for Bribri, 13.67 for Guarani, and 55.86 for Maya in test settings. Additionally, ChrF++ scores reached 50.29 for Bribri, 58.55 for Guarani, and 80.12 for Maya, showcasing its effectiveness in handling sentence transformation. These results highlight the potential of LLMs that can improve NLP tools for indigenous languages and help preserve linguistic diversity.

1 Introduction

Indigenous languages are an important part of human history and culture, but many are on the verge of disappearing. These languages hold unique knowledge and traditions that should be preserved for future generations. Thankfully, advancements in Natural Language Processing (NLP) offer new ways to protect and revitalize them.

For example, in New Zealand, technology is playing a key role in revitalizing the Maori language. Apps like 'Kōrerorero' are making it easier for people to learn and practice the language in their daily lives[1]. Similarly, in Canada, the FirstVoices app offers resources to support learning for more than 60 indigenous languages, helping to preserve and promote these rich cultural traditions[2].

The AmericasNLP 2025 Shared Task 2 (de Gibert et al., 2025) focuses on creating educational tools for Indigenous languages in the Americas, including Bribri, Guarani, Maya, and Nahuatl Omitlan. The initiative leverages NLP techniques to develop systems that can generate language learning exercises by transforming sentences based on grammatical changes, such as tense or type.

In this shared task, the provided dataset contains a source sentence and instruction that need to be applied to achieve the target sentence. The goal is to train a system capable of modifying the source sentences according to specified grammatical transformations. For instance, an example of sentence transformation in the Maya language,

Source: Táan u bin tu kool *(He is going to the field)*

Change(Instruction): TYPE:NEG

Target(Transformed): Ma' táan u bin ich kooli' *(He is not going to the field)*

Each of these languages presents unique linguistic characteristics. For example, Bribri is a tonal language with SOV(Subject-Object-Verb) word order supported by tools like morphological analyzers and electronic dictionaries (Coto-Solano et al., 2021). Guarani is a highly agglutinative language, where prefixes and suffixes are used to express grammatical information (Lucas et al., 2024).

[1]https://linguisticsnews.com/insight/case-study-the-evolution-of-indigenous-languages/

[2]https://autogpt.net/the-impact-of-ai-in-languages-preservation/

Proceedings of the Fifth Workshop on NLP for Indigenous Languages of the Americas (AmericasNLP), pages 119–125
May 4, 2025 ©2025 Association for Computational Linguistics

Maya languages exhibit fascinating linguistic features, such as aspectual marking instead of tense conjugation to express time-related information (Pugh et al., 2023).

The task of sentence transformation for Indigenous languages creates a unique challenge due to it's complex linguistic structures. To address these, the dataset was carefully preprocessed by cleaning text, standardizing formatting, and simplifying transformation tags into actionable instructions. Prompt design played a critical role, with zero-shot and few-shot prompts guiding models effectively in rewriting sentences based on linguistic instructions. Few-shot prompts consistently outperformed zero-shot prompts by providing examples for better learning. Large Language Models (LLMs) were fine-tuned using techniques like LoRA (Low-Rank Adaptation) and Bits-and-Bytes (BNB) quantization to optimize performance while reducing computational costs. Post-processing ensured concise outputs by extracting only the relevant transformed sentences. The results showed that Llama 3.2 achieved the best performance across Bribri, Guarani, and Maya languages, with high BLEU and ChrF++ scores on development and test datasets. Few-shot prompting proved particularly effective for low-resource languages, highlighting its advantage in multilingual NLP tasks.

The major contributions of our research work are as follows-

- We proposed an innovative sentence transformation system for Indigenous languages, utilizing LLMs for effective results.
- We executed a range of experiments on the dataset and presented a comprehensive analysis of their performance.

The experimentation details have been provided in the GitHub repository. [3]

2 Related Work

Indigenous languages are often low-resource, making them challenging for NLP systems that rely on extensive annotated data. Previous studies have showed the potential of NLP in preserving these languages by creating tools like machine translation systems and educational resources.

Leveraging pre-trained models like mBERT and XLM-R for cross-lingual knowledge transfer can help adapt high-resource language models to low-resource settings, enabling better sentence transformations (Pakray et al., 2025). In prior work organized by AmericasNLP, researchers demonstrated that GPT-4 and other large language models perform effectively in few-shot learning for low-resource languages (Ginn et al., 2024). Additionally, they highlighted data augmentation strategies that can address data scarcity and enhance model generalization in low-resource settings.

In a study, the author of the paper (Hammond, 2024) implemented a multilingual transformer-based model(mBERT) and an edit tree method to address the sentence transformation task, which performed poorly. Then, they applied a morphosyntactic similarity approach, which significantly improved performance by utilizing linguistic features. In another research work, the authors (Niklaus et al., 2019) introduced the idea of changing complex sentences into simple ones using recursive sentence simplification and a semantic hierarchy. In a separate study (Silfverberg et al., 2017), researchers proposed an efficient data augmentation technique by modifying morphological patterns, which helps with low-resource language with limited data.

The paper (Su et al., 2024) explores fine-tuning transformer models like NLLB-200, Claude 3 Opus and demonstrates their effectiveness in capturing sentence-level morphological inflections. For Maya, fine-tuning with data augmentation (using StemCorrupt) yielded the best performance. Another shared task paper by AmericansNLP explores sentence transformation using Pointer-Generator LSTM, Mixtral 8x7B (SICL[4] with LoRA), and GPT-4 (ICL[5]) (Bui and Von Der Wense, 2024). Also, they have proposed an ensemble method that outperforms single models by boosting accuracy by almost 4%.

An innovative approach by the authors combines rule-based NLP techniques with prompt-based methods leveraging large language models (LLMs) and POS[6] tagging(Vasselli et al., 2024). This approach balances general processing with language-specific customization for grammatical sentence transformation. Another study demon-

[3] https://github.com/mahshar-yahan/AmericansNLP-2025/tree/main/Shared%20Task-2

[4] SICL: Supervised In-Context Learning

[5] ICL: In-Context Learning

[6] POS: Parts of Speech

strates that minimal CSV-style prompting using large language models (LLMs) like GPT-4 and GPT-3.5 can achieve competitive performance in low-resource morphological tasks (Haley, 2024).

3 Dataset

We have utilized a dataset created for AmericasNLP 2025 Shared Task 2 (de Gibert et al., 2025), which aims to develop educational tools for Indigenous languages. The dataset includes four low-resource languages: Bribri, Guarani, Maya, and Nahuatl Omitlan. It is designed for sentence transformation tasks, where sentences are modified based on linguistic instructions such as changes in tense, aspect, polarity and so on. It includes 16 major categories with a total of 68 unique values across these categories. The dataset is divided into Train, Development (Dev), and Test sets, as shown in Table 1:

Split	Bribri	Guarani	Maya	Nahuatl Omitlan
Train	391	178	594	392
Dev	176	179	149	177
Test	120	364	310	121

Table 1: Language-wise distribution in the dataset

The relatively small size of the training data, particularly for some languages, presents a challenge for robust model training. The dataset also features a mix of simple and complex instructions, allowing for a wide array of sentence transformations to be applied. Table 2 offers some excellent examples to illustrate these transformations and their English equivalents.

4 Methodology

In this section, we have provided an overview of the methods and techniques applied to the dataset described earlier. Initially, the data was preprocessed, and the transformation tags were transferred to instruction. Subsequently, various LLMs were utilized to enhance performance. These models were fine-tuned and evaluated to optimize their effectiveness, as illustrated in Figure 1.

4.1 Data Preprocessing

Several preprocessing steps have been implemented on the given dataset of different language to achieve optimal outcomes. These steps include removing of unnecessary changes, standardizing text formatting and addressing inconsistencies in the data. Each step is designed to enhance the model's ability to process linguistic transformations effectively.

4.1.1 Removal of Unnecessary Changes

The dataset contains entries where the change column is tagged as NA, indicating that no modifications are required for the source sentence. These entries are removed to obtain meaningful transformation. This ensures that only actionable instructions are remained in the dataset. For example,
Before Removal: VOICE:MID, PERSON:NA
After Removal: VOICE:MID

4.1.2 Text Standardization

To ensure uniform formatting in the dataset, we have cleaned the text by removing punctuation, special characters, and unnecessary whitespace. This step helps reduce noise and improves the model's ability to focus on meaningful linguistic patterns. For instance in Bribri,
Before Removal: Ye' tö i kít
After Removal: Ye tö i kít *(Apostrophe removed)*
In the given example for cases English translation is *And here it is.* But in some cases, this preprocessing step may have impacted results, where apostrophes represent glottalization and differentiate minimal pairs.

4.2 Tag Simplification

This process simplifies complex tag combinations into clear, actionable instructions that are easy to understand. It helps the model interpret and apply transformations more effectively. For example, in the dataset, the Change field may contain multiple complex tags like TYPE:NEG, TENSE:PRF_REC.
Input Tags: TYPE:NEG, TENSE:PRF_REC
Simplified Instructions: Make the sentence negative and change to recent perfect tense.
This makes the dataset easier to work with and helps the model learn better. This ensures the model is trained on instructions it can accurately process and apply, resulting in more precise transformations.

4.3 Prompt Design

In this task, zero-shot-prompt and few-shot-prompt are utilized to rewrite sentences according to instructions. These prompts are structured to provide

Source *(Original Sentence)*	**Change** *(Instruction)*	**Target** *(Transformed Sentence)*
Kin in suut koonol merkaado *(I am returning to the market)*	ASPECT: INS	Je'el in suut koonol merkaado *(I will return to the market)*
Kin in suut koonol merkaado*(I am returning to the market)*	ASPECT:TER, TENSE: PAS_SIM	Ts'o'ok in suut koonol merkaado*(I have returned to the market)*

Table 2: Illustrative examples of single and multi-instruction sentence transformations in the Maya language

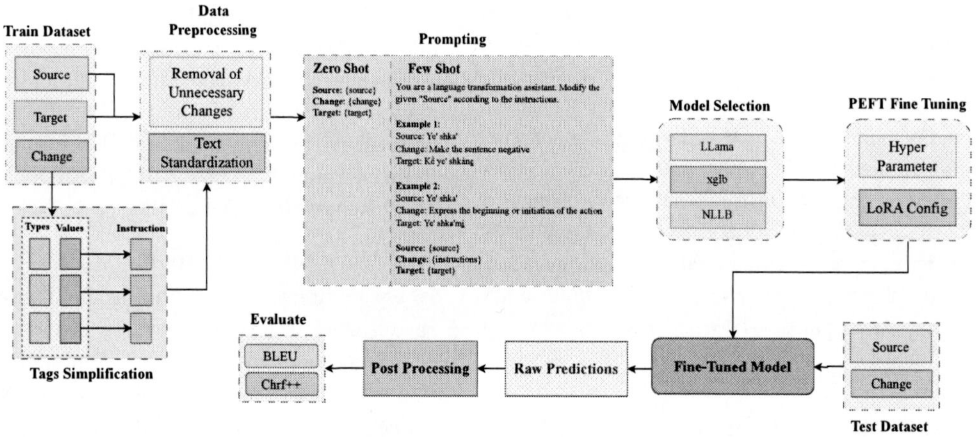

Figure 1: Methodological Workflow for Sentence Transformation in Indigenous Language Education Using Large Language Models

clear guidance to the model while ensuring consistency in the transformation process.

4.3.1 Zero Shot Prompt Design

These prompts are designed to evaluate the model's ability to perform translations and linguistic transformations without relying on specific training examples. The model is expected to independently generate the correct output based solely on the provided instruction. For instance, consider the following training prompt in Bribri:

Zero Shot Prompt
Source: Ye' shka'
Instruction: MODE:ADVERS
Target: Ye' shka'

In handling test data, a slightly modified version of the prompt is used to isolate the predicted sentence in the output: "Provide only the Target sentence, nothing else". This ensures that the generated output is concise and aligned with the task output.

4.3.2 Few Shot Prompt Design

Few-shot prompts incorporate multiple examples of source sentences paired with instructions and their corresponding target sentences. These examples act as references, helping the model learn transformation patterns and apply them accurately. For instance,

Few Shot Prompt:
Language: Bribri, Rewrite and change the Source sentence to the Target sentence according to the given instruction.
Example 1:
Instruction: Change to recent perfect tense. (*TENSE:PRF_REC*)
Source: Ye' shka'
Target: Ye' shké
Example 2:
Instruction: Make the sentence negative and change to recent perfect tense. (*TYPE:NEG, TENSE:PRF_REC*)
Source: Ye' shka'
Target: Ye' kë shkàne
Rewrite following sentence using instruction:
Instruction: Change to potential future tense and change to imperfective aspect. (*TENSE:FUT_POT, ASPECT:IPFV*)
Source: Ye' shka'
Target: Ye' shkömi

Language	Model	Prompt Type	Acc	BLEU	Chrf++
Bribri	Llama 3.1(8B-Instruct)	Zero Shot	1.79	2.74	11.28
	Llama 3.1(8B-Instruct)	Few Shot	5.11	12.73	50.22
	Llama 3.2(3B-Instruct)	Zero Shot	5.59	4.94	33.50
	Llama 3.2(3B-Instruct)	Few Shot	**6.21**	**22.36**	**50.46**
	Xglm 1.7B	Zero Shot	0.89	1.16	30.29
	Xglm 1.7B	Few Shot	2.51	13.56	29.19
Gurarani	Llama 3.1(8B-Instruct)	Zero Shot	6.47	3.16	29.56
	Llama 3.1(8B-Instruct)	Few Shot	9.01	18.34	28.15
	Llama 3.2(3B-Instruct)	Zero Shot	7.57	**24.14**	41.10
	Llama 3.2(3B-Instruct)	Few Shot	**10.53**	22.99	**58.30**
	Xglm 1.7B	Zero Shot	2.55	8.34	52.17
	Xglm 1.7B	Few Shot	4.19	6.24	48.17
Maya	Llama 3.1(8B-Instruct)	Zero Shot	8.29	17.11	56.56
	Llama 3.1(8B-Instruct)	Few Shot	10.11	19.56	68.15
	Llama 3.2(3B-Instruct)	Zero Shot	17.39	43.45	70.23
	Llama 3.2(3B-Instruct)	Few Shot	**21.31**	**57.16**	**82.48**
	Xglm 1.7B	Zero Shot	13.51	43.45	70.53
	Xglm 1.7B	Few Shot	1.16	11.23	40.44

Table 3: Performance Evaluation of Different Models and Zero-Shot and Few-Shot Prompt on the Dev Dataset for Bribri, Guarani, and Maya Languages using Accuracy, BLEU and ChrF++ Metrics

This approach bridges the gap between zero-shot learning and fully supervised training, making it highly effective for multilingual sentence transformation.

4.4 Train

The training process for sentence transformation task involves fine-tuning large language models (LLMs) such as Llama (Touvron et al., 2023), XGLM (Lin et al., 2021) and NLLB (Costa-Jussà et al., 2022) to accurately rewrite sentences based on instructions provided in the dataset. This task focuses on transforming sentences across different dimensions, such as tense, mood, aspect, voice, and negation.

To adapt pre-trained LLMs to the task-specific requirements, we have employed efficient fine-tuning techniques using LoRA (Low-Rank Adaptation) and quantization with Bits and Bytes (BNB). These methods allow us to optimize memory usage and computational efficiency while maintaining the model's performance. LoRA modifies only a subset of the model's parameters, making it ideal for tasks requiring domain-specific adjustments without retraining the entire model. BNB enables 4-bit quantization of model weights, significantly reducing memory consumption during training.

4.5 Post Processing

When using a casual language model for sentence transformation tasks, the generated output may include extra information beyond the desired target sentence. To address this, we have employed a simple linear search on the output to locate the keyword **"Target"**. Once the keyword is identified, everything following it is extracted as the final transformed sentence. This method ensures that only the relevant portion of the model's output is retained.

5 Results and Analysis

In this section, we have provided a comprehensive comparison of the performance across different approaches to large language models (LLMs) for different languages.

5.1 Parameter Setting

Table 4 shows parameter settings for different models.

In Table 4, *lr*, *optim*,*la* and *l4* represents *learning_rate*,*optimizer*, *lora_alpha* and *load_in_4bit* and respectively.

5.2 Evaluation Metrics

The performance of various models has been evaluated using the Bilingual Evaluation Under-

Model	lr	optim	la	l4
Llama 3.1 (8B-Instruct)	$3e^{-4}$	Paged Adamw	4	8
Llama 3.2 (3B-Instruct)	$2e^{-4}$	Paged Adamw	4	8
XGLM 1.7B	$2e^{-3}$	Adam	4	8

Table 4: Parameter settings for different models

study (BLEU) score, the Character-level F-score++ (ChrF++), and Accuracy metrics on the development and test dataset.

5.3 Comparative Analysis

From Table 3, we observed that Llama 3.2 (8B-Instruct) demonstrated the best performance for sentence transformation tasks in Bribri, Guarani, and Maya languages. For Bribri, it achieved the highest BLEU score of 22.36 and ChrF++ of 50.46 in few-shot settings on the development set. Similarly, for Guarani, it secured a BLEU score of 22.99 and ChrF++ of 58.35, while for Maya, it excelled with a BLEU score of 57.16 and ChrF++ of 82.48. In contrast, XGLM 1.7B performed poorly with significantly lower scores across all languages and settings. Few-shot prompting consistently outperformed zero-shot prompting for all models, demonstrating its advantage in low-resource language tasks. The submitted system using Llama 3.2 (8B-Instruct) performed well on the test sets, as shown in Table 5. It achieved competitive BLEU and ChrF++ scores, particularly for Maya, and secured 9th place on the leaderboard.

Language	Type	Evaluation Metrics		
		Acc	BLEU	Chrf++
Bribri	dev	6.21	22.36	50.46
	test	0.4167	19.51	50.29
	base	5.66	20.35	45.56
Gurarani	dev	10.53	22.99	58.30
	test	1.92	13.67	58.55
	base	22.78	34.99	78.72
Maya	dev	21.31	57.16	82.48
	test	13.55	55.86	80.12
	base	26.17	52.38	78.72

Table 5: The results of the submitted system on the development and test sets using Llama 3.2(3B-Instruct) Model

6 Conclusion

The research demonstrates the feasibility of using LLMs for sentence transformation tasks in Indigenous languages. The performance of the models, particularly when compared to a simple edit tree baseline, fell short across all tested languages. Factors such as excessive preprocessing, overly complex prompts, a small dataset size, and high out-of-vocabulary (<unk>) token rates in the model tokenizer may cause these challenges. Among the experimented models, Llama 3.2 is the most effective system. Few-shot prompting proved particularly advantageous for low-resource languages. However, this work provides valuable insights into the obstacles faced when applying LLMs to low-resource languages.

Limitations

Several limitations were identified in this study. First, the provided dataset is quite small, which impacted model generalization. The limited availability of annotated data particularly affected Guarani, where language-specific adaptations were not implemented due to time constraints. Computational constraints also restricted broader experimentation with larger-scale models or ensemble techniques. Addressing these limitations will be crucial for future advancements in Indigenous language processing.

Future Work

Future research should focus on advancing dataset quality and diversity through innovative data augmentation techniques, such as back-translation, contextual embedding-based augmentation, and syntax tree manipulation. Using methods like ensemble learning or hybrid modeling could also boost performance in sentence transformation tasks. Additionally, integrating neural morphology extensions to handle complex linguistic structures would improve sentence transformation tasks. Expanding this work to include more endangered languages could help preserve cultural heritage through NLP.

References

Minh Duc Bui and Katharina Von Der Wense. 2024. Jgu mainz's submission to the americasnlp 2024 shared task on the creation of educational materials for indigenous languages. In *Proceedings of the 4th Workshop on Natural Language Processing for Indigenous*

Languages of the Americas (AmericasNLP 2024), pages 195–200.

Marta R Costa-Jussà, James Cross, Onur Çelebi, Maha Elbayad, Kenneth Heafield, Kevin Heffernan, Elahe Kalbassi, Janice Lam, Daniel Licht, Jean Maillard, et al. 2022. No language left behind: Scaling human-centered machine translation. *arXiv preprint arXiv:2207.04672*.

Rolando Coto-Solano, Sharid Loáiciga, and Sofía Flores-Solórzano. 2021. Towards universal dependencies for bribri. In *Proceedings of the Fifth Workshop on Universal Dependencies (UDW, SyntaxFest 2021)*, pages 16–29.

Ona de Gibert, Raul Vazquez, Robert Pugh, Abteen Ebrahimi, Pavel Denisov, Ali Marashian, Enora Rice, Edward Gow-Smith, Juan C. Prieto, Melissa Robles, Rubén Manrique, Oscar Moreno Veliz, Ángel Lino Campos, Rolando Coto-Solano, Aldo Alvarez, Marvin Agüero-Torales, John E. Ortega, Luis Chiruzzo, Arturo Oncevay, Shruti Rijhwani, Katharina von der Wense, and Manuel Mager. 2025. Findings of the AmericasNLP shared tasks on machine translation, creation of educational material, and translation metrics for indigenous languages. In *Proceedings of the 5th Workshop on Natural Language Processing for Indigenous Languages of the Americas (AmericasNLP 2025)*, Albuquerque, New Mexico. Association for Computational Linguistics.

Michael Ginn, Ali Marashian, Bhargav Shandilya, Claire Post, Enora Rice, Juan Vásquez, Marie Mcgregor, Matthew Buchholz, Mans Hulden, and Alexis Palmer. 2024. On the robustness of neural models for full sentence transformation. In *Proceedings of the 4th Workshop on Natural Language Processing for Indigenous Languages of the Americas (AmericasNLP 2024)*, pages 159–173.

Coleman Haley. 2024. The unreasonable effectiveness of large language models for low-resource clause-level morphology: In-context generalization or prior exposure? In *The 4th Workshop on NLP for Indigenous Languages of the Americas*, pages 174–178. Association for Computational Linguistics (ACL).

Michael Hammond. 2024. The role of morphosyntactic similarity in generating related sentences. In *Proceedings of the 4th Workshop on Natural Language Processing for Indigenous Languages of the Americas (AmericasNLP 2024)*, pages 221–223.

Xi Victoria Lin, Todor Mihaylov, Mikel Artetxe, Tianlu Wang, Shuohui Chen, Daniel Simig, Myle Ott, Naman Goyal, Shruti Bhosale, Jingfei Du, et al. 2021. Few-shot learning with multilingual language models. *arXiv preprint arXiv:2112.10668*.

Agustín Lucas, Alexis Baladón, Victoria Pardiñas, Marvin Agüero-Torales, Santiago Góngora, and Luis Chiruzzo. 2024. Grammar-based data augmentation for low-resource languages: The case of guarani-spanish neural machine translation. In *Proceedings of the 2024 Conference of the North American Chapter of the Association for Computational Linguistics: Human Language Technologies (Volume 1: Long Papers)*, pages 6385–6397.

Christina Niklaus, Matthias Cetto, André Freitas, and Siegfried Handschuh. 2019. Transforming complex sentences into a semantic hierarchy. *arXiv preprint arXiv:1906.01038*.

Partha Pakray, Alexander Gelbukh, and Sivaji Bandyopadhyay. 2025. Natural language processing applications for low-resource languages. *Natural Language Processing*, 31(2):183–197.

Robert Pugh, Francis Tyers, and Quetzil Castañeda. 2023. Developing finite-state language technology for maya. In *Proceedings of the Workshop on Natural Language Processing for Indigenous Languages of the Americas (AmericasNLP)*, pages 30–39.

Miikka Silfverberg, Adam Wiemerslage, Ling Liu, and Lingshuang Jack Mao. 2017. Data augmentation for morphological reinflection. In *Proceedings of the CoNLL SIGMORPHON 2017 Shared Task: Universal Morphological Reinflection*, pages 90–99.

Jim Su, Justin Ho, George Broadwell, Sarah Moeller, and Bonnie Dorr. 2024. A comparison of fine-tuning and in-context learning for clause-level morphosyntactic alternation. In *Proceedings of the 4th Workshop on Natural Language Processing for Indigenous Languages of the Americas (AmericasNLP 2024)*, pages 179–187.

Hugo Touvron, Thibaut Lavril, Gautier Izacard, Xavier Martinet, Marie-Anne Lachaux, Timothée Lacroix, Baptiste Rozière, Naman Goyal, Eric Hambro, Faisal Azhar, et al. 2023. Llama: Open and efficient foundation language models. *arXiv preprint arXiv:2302.13971*.

Justin Vasselli, Arturo Martínez Peguero, Junehwan Sung, and Taro Watanabe. 2024. Applying linguistic expertise to llms for educational material development in indigenous languages. In *Proceedings of the 4th Workshop on Natural Language Processing for Indigenous Languages of the Americas (AmericasNLP 2024)*, pages 201–208.

Leveraging Large Language Models for Spanish-Indigenous Language Machine Translation at AmericasNLP 2025

Mahshar Yahan, Dr. Mohammad Amanul Islam
Department of Computer Science and Engineering
Uttara University, Bangladesh
mahshar@uttara.ac.bd, amanul.islam@uttarauniversity.edu.bd

Abstract

This paper presents our approach to machine translation between Spanish and 13 Indigenous languages of the Americas as part of the AmericasNLP 2025 shared task. Addressing the challenges of low-resource translation, we fine-tuned advanced multilingual models, including NLLB-200 (Distilled-600M), Llama 3.1 (8B-Instruct) and XGLM 1.7B, using techniques such as dynamic batching, token adjustments, and embedding initialization. Data preprocessing steps like punctuation removal and tokenization refinements were employed to achieve data generalization. While our models demonstrated strong performance for Awajun and Quechua translations, they struggled with morphologically complex languages like Nahuatl and Otomí. Our approach achieved competitive ChrF++ scores for Awajun (35.16) and Quechua (31.01) in the Spanish-to-Indigenous translation track (Es→Xx). Similarly, in the Indigenous-to-Spanish track (Xx→Es), we obtained ChrF++ scores of 33.70 for Awajun and 31.71 for Quechua. These results underscore the potential of tailored methodologies in preserving linguistic diversity while advancing machine translation for endangered languages.

1 Introduction

Nearly half of the world's 7,000 languages are currently endangered[1]. Experts predict that around 1,500 of these languages could vanish by the end of this century due to factors like globalization, economic growth, and insufficient support for Indigenous languages[2]. Indigenous languages are not just cultural gems but also hold unique perspectives and knowledge. The United Nations has declared 2022–2032 as the International Decade of Indigenous Languages, highlighting the urgency of this issue (Boodeea et al., 2025).

Machine Translation (MT) presents significant challenges, particularly in low-resource settings. Limited data availability, the presence of diverse dialects, and complex linguistic structures such as polysynthesis significantly increase the challenges. However, recent improvements in neural machine translation (NMT) and multilingual learning have shown promise. For example, models like Meta's NLLB-200 (Distilled-600M)(Costa-Jussà et al., 2022) and fine-tuned methods using Low-Rank Adaptation(LoRA) (Hu et al., 2022) have worked well in low-resource settings, improving translation accuracy while helping preserve languages with the involvement of Indigenous communities.

The AmericasNLP 2025 Shared Task focuses on translating between Spanish and 13 Indigenous languages, such as Quechua, Guarani, and Wayuunaiki. This project uses advanced MT techniques and works closely with Indigenous communities to create accurate and culturally respectful translation models. By using advanced techniques like improved tokenization and batching, the initiative aims to build strong MT systems that respect linguistic diversity while pushing forward the field of computational linguistics.

This task is an important step towards using technology to bridge cultural gaps, ensuring that Indigenous voices are heard and preserved for future generations.

The implementation details have been provided in a GitHub repository[3].

2 Related Work

MT has emerged as a promising solution for low-resource languages. Fine-tuning large language models and innovative tokenization strategies have played a big role in these improvements. However, challenges such as limited training data, linguistic

[1] https://www.science.org/content/article/languages-are-being-wiped-out-economic-growth

[2] https://www.anu.edu.au/news/all-news/1500-endangered-languages-at-high-risk

[3] https://github.com/mahshar-yahan/AmericansNLP-2025/tree/main/Shared%20Task-1

Proceedings of the Fifth Workshop on NLP for Indigenous Languages of the Americas (AmericasNLP), pages 126–133
May 4, 2025

diversity, and issues like overgeneration continue to hinder the development of robust systems.

Recent Advancements
Recent advancements in multilingual models have significantly improved translation quality for low-resource languages. (Costa-Jussà et al., 2022) introduced NLLB-200 (Distilled-600M), a massively multilingual model trained on 200 languages, demonstrating the effectiveness of fine-tuning for low-resource settings. A recent study further highlighted the potential of NLLB-200 (Distilled-600M) by showing that fine-tuning this model can substantially improve translation quality for specific language pairs, such as Spanish to Quechua and Spanish to Guarani (Gilabert et al., 2024). Additionally, LoRA-based approaches (Hu et al., 2022) have shown promise by enabling efficient parameter updates in large language models without requiring extensive computational resources. Notably, leveraging LoRA has led to a performance improvement of 14.2%.

Tokenization Strategies
Indigenous languages often exhibit agglutinative or polysynthetic structures that challenge standard tokenization methods. (Attieh et al., 2024) compared various tokenization strategies, including SentencePiece and BPE-MR. They found that BPE-MR performs better for morphologically rich languages by preserving meaningful subword units. Our approach inspired upon these findings by tailoring tokenization strategies to the linguistic characteristics of AmericasNLP languages.

Overgeneration issues
Overgeneration is a well-documented issue in machine translation systems, where models produce excessively long or redundant outputs that compromise translation quality. Prior work has addressed this problem through evaluation metrics and architectural modifications. For instance, LAAL (Length-Adaptive Average Lagging) provides unbiased metrics to measure overgeneration during simultaneous translation tasks (Papi et al., 2022). Additionally, methods such as beam search optimization (Cohen and Beck, 2019) have been proposed to mitigate excessive output length.

Addressing Similar Challenges
MMTAfrica (Emezue and Dossou, 2022) employs backtranslation and reconstruction techniques to enhance multilingual translations for African languages. Similarly, we have utilized backtranslation in our system, enabling each of our models to translate between Spanish and Indigenous languages bidirectionally. On the other hand, ModeLing (Chi et al., 2024) is a benchmark dataset designed to evaluate linguistic reasoning in low-resource settings. This work focused on phenomena such as possessive morphology and word order variation. ModeLing provides insights into linguistic challenges similar to those faced in AmericasNLP.

3 Dataset

The dataset provided by AmericasNLP 2025 in Shared Task 1 (de Gibert et al., 2025) focuses on MT between Spanish and 13 Indigenous languages of the Americas: Awajun (agr), Aymara (ayr), Bribri (bzd), Asháninka (cni), Chatino (ctp), Guarani (grn), Wayuunaiki (guc), Wixarika (hch), Nahuatl (nah), Otomí (oto), Quechua (quy), Raramuri (tar) and Shipibo-Konibo (shp). It is divided into training, development, and test sets. Training samples vary from 3,883 (Asháninka) to 125,008 (Quechua), while development sets contain between 599 and 6,635 samples per language. The test set is mostly balanced, with 1,003 samples per language, except for Awajun (358) and Wayuunaiki (498). The dataset supports two translation sub tasks: Spanish to Indigenous languages (Es→Xx) and Indigenous languages to Spanish (Xx→Es). Across all datasets, we identified an average of approximately 765 new words per language that were not present in the initial vocabulary of the NLLB-200(Distilled-600M) tokenizer (Costa-Jussà et al., 2022), which we used for this task. Among the provided datasets, we have utilized all except Chatino and Rarámuri. Here the number of train, development, and test datasets for different subtasks is shown in the table 1.

4 Methodology

In this section, we explain the process of translating a sentence into a specific language. Here, we will discuss both sub-tracks of AmericasNLP 2025 Shared Task 1, where Spanish is translated to Indigenous languages and vice versa. Additionally, we will see how to handle unknown words while training the model for a new language. Also we explore how sentence length can help reduce translation errors.

[5] https://en.wikipedia.org/wiki/Wayuu_language
[6] https://en.wikipedia.org/wiki/Aymara_language

Language	Train	Dev	Test
agr	21,964	1,018	358
ayr	6,531	996	1,003
bzd	7,508	996	1,003
cni	3,883	883	1,003
ctp	357	499	1,000
grn	26,032	995	1,003
guc	59,715	6,635	498
hch	8,966	994	1,003
nah	16,145	672	1,003
oto	4,889	599	1,003
quy	125,008	996	1,003
shp	14,592	996	1,003
tar	14,720	995	1,003

Table 1: Language Data Across Stages

4.1 Data Preprocessing

Data preprocessing is a crucial step in preparing the dataset for MT. In this step, we have cleaned and standardized text to improve model performance and ensure consistency across languages.

4.1.1 Punctuation Removal

In this step, we remove punctuation marks to ensure uniformity across the dataset. The removal of punctuation helps in the tokenization process as it reduces unnecessary symbols. We used the *MosesPunctNormalizer* (Koehn et al., 2007) function from the *sacremoses* (Face, 2018) library for normalization. For example,

Before Removal: Tujash, senchi nampekaju, nunik jiyanitan nagkamawag, senchi maninau.

After Removal: Tujash senchi nampekaju nunik jiyanitan nagkamawag senchi maninau.

4.1.2 Whitespace and Character Cleaning

Whitespace inconsistencies were addressed by removing extra spaces and ensuring proper formatting. Leading and trailing spaces were trimmed, and multiple spaces were condensed into one. Additionally, invalid characters were identified and removed to avoid errors during tokenization. In the following example an unnecessary extra space before a fullstop is removed,

Before Cleaning: Nuniamuik pishak najaneaku .

After Cleaning: Nuniamuik pishak najaneaku.

4.1.3 Lowercasing

All text was converted to lowercase for consistency unless case sensitivity was required. However, sometimes capitalization is important, like for proper nouns, acronyms, or special terms. In those cases, we keep the original case instead of converting everything to lowercase. To ensure accurate handling of case-sensitive words, we utilized the SpaCy library (Honnibal et al., 2020) for Spanish text processing. SpaCy's built-in Named Entity Recognition (NER) capabilities allowed us to identify and retain the original case for entities like names, locations, and other significant terms. For instance,

Before: Etsa wantintuk yumijau

After: etsa wantintuk yumijau

4.1.4 Handling Unknown Tokens

Unknown tokens are words or symbols not present in the tokenizer's vocabulary. To address this, we introduced <unk> tokens to represent out-of-vocabulary items. During preprocessing, texts containing unknown tokens were flagged for review, allowing us to refine the vocabulary or handle these cases systematically. For instance, rare Indigenous words were either added to the tokenizer or mapped to <unk> during training. This strategy minimized disruptions caused by unseen words while maintaining translation quality.

4.2 Token Adjustment

Since some languages are new to the model, we need to adjust the tokenization process to fit them. This step is essential for helping the model generalize and properly understand Indigenous languages. By doing this, we can improve translation quality and ensure the model handles these languages more effectively.

4.2.1 Adding New Language Tokens

To add new languages in the translation model, we introduced special language tokens. These tokens help the model recognize the source and target languages during both training and inference. The token addition process involved updating the tokenizer's vocabulary and mappings to integrate these new tokens seamlessly. Each language was assigned a unique token, such as <agr_Latn> for Awajun and <spa_Latn> for Spanish. These tokens were added to sentences during training to clearly specify the language. For example:

Before: Yama nagkamchamunmak Chijajai, Timantim, Sukuyá.

After: <agr_Latn>Yama nagkamchamunmak Chijajai, Timantim, Sukuyá.

Language	Closest Supported Language	Basis for Similarity
agr_Latn (Awajun)	quy_Latn (Quechua)	Geographic proximity in Peru and shared agglutinative morphology (Goulder, 2005).
bzd_Latn (Bribri)	grn_Latn (Guarani)	Both are polysynthetic languages with tonal systems in Central and South America (Kann et al., 2022).
cni_Latn (Asháninka)	quy_Latn (Quechua)	Regional proximity in Peru and shared syntactic traits (Goulder, 2005; Bustamante et al., 2020).
guc_Latn (Wayuunaiki)	grn_Latn (Guarani)	Polysynthetic structure and noun incorporation in northern South America.[5]
hch_Latn (Wixarika)	quy_Latn (Quechua)	Shared agglutinative features despite different language families (Goulder, 2005).
nah_Latn (Nahuatl)	ayr_Latn (Aymara)	Typological similarities like agglutination and SOV word order due to historical interactions.[6]
oto_Latn (Otomí)	ayr_Latn (Aymara)	Borrowing from Nahuatl and typological resemblance to Aymara.[6]
shp_Latn (Shipibo-Konibo)	quy_Latn (Quechua)	Shared Amazonian influences and agglutinative morphology (Goulder, 2005; Bustamante et al., 2020).

Table 2: Mapping of Embedding Initialization for Unsupported Languages Based on Linguistic Similarity using NLLB-200 (Distilled-600M)

4.2.2 Embedding Initialization

The NLLB-200 (Distilled-600M) (Costa-Jussà et al., 2022) model directly supports three Indigenous languages: Aymara (ayr_Latn), Guarani (grn_Latn), and Quechua (quy_Latn). However, when extending the model to new languages that are not explicitly supported, embeddings are initialized using representations from linguistically similar languages. For example, Awajun (agr_Latn) uses Quechua(quy_Latn) embeddings due to linguistic similarities. This approach leverages existing knowledge, reducing training time and improving convergence. Using PyTorch, the embedding layer is resized, and new token IDs are mapped to pre-trained embeddings, ensuring compatibility while preserving prior representations. This method enables efficient extension to low-resource languages.

In comparison, models like LLaMA 3.1 (Touvron et al., 2023) and XGLM (Lin et al., 2021) offer multilingual capabilities but do not directly support Indigenous languages. LLaMA 3.1 focuses on eight high-resource languages, such as Spanish and Hindi. XGLM uses a balanced multilingual corpus but lacks direct support for low-resource Indigenous languages.

4.3 Fine Tuning Process

The fine-tuning process was conducted separately for Task 1 (Es→Xx) and Task 2 (Xx→Es) using NLLB-200(Distilled-600) (Costa-Jussà et al., 2022), LLaMA 3.1 (Touvron et al., 2023), and XGLM (Lin et al., 2021) models. Each model was adapted to the specific translation direction by leveraging its pre-trained multilingual capabilities.

For NLLB, the training process involved freezing encoder layers to reduce computational overhead while updating decoder layers for task-specific adaptation. The model was fine-tuned using a custom training loop with Adafactor optimizer and a constant learning rate scheduler with warm-up steps. Training batches were dynamically generated, ensuring source-target alignment through language-specific tokens. Periodic checkpoints were saved, and the best-performing model was selected based on ChrF++ scores on the development set. Language-specific tokens (e.g., spa_Latn for Spanish and agr_Latn for Awajun) were used to guide the model during training and evaluation.

For LLaMA 3.1 and XGLM, we followed a similar fine-tuning strategy but incorporated the parameter-efficient technique LoRA. This method allowed us to train adapter layers in self-attention blocks while freezing most of the model's parameters. Dynamic batching was employed, where language pairs were randomly selected for each batch. It allowed the model to learn from diverse linguistic contexts and improve generalization across languages. Mixed-precision training was employed to further optimize GPU utilization. Both models were fine-tuned using the same bilingual datasets but with task-specific configurations for each translation direction.

4.4 Post Processing

To ensure the translated text remains concise and relevant, we first determined the length of the original sentence and compared it to the length of the translated output. If the translated text was more than twice the length of the original, we retained only the first 1.25 times the original length. Since we used a causal learning model, it sometimes generated extra information. This method helped control excessive output while maintaining translation quality.

5 Results and Analysis

The evaluation of our system in the AmericasNLP 2025 Shared Task on MT revealed mixed results across languages for both Track 1 (Spanish to Indigenous languages) and Track 2 (Indigenous languages to Spanish) will be discussed in this section. Our experiments utilized fine-tuned versions of NLLB-200 (Distilled-600M) (Costa-Jussà et al., 2022), XGLM 1.7B (Lin et al., 2021), and Llama 3.1(8B-Instruct) (Touvron et al., 2023), focusing on multilingual setups to optimize performance across diverse linguistic structures. The test results of the submitted system using NLLB-200 (Distilled-600M) are presented in Table 6.

5.1 Hyper Parameter Setting

Table 5 shows parameter settings for different models.

In Table 5, *lr*, *optim,la* and *l4* represents *learning_rate,optimizer*, *lora_alpha* and *load_in_4bit* and respectively.

5.2 Evaluation Metrics

The performance of various models has been evaluated using the Bilingual Evaluation Understudy (BLEU) score, the Character-level F-score (ChrF), and the Character-level F-score++ (ChrF++) metrics on the development and test dataset.

5.3 Comparative Analysis

In this subsection, we provide a detailed analysis of the performance of different models across both development and test datasets for the submitted languages. Using Table 3 and Table 4, which present development results, and Table 6, summarizing test results, we analyze the performance of submitted models across languages. This comparison helps identify trends and determine which models perform better for specific languages in both tracks.

5.3.1 Track 1 (Es→Xx)

NLLB-200 (Distilled-600M) consistently outperformed LLaMA 3.1 and XGLM across all languages on both development and test datasets. While all models performed below baseline, notable trends were observed in Awajun (agr) and Quechua (quy), where results approached the baseline. For the test data, NLLB-200 achieved the highest ChrF++ scores, with 35.16 for agr and 31.01 for quy, demonstrating its ability to handle low-resource Indigenous languages. On the development data, agr and quy also performed well, with ChrF++ scores of 31.55 and 40.01, respectively, showing consistency across datasets.
LLaMA 3.1 exhibited moderate performance for agr on development data (25.17 ChrF++) but struggled with other languages, including quy (13.74 ChrF++). XGLM performed the weakest overall, with ChrF++ scores of 20.44 for agr and only 9.45 for quy on development data, indicating significant challenges in adapting to low-resource settings. However, even in NLLB-200 (Distilled-600M), the best-performed model also showed poor performance relative to the baseline, particularly for morphologically complex languages like Nahuatl (ChrF++: 13.88 vs. baseline 26.36) and Wayuunaiki (ChrF++: 14.40 vs. baseline 24.74) on test results. These results highlight challenges in handling linguistic diversity despite leveraging advanced models.

5.3.2 Track 2 (Xx→Es)

The performance of NLLB-200, LLaMA 3.1, and XGLM in Track 2 was evaluated using ChrF++

Language	NLLB-600M		Llama 3.1 (8B-Instruct)		XGLM 1.7B	
	BLEU	**ChrF++**	**BLEU**	**ChrF++**	**BLEU**	**ChrF++**
	BLEU	ChrF++	BLEU	ChrF++	BLEU	ChrF++
agr	5.97	31.55	5.11	25.17	3.25	20.44
aym	4.03	30.11	4.09	28.13	2.51	22.45
bzd	3.63	16.25	2.72	15.19	1.85	12.37
cni	2.35	24.24	2.02	22.46	1.45	18.92
grn	3.44	19.53	2.57	20.13	1.83	16.24
guc	1.11	17.56	0.56	11.44	0.32	8.76
hch	8.66	28.17	6.79	24.21	4.32	19.87
nah	1.13	14.64	0.93	10.29	0.61	7.85
oto	0.62	15.12	0.23	6.43	0.15	4.21
quy	2.43	40.01	1.16	13.74	0.78	9.45
shp	1.30	18.12	1.01	9.76	0.67	6.32

Table 3: Comparison of BLEU and ChrF++ scores of development data across different models and languages of Es to Xx(Track 1).

Language	NLLB-600M		Llama 3.1 (8B-Instruct)		XGLM 1.7B	
	BLEU	**ChrF++**	**BLEU**	**ChrF++**	**BLEU**	**ChrF++**
agr	11.12	32.80	9.45	28.17	6.73	23.54
aym	8.82	31.72	7.21	26.85	5.34	22.16
bzd	4.31	26.74	3.52	22.18	2.65	18.72
cni	2.85	21.20	2.31	17.65	1.74	14.84
grn	8.62	32.07	7.15	27.26	5.17	22.45
guc	2.22	12.58	1.78	10.46	1.33	8.81
hch	3.69	23.36	3.05	19.48	2.21	16.35
nah	7.22	26.89	5.86	22.41	4.33	18.82
oto	1.50	19.01	1.23	15.84	0.90	13.31
quy	8.76	33.83	7.18	28.76	5.26	23.68
shp	7.22	27.33	5.87	23.23	4.33	19.13

Table 4: Comparison of BLEU and ChrF++ scores of development data across different models and languages of Xx to Es(Track 2).

Model	lr	optim	la	l4
NLLB-200 (Distilled-600M)	$2e^{-4}$	Ada Factor	-	-
Llama 3.1 (8B-Instruct)	$3e^{-3}$	Paged Adamw	4	8
XGLM 1.7B	$3e^{-3}$	Adam	4	8

Table 5: Parameter settings for different models

scores on both development and test datasets. Similarly, as track 1 Awajun (agr) and Quechua (quy) showed results approaching the baseline, demonstrating better adaptability compared to other languages.

On the development data, NLLB-200 outperformed the other models across all languages. It achieved ChrF++ scores of 32.80 for agr and 33.83 for quy, showcasing its strong multilingual capabilities. LLaMA 3.1 followed with moderate performance, scoring 28.17 ChrF++ for agr and 22.86 ChrF++ for quy, indicating some adaptability to low-resource languages in this track. XGLM exhibited weaker performance overall, with ChrF++ scores of 23.54 for agr and 20.36 for quy, reflecting its challenges in handling complex linguistic diversity.

On the test data, NLLB-200 maintained its dominance, achieving ChrF++ scores of 33.70 for

Language	Es to Xx (Track 1)			Xx to Es (Track 2)		
	BLEU	ChrF	ChrF++	BLEU	ChrF	ChrF++
agr	7.82	40.10	35.16[1]	13.21	36.11	33.70[2]
aym	1.96	31.61	27.72[1]	5.89	27.53	25.78[1]
bzd	4.55	21.68	22.77[1]	5.87	27.53	26.22[2]
cni	2.43	26.96	23.17[1]	3.06	21.34	20.13[2]
grn	3.46	17.84	16.21[2]	15.14	26.15	24.70[2]
guc	0.11	15.86	12.83[2]	3.14	16.19	14.40[2]
hch	11.07	30.47	26.77[1]	3.98	23.69	22.02[2]
nah	0.65	15.73	12.64[2]	4.00	15.40	13.88[2]
oto	0.76	14.16	12.02[1]	1.50	19.91	17.80[1]
quy	3.07	36.14	31.01[2]	10.60	33.26	31.71[2]
shp	0.37	14.94	12.76[2]	8.94	32.58	30.83[2]

Table 6: Translation Evaluation Metrics for submitted test languages using NLLB-200 (distilled-600M)

agr and 31.71 for quy, coming close to the baseline scores of 38.39 (agr) and 37.18 (quy). These results highlight NLLB-200's ability to generalize well across datasets. However, even NLLB-200 struggled with morphologically complex languages like Nahuatl (nah), scoring only 13.88 ChrF++, which is below its baseline of 26.36 ChrF++.

Overall, NLLB-200 delivered solid results in both tracks for Awajun (agr), indicating that the token adjustments effectively compensated for the model's lack of direct understanding of the language. This demonstrates the adaptability of NLLB-200 in handling low-resource languages through fine-tuning. LLaMA 3.1 exhibited moderate potential, particularly for Awajun (agr) and Quechua (quy), suggesting that further fine-tuning could enhance its performance in these languages. However, all models, including NLLB-200, showed relatively poor performance compared to the baseline for morphologically complex languages like Nahuatl (nah) and Otomí (oto), highlighting the challenges posed by such linguistic diversity.

6 Conclusion

This research work on MT provided valuable insights into the challenges and potential of translating between Spanish and Indigenous languages. Our approach incorporated techniques like token adjustments and dynamic batching to address linguistic diversity and complex grammatical structures. The results highlighted both the strengths and limitations of our models. While Awajun and Quechua showed decent performance, most other languages underperformed against the baseline, revealing gaps in handling morphosyntactic complexities. This study shows the importance of developing tailored strategies for Indigenous languages, which often feature unique linguistic phenomena such as polysynthesis and agglutination.

7 Limitations

Our models struggled to consistently outperform the baseline in most languages, likely due to difficulties in handling complex grammar and sentence structures. Training large models like NLLB-200 (Distilled-600M) and Llama required powerful GPUs, which were not fully available. This constraint impacted critical processes such as hyperparameter tuning and token adjustments, which are essential for optimizing performance. Additionally, the reduced training duration (limited to 5 epochs) further hindered the models' ability to fully adapt to the linguistic intricacies of the target languages.

8 Future Work

Future efforts will focus on addressing the challenges identified in this study to improve translation quality for Indigenous languages. First, increasing training epochs and leveraging more powerful computational resources will allow for better fine-tuning of large models. Exploring transfer learning from linguistically similar languages may also enhance performance for underperforming cases like Guarani and Nahuatl. Another key area for improvement is the development of specialized architectures or fine-tuning strategies tailored to polysynthetic and agglutinative languages. Finally, expanding the dataset with diverse linguistic phenomena and experimenting with ensemble methods could further enhance translation accuracy and robustness across all languages.

References

Joseph Attieh, Zachary Hopton, Yves Scherrer, and Tanja Samardzic. 2024. System description of the nordicsalps submission to the americasnlp 2024 machine translation shared task. In *Proceedings of the 4th Workshop on Natural Language Processing for Indigenous Languages of the Americas (AmericasNLP 2024)*, pages 150–158.

Zaheenah Beebee Jameela Boodeea, Sameerchand Pudaruth, Nitish Chooramun, and Aneerav Sukhoo. 2025. Automatic translation between kreol morisien and english using the marian machine translation framework. In *Informatics*, volume 12, page 16. MDPI.

Gina Bustamante, Arturo Oncevay, and Roberto Zariquiey. 2020. No data to crawl? monolingual corpus creation from pdf files of truly low-resource languages in peru. In *Proceedings of the Twelfth Language Resources and Evaluation Conference*, pages 2914–2923.

Nathan A Chi, Teodor Malchev, Riley Kong, Ryan A Chi, Lucas Huang, Ethan A Chi, R Thomas McCoy, and Dragomir Radev. 2024. Modeling: A novel dataset for testing linguistic reasoning in language models. *arXiv preprint arXiv:2406.17038*.

Eldan Cohen and Christopher Beck. 2019. Empirical analysis of beam search performance degradation in neural sequence models. In *International Conference on Machine Learning*, pages 1290–1299. PMLR.

Marta R Costa-Jussà, James Cross, Onur Çelebi, Maha Elbayad, Kenneth Heafield, Kevin Heffernan, Elahe Kalbassi, Janice Lam, Daniel Licht, Jean Maillard, et al. 2022. No language left behind: Scaling human-centered machine translation. *arXiv preprint arXiv:2207.04672*.

Ona de Gibert, Raul Vazquez, Robert Pugh, Abteen Ebrahimi, Pavel Denisov, Ali Marashian, Enora Rice, Edward Gow-Smith, Juan C. Prieto, Melissa Robles, Rubén Manrique, Oscar Moreno Veliz, Ángel Lino Campos, Rolando Coto-Solano, Aldo Alvarez, Marvin Agüero-Torales, John E. Ortega, Luis Chiruzzo, Arturo Oncevay, Shruti Rijhwani, Katharina von der Wense, and Manuel Mager. 2025. Findings of the AmericasNLP shared tasks on machine translation, creation of educational material, and translation metrics for indigenous languages. In *Proceedings of the 5th Workshop on Natural Language Processing for Indigenous Languages of the Americas (AmericasNLP 2025)*, Albuquerque, New Mexico. Association for Computational Linguistics.

Chris C Emezue and Bonaventure FP Dossou. 2022. Mmtafrica: Multilingual machine translation for african languages. *arXiv preprint arXiv:2204.04306*.

Hugging Face. 2018. Sacremoses: A python port of moses tokenizer.

Javier García Gilabert, Aleix Sant, Carlos Escolano, Francesca De Luca Fornaciari, Audrey Mash, and Maite Melero. 2024. Bsc submission to the americasnlp 2024 shared task. In *Proceedings of the 4th Workshop on Natural Language Processing for Indigenous Languages of the Americas (AmericasNLP 2024)*, pages 143–149.

Paul Goulder. 2005. The languages of peru: Their past, present, and future survival. *EnterText*, 2(2).

Matthew Honnibal, Ines Montani, Sofie Van Landeghem, and Adriane Boyd. 2020. spacy: Industrial-strength natural language processing in python. Version 3.0.

Edward J Hu, Yelong Shen, Phillip Wallis, Zeyuan Allen-Zhu, Yuanzhi Li, Shean Wang, Lu Wang, Weizhu Chen, et al. 2022. Lora: Low-rank adaptation of large language models. *ICLR*, 1(2):3.

Katharina Kann, Abteen Ebrahimi, Manuel Mager, Arturo Oncevay, John E Ortega, Annette Rios, Angela Fan, Ximena Gutierrez-Vasques, Luis Chiruzzo, Gustavo A Giménez-Lugo, et al. 2022. Americasnli: Machine translation and natural language inference systems for indigenous languages of the americas. *Frontiers in Artificial Intelligence*, 5:995667.

Philipp Koehn, Hieu Hoang, Alexandra Birch, Chris Callison-Burch, Marcello Federico, Nicola Bertoldi, Brooke Cowan, Wade Shen, Christine Moran, Richard Zens, Chris Dyer, Ondřej Bojar, Alexandra Constantin, and Evan Herbst. 2007. Moses: Open source toolkit for statistical machine translation. In *Proceedings of the 45th Annual Meeting of the Association for Computational Linguistics Companion Volume Proceedings of the Demo and Poster Sessions*, pages 177–180.

Xi Victoria Lin, Todor Mihaylov, Mikel Artetxe, Tianlu Wang, Shuohui Chen, Daniel Simig, Myle Ott, Naman Goyal, Shruti Bhosale, Jingfei Du, et al. 2021. Few-shot learning with multilingual language models. *arXiv preprint arXiv:2112.10668*.

Sara Papi, Marco Gaido, Matteo Negri, and Marco Turchi. 2022. Over-generation cannot be rewarded: Length-adaptive average lagging for simultaneous speech translation. *arXiv preprint arXiv:2206.05807*.

Hugo Touvron, Thibaut Lavril, Gautier Izacard, Xavier Martinet, Marie-Anne Lachaux, Timothée Lacroix, Baptiste Rozière, Naman Goyal, Eric Hambro, Faisal Azhar, et al. 2023. Llama: Open and efficient foundation language models. *arXiv preprint arXiv:2302.13971*.

Findings of the AmericasNLP 2025 Shared Tasks on Machine Translation, Creation of Educational Material, and Translation Metrics for Indigenous Languages of the Americas

Ona de Gibert[~*] **Robert Pugh**[♣*] **Ali Marashian**[♯*] **Raúl Vázquez**[~] **Abteen Ebrahimi**[♯]
Pavel Denisov[♠] **Enora Rice**[♯] **Edward Gow-Smith**[γ] **Juan C. Prieto**[β] **Melissa Robles**[β]
Rubén Manrique[β] **Oscar Moreno Veliz**[⋈] **Ángel Lino Campos**[⋈] **Rolando Coto-Solano**[♡]
Aldo Alvarez[Ω] **Marvin Agüero-Torales**[△▽] **John E. Ortega**[α] **Luis Chiruzzo**[◇]
Arturo Oncevay[⋈] **Shruti Rijhwani**[℧] **Katharina von der Wense**[♯†] **Manuel Mager**[‡†]

[~]University of Helsinki [♣]Indiana University, Bloomington [♯]University of Colorado Boulder
[♠]Fraunhofer IAIS [γ]University of Sheffield [β]Universidad de Los Andes
[⋈]Pontificia Universidad Católica del Perú [♡]Dartmouth College [△]Universidad de Granada, Spain
[Ω]Universidad Nacional de Itapua, Paraguay [▽]Global CoE of Data Intelligence, Fujitsu
[◇]Universidad de la República, Uruguay [α]Northeastern University [℧]Google DeepMind
[†]Johannes Gutenberg University Mainz [‡]Amazon

Abstract

This paper presents the findings of the AmericasNLP 2025 Shared Tasks: (1) machine translation for truly low-resource languages, (2) morphological adaptation for generating educational examples, and (3) developing metrics for machine translation in Indigenous languages. The shared tasks cover 14 diverse Indigenous languages of the Americas. A total of 12 teams participated, submitting 27 systems across all tasks, languages, and models. We describe the shared tasks, introduce the datasets and evaluation metrics used, summarize the baselines and submitted systems, and report our findings.

1 Introduction

The recent rapid progress in Natural Language Processing (NLP), significantly accelerated by the improved architectures, training methods, and the rise of Large Language Models (LLMs), has primarily benefited *high-resource languages*, languages that have large amounts of digital text available such as English or French. In contrast, languages with low amounts of data, known as *low-resource languages*, still face considerable challenges in terms of both data availability and the development of appropriate models (e.g., Ignat et al., 2024). Low-resource languages that are native to a specific region, or *Indigenous languages*, remain challenging for even the most novel NLP techniques (Mager et al., 2024; Weerasinghe et al., 2025; Hettiarachchi et al., 2025).

Figure 1: Map of Central and South America presenting an approximate distribution of where each Indigenous language covered by the three Shared Tasks is spoken.

To address these disparities, the Workshop on NLP for Indigenous Languages of the Americas (AmericasNLP) was established with the goal of advancing NLP research for Indigenous languages from the American continent.

Building on the success of last year's Shared Tasks (ST) (Ebrahimi et al., 2024; Chiruzzo et al., 2024), the 2025 edition expands its scope with three STs designed to address critical challenges in working with Indigenous languages. Many of the languages included in the STs are polysynthetic, agglutinative or tonal languages, features which are not mutually exclusive. In addition, they often lack a standardized orthography, exhibit dialectal vari-

*In order, the main organizers for shared tasks 1, 2, and 3.

† Irrespective of Manuel Mager's listed affiliation, this work is independent of his employment at Amazon.

Proceedings of the Fifth Workshop on NLP for Indigenous Languages of the Americas (AmericasNLP), pages 134–152
May 4, 2025

ation and frequent code-switching with dominant regional languages (Mager et al., 2019).

The goal of this effort is not only to advance methodologies for low-resource settings but also to support the development of tools for language learning, preservation, and revitalization. Moreover, we expect to develop technologies that can include the native speakers of these languages in the recent developments in our field. This year's STs include:

- **ST1: Machine Translation (MT) for low-resource languages**, translating between Spanish and 13 Indigenous languages with limited parallel data. This year, it features two new languages (Awajun and Wayuunaiki), and a new translation direction (into Spanish).
- **ST2: Morphological adaptation to generate educational examples** transforming sentences to create grammar exercises for language learners. This year, we include Nahuatl as an additional language.
- **ST3: Developing metrics for MT in Indigenous languages** designing evaluation metrics suited to the linguistic properties of low-resource languages. The first edition of its kind.

Across all tasks, languages, and models, a total of 12 teams participated, submitting 27 systems. The consistent interest from the community highlights the continued interest in developing NLP tools for Indigenous languages.

We publicly release the training and development data through our GitHub repository.[1]

2 Languages

The STs feature 14 Indigenous languages spoken across North, Central, and South America, listed in Table 1. These languages differ in language family, number of speakers, geographical distribution, and resource availability; reflecting their diversity. They vary in their levels of official recognition, and in many cases, speaker population data is based on outdated census information. Figure 1 shows the approximate geographical distribution of the languages included in the tasks. Below, we briefly introduce each of the languages.

[1] https://github.com/AmericasNLP/americasnlp2025/

Language	Family	ISO 639-3	Glottolog	ST
Asháninka	Arawak	cni	asha1243	1
Awajun	Chicham	agr	agua1253	1
Aymara	Aymaran	aym	nucl1667	1
Bribri	Chibchan	bzd	brib1243	1,2,3
Chatino	Oto-Manguean	ctp	chat1268	1
Guarani	Tupi-Guarani	grn	para1311	1,2,3
Maya	Mayan	yua	yuca1254	2
Nahuatl	Uto-Aztecan	nah	azte1234	1,2,3
Otomí	Oto-Manguean	oto	otom1300	1
Quechua	Quechuan	quy	ayac1238	1
Rarámuri	Uto-Aztecan	tar	tara1321	1
Shipibo-Konibo	Panoan	shp	ship1253	1
Wayuunaiki	Arawak	guc	wayuu1243	1
Wixarika	Uto-Aztecan	hch	huic1243	1

Table 1: Languages of the Shared Tasks, their language families, ISO 639-3 and Glottolog codes, and Shared Tasks were they are included.

Asháninka (aka *Campa*) is an Arawakan language spoken primarily in Peru and Brazil by approximately 74,500 speakers. It is agglutinative and polysynthetic and has a Verb-Subject-Object (VSO) word order.

Awajun (aka *Aguaruna*) is a Chicham language spoken in northern Peru, by around 53,400 speakers. It follows a Subject-Object-Verb (SOV) and has rich morphology that consists of agglutinative suffixes. We use the Marañón variant.

Aymara is an Aymaran language spoken in the Andean regions of Bolivia and Peru, with approximately 1.7 million speakers. It is recognized for its agglutinative morphology and polysynthetic nature, typically following a SOV word order. We use Central Aymara variant, spoken in Aymara La Paz.

Bribri is a Chibchan language spoken in southern Costa Rica, by an estimated 7,000 people. The language exhibits morphological ergativity and is tonal, with SOV word order. We use the Amburi variant.

Chatino refers to a group of indigenous Mesoamerican languages within the Zapotecan branch of the Oto-Manguean family, spoken in Oaxaca, Mexico. These languages are tonal and have complex systems of verbal inflection. We use the San Juan Quiahije variant, spoken by about 5,000 people.

Guarani is a Tupi–Guarani language spoken mainly in Paraguay, where it is one of the official languages, as well as in parts of Bolivia, Argentina, and Brazil. It has approximately 6.5 million speakers. It is an agglutinative language. We use the Paraguayan variant, except the training data for ST1, which consists of a mix of dialects.

Maya is a Mayan language spoken on the Yucatán Peninsula of Mexico, northern Belize, and parts of Guatemala, with approximately 800,000 speakers. It is characterized by its use of glottalized consonants and a Verb-Subject-Object (VSO) word order. We use the Yucatec Maya variant.

Nahuatl Nahuatl is a group of related Uto-Aztecan languages spoken throughout Mexico and in parts of Central America, with approximately 1.6 million speakers in total. There are over 30 variants of the language. It is polysynthetic and agglutinative.

For ST1, we use a diverse set of variants, including colonial-era written Nahuatl, for training (from the Axolotl corpus (Gutierrez-Vasques et al., 2016)) and Huasteca Nahuatl for ST1 evaluation as well as for ST3. ST2 focuses on Western Sierra Puebla Nahuatl, a relatively understudied Nahuatl variety.

Otomí (aka *Hñähñu*[2]) is an Oto-Manguean language spoken in central Mexico by about 300,000 people. It has nine variants. Otomí languages are tonal and exhibit a complex system of verb inflection, typically following SVO word order. We focus on the Ixtenco Otomí (OTX), a variant with less than 460 speakers, in the Mexican state of Tlaxcala.

Quechua is a family of languages spoken across the Andean regions of Argentina, Bolivia, Chile, Colombia, Ecuador, and Peru, with approximately 7.2 million speakers. It is recognized as an official language in Peru and Bolivia and is known for its agglutinative structure and SOV word order. We use the Quechua Ayacucho variant, although the training data also includes text in Quechua Cuzco.

Rarámuri (aka *Tarahumara*) is a Uto-Aztecan language spoken in northern Mexico, by around 70,000 speakers. It is polysynthetic and agglutinative. We use the highlands variant.

Shipibo-Konibo is a Panoan language spoken in Peru by approximately 26,000 people. It is characterized by its agglutinative morphology and predominantly SOV word order and uses postpositions.

[2]Other names for the language are used, depending on the language variant.

Wayuunaiki is an Arawakan language spoken in northern Colombia and Venezuela, primarily by the Wayuu community, with about 420,000 speakers. It is an agglutinative language with a predominant SOV word order.

Wixarika (aka *Huichol*) is a Uto-Aztecan language spoken in Mexico, by approximately 35,000 speakers. It is official in Mexico with four variants. It is an agglutinative morphology with strong polysynthetic characteristics and follows the SOV word order. We use the Nayarit version, spoken in Zoquipan.

3 ST1: A ST on Machine Translation on Truly Low-resource Languages

Description Low-resource MT (Haddow et al., 2022) is mainly characterized by the limited availability of parallel corpora, but it also faces additional challenges, such as the scarcity of monolingual data and issues related to data quality.

This task focuses on translation between Spanish and 13 indigenous languages. Now in its fourth iteration (Mager et al., 2021; Ebrahimi et al., 2023, 2024), it continues to push the boundaries of MT for these languages, emphasizing generalization strategies for low-resource MT and the creation of new linguistic resources to support these efforts.

For this year's edition, we introduce two new languages (Awajun, Wayuunaiki) for the ST1 task and expand the ST to cover both translation into an Indigenous language from Spanish (Track 1), as well as translation from an Indigenous language into Spanish (Track 2). These two translation directions are organized as separate tracks within the ST. Furthermore, following the spirit of open science, this year we only take into account submissions which rely solely on open-source weights for the final ranking.

Data Table 7 in the Appendix shows our data statistics. We use the same training data as in previous editions for the repeating languages. This consists of the organizers' collection of parallel sentences, and the data collected by Vázquez et al. (2021) and De Gibert et al. (2023), a combination of scraped sources, and synthetically generated data, obtained through back-translation.

For Wayuunaiki, the train dataset was derived from the work of Prieto et al. (2024), with a thorough curation and selection of the data. It was compiled from grammar books, the Bible, short stories, a dictionary and the Colombian constitution, with a total of 59,715 sentences. To process this data, different extraction techniques were applied based on the structure of each source. Web scraping was used for highly structured texts like the Bible, ensuring precise verse alignment. For more complex sources, such as grammar books and linguistic studies, GPT-4 was used to identify sections of the text containing translated sentences, extracting and tabulating them into a standardized format. In cases were texts were available only as scanned documents or unstructured PDFs, OCR combined with GPT-4 processing enabled the retrieval of bilingual content. Finally, a manual review process was conducted across all sources to filter incomplete translations and correct formatting inconsistencies.

For Awajun, the main part of the training data was extracted from various web sources such as poems, stories, laws, protocols, guidelines, handbooks, the Bible, and news published by Ojo Público,[3] a news media organization that supported the first iteration of the dataset (Moreno et al., 2024). An official translator validated all sources for the corpora to ensure the same dialect is used. Only a few of the sources were aligned automatically, using line breaks and sentence length heuristics as reference, while most of the sources were aligned manually to retain the quality of the translations.

For development and evaluation, we use the AmericasNLP 2021 data (Mager et al., 2021), a multi-way parallel dataset of the XNLI (Conneau et al., 2018) test set into 10 languages of the Americas (Asháninka, Aymara, Bribri, Guarani, Nahuatl, Otomí, Quechua, Rarámuri, Shipibo-Konibo, and Wixarika). The Chatino data comes from Mexican court proceedings. For an in-depth review of the development and evaluation data, please refer to Ebrahimi et al. (2022, 2024) and Mager et al. (2021).

For the new languages, the Wayuunaiki development set is sourced from the work of Prieto et al. (2024), while the test set is created by translating the first 95 pages of the book *Journey to the Center of the Earth* by Verne (1874), with an average of 150 words per page. To uphold high ethical standards, we ensured that translators received fair compensation. The test set also includes the translation of the short story *Benjamin Bunny* by Potter (1904). In the case of Awajun, the development set was split from the available training data. We compile a small test set that contains translations provided by a professional translator in texts extracted from news within the Territorio Amazonas domain, and another portion of the test set are examples extracted from a dictionary by Espejo Apikai et al. (2021) not processed for the train or development set.

Metrics We use ChrF++ (Popović, 2017) as the main metric of the task, although we also report BLEU (Papineni et al., 2002).

ChrF++ is an overlap-based metric at the character-level, which is more suitable than BLEU for our task since most languages are morphologically rich, and BLEU often penalizes morphological variants (Chauhan et al., 2023). The final score for each submission (ChrF++ column in Table 8) is calculated by taking an average over all thirteen languages; if there is no model output for a given language, the score is taken as 0.

Baselines For our baseline, we follow the training set-up of "Submission 3" to the 2023 edition of the ST by Gow-Smith and Sánchez Villegas (2023). We extend the embedding matrix of NLLB-200-distilled-1.3B[4] with language tags for the languages not already covered, and finetune on the task data as well as additional training sources. We finetune two separate models for Track 1 and 2. See the original paper for further training details, our only modification for this year is the addition of the two new languages. We choose the best checkpoint based on the highest average ChrF++ across all languages.

Aiming to assess the current performance of LLMs on the task languages, we also implemented a fine-tuned a LLaMA3.2 model (Dubey et al., 2024) [5] using Low-Rank Adaptation (LoRA) adapters (Hu et al., 2022). This baseline performed poorly, only managing to copy the source sentence; however, we do not rule out the possibility of bugs in our implementation.

Submitted Systems For this year's ST1 we recieved a total of 5 submissions by 3 different teams. Below, we briefly describe each team's participation:

- **George Mason University (GMU)** (Hus et al., 2025): this team submits two systems

[3]https://ojo-publico.com/

[4]facebook/nllb-200-distilled-1.3B

[5]meta-llama/Llama-3.2-3B-Instruct

TEAM	AGR	AYM	BZD	CNI	CTP	GRN	GUC	HCH	NAH	OTO	QUY	SHP	TAR
						TRACK 1: SPA-XXX							
Baseline	**36.76**	**31.21**	**25.52**	**24.39**	**36.53**	**35.68**	**24.18**	**28.26**	**22.42**	**12.78**	31.88	**25.76**	**15.96**
GMU	35.09	22.91	22.51	22.22	13.33	29.95	22.93	26.14	20.33	11.31	**32.70**	19.46	13.89
Syntax Squad	35.16	27.72	22.77	23.17	-	16.21	12.83	26.77	12.64	12.02	31.01	12.76	-
UCSP	-	-	-	-	-	-	-	-	-	-	16.75	-	-
						TRACK 2: XXX-SPA							
Baseline	**38.39**	**35.60**	**30.14**	**24.86**	**35.84**	**35.91**	**24.74**	**26.33**	**26.36**	**20.81**	**37.18**	**47.81**	18.75
GMU	36.59	26.09	27.86	22.44	26.16	33.84	23.93	24.37	25.58	18.24	33.02	38.01	**19.72**
Syntax Squad	33.70	25.78	26.22	20.13	-	24.70	14.40	22.02	13.88	17.80	31.71	30.83	-
UCSP	-	-	-	-	-	-	-	-	-	-	17.87	-	-

Table 2: The best CHRF++ scores for ST1 for each team (across all submitted systems) across all languages. Bold values represent the best performing system overall, while underlined values are the best performing submission to this year's shared task.

for all language pairs in both tracks. First, they finetune NLLB-200-3.3B with the provided data for each language pair separately. Then, they prompt GPT-4o-mini model with external knowledge coming from bilingual dictionaries (a translation word is provided for each word of the sentence), two sample parallel sentences (few-shot approach), a full grammar book on the Indigenous language and a suggested translation, which is the generated hypothesis of the first NLLB-based system. Since GPT4-0-mini is a closed-source model, we only use their NLLB-based approach for the ranking. GMU is the only team to submit entries for all language pairs.

- **Syntax Squad** (Yahan and Amanul Islam, 2025): this team submits one system for 11 language pairs in both tracks and one extra system for translation from Spanish into Aymara. They perform data normalization and then finetune NLLB-200-600M, LLaMA 3.1 8B Instruct, XGLM 1.7B (Lin et al., 2021). They submitt their NLLB-based model, which outperforms the other two in the develoment set.

- **Universidad Católica San Pablo (UCSP)** (Congora et al., 2025): this team participates in the task for Quecha translation from/into Spanish. They dedicate efforts to data collection and data cleaning. Furthermore, they expand their datasets by generating synthetic sentences via the replacement of subjects and verbs in the sentences. They use two methods: Wordnet, which is deemed unsatisfactory, and an LLM (Phi3-mini for English and Phi3.5 for Spanish). Then, they train two different architectures on the augmented dataset: transformer-base (Vaswani et al., 2017) and mT5-small (Xue et al., 2021).

Results The best performance per language for each team is shown in Table 2. In the Appendix, Table 8 provides the official ranking of the ST, which excludes closed-source models, and Table 9 reports the complete results for all submissions and teams. The baseline is hard to beat in both tracks. In both tracks, GMU is the only team to beat it for any language. The strong performance of the baseline indicates the importance of multilingual training, as NLLB is finetuned across all language pairs simultaneously, unlike GMU's NLLB-based submission, which is finetuned on each language individually.

In Track 1 (SPA→XXX), GMU's NLLB-based submission achieves the highest average performance, with a ChrF++ score of 21.95, closely followed by Syntax Squad (17.93) and GMU's GPT-based system (18.81). GMU surpasses the baseline only for Quechua, achieving a +0.82 gain in ChrF++. While Syntax Squad performs well overall, its results are notably weaker for Guarani, Wayuunaiki, Nahuatl, and Shipibo-Konibo.

In Track 2, the best-performing model is also GMU's NLLB-based submission, with an average ChrF++ score of 26.62, slightly ahead of their own GPT-based system (26.41), which performs significantly worse for Chatino. They surpass the baseline for Rarámuri, achieving a +0.97 gain in ChrF++. Overall, GPT-based models appear effective at post-grammar correction for Spanish, but show weaker performance for the Indigenous language targets.

Submissions for Quechua from UCSP underper-

Language	Num. Sentences	Textual features			Grammatical changes	
	(train-dev-test)	Words/Sent	Chars/Word	TTR	Changes/Sent	Num Changes
Nahuatl	391-176-120	3.05	7.69 (20)	0.06	3.5	47
Maya	584-149-310	5.48	4.66 (14)	0.03	1.1	34
Bribri	309-212-480	3.75	3.39 (8)	0.02	2.8	28
Guarani	178-79-364	3.92	6.17 (14)	0.07	1.0	19

Table 3: A comparison of descriptive statistics of the corpora for ST2, calculated on the combination of the train and dev sets. Included features about the text are the average sentence length, average word length, the length of the longest word (in parentheses after the average word length), and the type-token ration for the corpus. With respect to the "Grammatical features", we report the average number of requested grammatical changes per sentence, as well as the total number of unique grammatical changes (i.e. feature-value pairs) in the entire corpus.

form when compared to other submissions, suggesting that training models from scratch has stopped being the most effective approach in low-resource settings.

Findings MT where the target is an Indigenous language appears to have reached a performance plateau. Improvements in the AmericasNLP workshop seem to be difficult given current data limitations. While this may not be the case in general, the most effective strategy in the AmericasNLP workshop remains to be the finetuning of a highly multilingual pretrained model (such as NLLB). In contrast, for translations where the target langauge is a high-resource language like Spanish, LLMs can provide a boost in performance. This is likely due to their extensive pretraining and a stronger representation of the higher-resource target language. However, whether the performance gains justify the practical costs of running these models remains an open question.

4 ST2: A ST on Morphological Adaptation to Generate Educational Examples

Description Language education initiatives, which are critical to many language revitalization efforts, require educational materials that are costly and time-consuming to create.

This task focuses on generating grammar exercises for learners of four Indigenous languages. In its first edition (Chiruzzo et al., 2024), the task involved automatically transforming a given base sentence by modifying its tense, aspect, or other morphosyntactic features into a target sentence. These sentences can later be used to create educational materials for language learners. This year's edition features the addition of an endangered variety of Nahuatl.

Data Four languages are included in this year's task: Bribri, Guarani, and Maya, which were all included in last year's task, and a new addition, Nahuatl. Since the data for the first three languages is the same as in last year's task, we refer the reader to Chiruzzo et al. (2024) for details.

Mexico's *Instituto Nacional de Lenguas Indígenas* (INALI) recognizes 30 Nahuatl varieties (INALI, 2012). The variant included in ST2 is commonly referred to as Western Sierra Puebla Nahuatl or Zacatlán-Ahuacatlán-Tepetzintla Nahuatl (*Náhuatl de la Sierra Oeste de Puebla*, ISO-639-3: `nhi`), spoken in the northwestern sierra region of the state of Puebla, Mexico by less than 20,000 people. This Nahuatl variety is relatively understudied, with most linguistic work, such as a short unpublished grammar and some examination of morphological and phonological phenomena, focusing on the subvariety spoken in the community of San Miguel Tenango, Zacatlán (Schroeder and Tuggy, 2010; Schroeder, 2014, 2015) or the municipality of Ahuacatlán (Sasaki, 2014).

The sentences used (see. Table 3) for the ST come from the community of Omitlán, Tepetzintla, where the specific Nahuatl communalect has been less studied, though it has been included in some recent computational work for the variety, such as a morphological analyzer (Pugh and Tyers, 2021b) and a Universal Dependencies treebank (Pugh et al., 2022). The base sentences are a part of a currently-unreleased corpus of grammatical example sentences, and the transformed sentences were verified by a native-speaking expert from the community.

The set of features used to annotate the Nahuatl data were:

- **Person and number**: Person/number of the subject, object, and indirect object of the Verb, and the possessor of the Noun in the sentence.

System Name	Bribri	Maya	Guarani	Nahuatl	Avg	Rank
NAIST	**41.25**	42.90	32.69	**17.50**	33.59	1◊
JHU_1	22.71	**63.87**	**43.68**	3.33	33.40	2◊
JHU_4	18.75	60.00	40.93	1.67	30.34	3
JHU_2	20.21	59.35	38.19	3.33	30.27	4
JHU_5	15.83	59.03	41.21	2.50	29.64	5
JHU_3	20.21	56.77	38.74	1.67	29.35	6
Syntax Squad	0.42	13.55	1.92	0.00	3.97	8
JHU_6	5.42	9.68	6.32	0.00	5.35	7
FPUNApy	0.00	0.00	8.52	0.00	2.13	9
IUNLP	0.00	2.26	3.85	0.00	1.53	10
RaaVa	1.25	0.00	2.20	0.00	0.86	11
Vasselli et al. (2024)	54.17	53.55	36.81	-	-	-
Baseline	5.66	26.17	22.78	0.00	13.65	-

Table 4: Final Accuracy results table for ST2. Note that while 6 teams submitted results on the test set, only 2 teams submitted system description papers, therefore we only describe the systems for two of the teams (NAIST and JHU). We also report the results from the previous year's winning system and the edit-tree baseline. The overall accuracy difference between ranks 1 and 2 is not significant (see ◊).

Person and number are represented together: 1_SG, 1_PL, 2_SG, 2_PL, 3_SG, 3_PL.

- **Tense**: Past, Present or Future (PRE_SIM, PAS_SIM, FUT_SIM, respectively).
- **Aspect**: Perfective (PERFV) and Imperfective (IMPFV) aspects occur with the past tense, and the Durative (DUR) aspect can occur with Past, Present, or Future tenses.
- **Mood**: Optative (OPT), Imperative (IMP, Conditional (COND), Interrogative (INT), or Indicative (NA).
- **Transitivity**: Nahuatl uses indefinite object prefixes to reduce the valency of a verb (e.g. *nechinnextiliah* "They show them to me" vs. *tetlanextiliah* "They show things to people"). When the valency is reduced by one of these morphemes, the transformation contains the tag TRANSITIV:ITR.
- **Purposive**: Nahuatl verbs can take a Purposive suffix indicating directionality of motion, e.g. "Go and do VERB". This directionality can be either away from (VET) or toward (VEN) the speaker.
- **Honorific**: Nahuatl varieties have as many as four levels of honorifics (Hill and Hill, 1978), though we only include the first in our dataset since it is the most common.
- **Polarity**: Positive or negative.

Metrics The main metric of this task is accuracy (fraction of times the system output matches the expected output). Systems for every language are evaluated separately, in addition to the overall average score, which is used to determine the shared task's winner.

Baselines This year, the baseline was the same as last year's, namely a simplified adaptation of the Prefer Observed Edit Trees (POET) method, which involves learning the edit operations required to convert a source string into a target string (Kann and Schütze, 2016). Learning is performed by calculating the edit tree for each pair of source and target sentences in the training data, and counting the total number of each edit tree associated with the specific grammatical change. During testing, the edit trees for the given grammatical change are applied to the given source sentence in order of decreasing frequency until the succeeding edit tree is found. If no such tree is found, the source sentence is returned as the output.

Submitted Systems We received 11 submissions from 6 teams for the task, but unfortunately only three teams submitted system description papers. Given the lack of description papers from the other 3 teams, we are unable to discuss their submissions.

- **NAIST**: The NAIST submission (Vasselli et al., 2025) developed three different systems: example-based LLM prompting system with additional synthetic data, a transformation-based prompting system where each token is annotated according to its required operation to achieve the sentence-level transformation, and, for Nahuatl, a purely rule-based system which heuristically assigns part-of-speech tags and uses them to infer grammatical features.

- **JHU**: There were a total of six JHU submissions (Lupicki et al., 2025). The submitted systems include multiple variations of prompt-engineering with LLMs, including experimenting with chain-of-thought, few-shot prompting, using additional linguistic data such as parts of speech and a reference book (for Maya, Bribri, and Guarani), and ensembling multiple LLM-based systems. Additionally, they train a pointer generator LSTM model.

- **Syntax Squad**: This team investigated LoRA fine-tuning of LLMs, namely Llama models and XGLM, for the sentence transformation task. The process also involved some text preprocessing, such as removing punctuation and diacritics, and post-processing of the LLM output. They did not describe results for the Nahuatl data.

Results The results of all submissions are listed in Table 4. Two of the three submitted system descriptions correspond to the two highest-performing submissions. The JHU team achieved the best performance for Maya and Guarani with their ensemble method, surpassing the last year's best-performing system on the same data. NAIST achieved the best score for both Bribri (41.25% acc.) and Nahuatl (17.5%), though their system did not outperform last year's winning system for Bribri, a fact the authors attribute to their application of transformations all at once, instead of incrementally as was done in last year's winning system. On the other hand, JHU system 1 had the best performance for Maya (63.87% acc.) and Guarani (43.67% acc.). The overall difference between NAIST and JHU System 1 is not significant[6] we decided for having both teams as winners of this years edition. It is also important to notice the poor performance of most teams on Nahuatl, with 5 submitted systems achieving 0% accuracy, and all, except for NAIST, achieveing less than 4% acc.

The Syntax Squad submission underperformed the baseline for all languages. While it warrants further investigation, it is likely that the dataset sizes were too small to effectively fine-tune the LLMs for this task. Furthermore, they highlight the potential negative impact of excessive preprocessing of the text. For example, for languages like Maya where changes in tone can indicate a change in Voice (one of the features in the Maya dataset), removing this may introduce unwanted noise and make it more challenging for a model to learn the necessary sentence transformations.

Findings For the three languages represented in last year's shared task, we saw year-over-year improvements in the best-performing system for two (Maya and Guarani). None of the submitted systems improved on last year's best performing system on the Bribri data.

Interestingly, Nahuatl proved to be quite challenging, with all teams achieving their lowest score on the Nahuatl data. The best performance on this data was achieved with the purely rules-based system. We suspect that this is due to a combination of lack of representation of the Western Sierra Puebla variety in LLM training data, and a number of language- and dataset-specific features, e.g. longer words, many grammatical transformations per sentence, the largest number of unique grammatical transformations compared to the other languages in the shared task (see Table 3 for details).

While the trend of leveraging pretrained LLMs via prompt engineering and reference data continues to show promise for some languages, the results on the Nahuatl data show that knowledge-based approaches still merit attention, particularly when dealing with complex tasks and data (multiple interacting grammatical transformations, complex morphology with long words) and/or languages with minimal resources (both with respect to LLM training data as well as reference materials and digital dictionaries).

5 ST3: A ST on Creating Metrics for Machine Translation in Indigenous Languages

Description Automatic metrics are a crucial alternative to human evaluation for efficiently evaluating the output of MT systems. However, indigenous languages present unique challenges that standard metrics are not designed to handle. MT evaluation commonly relies on two types of automatic

[6]Average sample-wise accuracy values with 95% confidence intervals, calculated with the bootstraping approach (Ferrer and Riera), are 36.97 [34.46, 39.56] for the NAIST system, and 36.89 [34.30, 39.48] for the JHU_1 system

Language	Num. Sentences	Textual features		
	(dev-test)	Words/Sent	Chars/Word	TTR
Nahuatl	100-200	6.68-6.78	8.27-7.83	0.27-0.23
Bribri	100-200	12.23-11.23	4.78-4.7	0.16-0.14
Guarani	100-200	6.24-6.36	7.94-7.43	0.28-0.24

Table 5: Data statistics for ST3. The textual statistics are for the reference translations, for dev and test sets. We report the average sentence length, average word length, and the type-token ration for the corpus. Overall, 300 sentence pairs were annotated for each language.

metrics: overlap-based and neural. Overlap-based metrics, such as BLEU and ChrF , are less effective for Indigenous languages as these languages often lack standardized orthographies and exhibit polysynthetic structures, making exact word or (to a lesser degree) character overlap unreliable. The limitations of BLEU are well documented (Mathur et al., 2020), and the overreliance of the MT community can potentially negatively affect MT development (Kocmi et al., 2021). Neural metrics, such as COMET (Rei et al., 2020), are also limited because they rely on pretrained models trained on large datasets that rarely include low-resource languages. In the first edition of its kind, this task consists in building metrics to evaluate the quality of translations from Spanish into three Indigenous languages: Guarani, Bribri, and Nahuatl.

Data For each language, a set of 100 sentence pairs are selected from the submissions to AmericasNLP 2024 MT ST, from multiple systems. Although the initial pool of sentences are selected randomly, it is important to select pairs of varying quality to ensure that the metrics can effectively distinguish these differences in quality. We use ChrF++ as a proxy of the quality of submissions, and for a portion of sentences we also include the gold translations [7]. The same set of Spanish sentences were used for all the languages. For the test data, we repeated this process. These sentences were then given to annotators for the human judgment. The annotators are asked to rate each translation on a 5-point scale on two axes: semantics and fluency (Koehn and Monz, 2006). As bilingual speakers, the annotators have access to the source sentence in Spanish, and a candidate translation in the target Indigenous language. Table 5 reports the textual statistics for dev and test sets.

[7]Note that using ChrF++ as a metric could introduce bias. We use ChrF++ mainly to detect the "best" and "worst" translations, but for the majority of Spanish sentences we include random translations. Also, since most of the systems are of lower quality, we expect the introduced bias to be negligible.

Metrics The winning submission will be the one with the highest correlation with the ratings on a held-out test set of size 200. We employ Pearson correlation coefficient as the main evaluation metric, but also report Spearman correlation values. We choose Pearson over Spearman as it measures the linearity of the relationship. Linear metrics are preferred since they offer greater interpretability.

Baselines We use BLEU and Chrf++ as our automatic baselines. ChrF++ is character-based and is shown to correlate better than BLEU with morphologically-rich languages. ChrF outperforms BLEU on non-standardized orthographies as well (Aepli et al., 2023). Therefore, we consider it as the main baseline to beat.

Submitted Systems This ST got a total of 11 submissions by 3 different teams. We only have the descriptions of two of these teams. Below is a concise overview of each team's contribution.

- **Tekio**: The submission of R. Krasner et al. (2025) relies mainly on finetuning Language-agnostic BERT Sentence Encoder (LaBSE; (Feng et al., 2022)) to develop better semantic representations for Indigenous languages. They use the data for the MT ST for contrastive alignment in the finetuning. This finetuned LaBSE is the backbone of four metrics: 1) YiSi-1 (Lo, 2019, 2020) is an MT quality metric that needs representations to evaluate semantic similarity. In the first submission, for each language, they chose the top three intermediate layers based on the performance on the development set and averaged their token embeddings. 2) The same as #1, but they use the three layers that that did best on average for all the languages to avoid overfitting. 3) COMET Estimator Model (Rei et al., 2020) with the finetuned LaBSE as the pretrained model and mean absolute error (MAE) as the loss function. 5-fold cross-validation is

Method	Guarani Spearman	Guarani Pearson	Bribri Spearman	Bribri Pearson	Nahuatl Spearman	Nahuatl Pearson	Average Spearman	Average Pearson
ChrF++	<u>0.6725</u>	0.6263	0.4517	0.3823	**0.6783**	0.5549	0.6008	0.5212
BLEU	0.4676	0.4056	0.4518	0.3456	0.3541	0.4061	0.4245	0.3857
Tekio_1	0.6611	0.7196	<u>0.5622</u>	0.6244	0.668	0.6115	**0.6304**	0.6518
Tekio_2	0.6611	0.7196	0.5569	0.63	0.6132	0.5845	0.6104	0.6447
Tekio_3	0.5597	<u>0.7209</u>	0.4892	0.6261	0.4963	0.529	0.5151	0.6254
Tekio_4	0.5605	**0.7234**	0.4909	0.6268	0.5036	0.5351	0.5183	0.6285
RaaVa_1	0.6723	0.6249	0.5356	0.4223	<u>0.6766</u>	0.5657	<u>0.6282</u>	0.5377
RaaVa_2	0.6516	0.6776	**0.5755**	0.5662	0.6145	0.5921	0.6139	0.612
RaaVa_3	0.656	0.7038	0.4829	0.5931	0.6364	0.6263	0.5918	0.6411
RaaVa_4	0.656	0.7038	0.4829	0.5931	0.6364	0.6263	0.5918	0.6411
RaaVa_5	0.6526	<u>0.7209</u>	0.5379	**0.654**	0.6195	**0.6362**	0.6033	**0.6704**
RaaVa_6	0.6429	0.6964	0.5332	<u>0.6523</u>	0.6132	<u>0.6351</u>	0.5965	<u>0.6613</u>
LexiLogic	**0.6811**	0.6529	0.5021	0.3763	0.6717	0.5504	0.6183	0.5265

Table 6: Final results for ST3. The best score for each column is bolded, while the second best score is underlined. The difference between RaaVa_3 and RaaVa_4 is minuscule and can only be seen in the later decimals.

used on all the available annotated scores. 4) The same as #3, but with mean squared error (MSE) as the loss function.

- **RaaVa**: The submission of Raja and Vats (2025) combines various linguistic and computational features, including lexical similarity via Levenshtein distance (Levenshtein et al., 1966), phonetic similarity using Metaphone (Philips, 1990) and Soundex encoding (Russell, 1918), semantic similarity through LaBSE sentence embeddings, and fuzzy token matching to account for morphological variations (Kondrak, 2005). They submit 6 systems: 1) this system integrates character-level lexical overlap via Jaccard similarity with phonetic similarity from Metaphone encodings. 2) Lexical (Damerau-Levenshtein edit distance), phonetic (Metaphone encodings), and semantic similarity (LaBSE sentence encoding) are linearly combined with fixed weights. 3) This system incorporates four similarity metrics, adding fuzzy similarity to the lexical, phonetics, and semantic similarities. Again, the final metric is a weighted average of the individual metrics. 4) Two separate linear regression models are trained for semantic and fluency, based on the four similarity metrics of #3. The regression models are trained on the development sets. 5) Same as #4 but a Ridge regression is used for semantic similarity estimation, while Random Forest regression is used to model fluency. 6) Same as #5, but a Gradient Boosting Regressor (GBR, (Zemel and Pitassi, 2000)) is trained to model fluency.

Results Table 6 shows the final correlation scores for the submitted systems. Overall, RaaVa_5 has the best Pearson performance and is the winner of the shared task, while RaaVa_6 follows closely as the second best system. Tekio_1 has the best Spearman correlation on average, and the third best according to Pearson. None of the systems beat ChrF++ on Spearman for Nahuatl.

Findings In our schema, we weigh fluency and adequacy the same, which could partially explain the superior performance of RaaVa_5 and RaaVa_6 that model those two aspects separately. RaaVa_5 increases the Pearson correlation by 0.149 on average. It must be noted that this framework of human judgment for MT has drawn criticisms (Graham et al., 2013). We adopt this schema for its simplicity for annotators and consistency with previous iterations of MT shared task, but this could potentially change in future iterations.

Table 10 demonstrates the correlation scores of each submitted system with semantics and fluency. Tekio_1 has the highest overall correlation with semantics at 0.6446, while RaaVa_5 is a close second at 0.6432. However, RaaVa_5 has a much higher correlation with fluency than Tekio_1.

The baseline performance on Bribri is relatively poor, hinting that string-based methods are particularly lacking for this language. However, it is important to note that Bribri has much longer sentences in terms of number of words in our study (Table 5). It sees the biggest boost in performance (+0.27) among the three languages. In contrast, Guarani and Nahuatl exhibit more modest gains (+0.1 and +0.08, respectively) but have stronger baseline results. The agglutinating morphology of Nahuatl could in part explain the strong performance of ChrF++ (Pugh and Tyers, 2021a), whereas Bribri is a fusional language. Taken together, the results suggest that neural approaches hold significant potential for Indigenous languages. This corroborates the findings of Aepli et al. (2023) where neural models based on COMET far outperformed string-based baselines for language variations with non-standardized orthographies.

6 Conclusions

We have introduced the three STs held this year at the AmericasNLP workshop: (1) MT for truly low-resource Languages, (2) morphological adaptation for generating educational examples, and (3) metric development for MT in Indigenous languages. Overall, 12 teams participated across a total of 27 submissions.

In the MT task, the baseline (a 1.3B encoder-decoder model) proves hard to beat for translation from Spanish. The new translation direction into Spanish benefits from the use of GPT-based models. This highlights both the limitations imposed by the current available data and the strength of well-adapted, smaller-scale approaches. For the task on generating examples for educational material, while the use of LLMs through prompt engineering and reference-based approaches proves effective for certain languages, our results suggest that knowledge-based methods still hold value, especially for morphologically complex, low-resource languages and tasks involving multiple interacting grammatical phenomena. In the metrics ST, we find that neural methods far outperform the string-based baselines; in spite of the amount of available data that limits the performance of neural models.

These shared tasks contribute to the broader NLP community by advancing methods specific to highly diverse, underrepresented languages. They also provide publicly available datasets, tools, and benchmarks that serve both academic research and community-driven language technology efforts.

Acknowledgements

We would like to thank all teams for their participation, to all reviewers, and all the community that has supported us for this shared task. We want to specially thank to our annotators Wayuunaiki Language Translation Services S.A.S, María Ximena Juárez Huerta, Ángeles Márquez Hernandez, Luis Samuel Santiago Melchor, Blanca Estela Huerta Acosta, Heber Jabdiel Almaraz Miranda, Yanua Liseth Atamain Uwarai, Amanda Domínguez Galeano, Alex Agustin González Diaz, and Rosana Andrea Alvarez Meza.

This project has benefited from financial support to Ona de Gibert by the European Union's Horizon Europe research and innovation programme under Grant agreement No 101070350 and from UK Research and Innovation (UKRI) under the UK government's Horizon Europe funding guarantee [grant number 10052546].

Ethical statement

All AmericasNLP shared tasks are community-based efforts, and therefore they have a close relationship with the native speakers of all communities. We follow the consensus principles in the NLP field when working with indigenous communities (Bird, 2020; Mager et al., 2023): performing consultation with native speakers and communities for each of the languages; we aim to respect the local culture; we also involve native speakers in the scientific work; and we share and distribute the data and research openly. We also want to emphasize that the systems in this exercise are scientific experiments, are not production-ready, and should not be used to solve real-world problems. We also encourage all participating teams to share their systems, model weights, and additional data, so that the advances can be used at the discretion of each community. For ST1, in some languages, the Bible is used as part of the training data. However, we tried to reduce its usage to a minimum, and never used it for testing, as we aim to have as unbiased a benchmarking set as possible (Hutchinson, 2024). Finally, all translators and manual annotators were paid above the average teacher's salary, depending on their country of origin.

References

Noëmi Aepli, Chantal Amrhein, Florian Schottmann, and Rico Sennrich. 2023. A benchmark for evaluating machine translation metrics on dialects without standard orthography. In *Proceedings of the Eighth Conference on Machine Translation*, pages 1045–1065, Singapore. Association for Computational Linguistics.

Željko Agić and Ivan Vulić. 2019. JW300: A wide-coverage parallel corpus for low-resource languages. In *Proceedings of the 57th Annual Meeting of the Association for Computational Linguistics*, pages 3204–3210, Florence, Italy. Association for Computational Linguistics.

Steven Bird. 2020. Decolonising speech and language technology. In *Proceedings of the 28th International Conference on Computational Linguistics*, pages 3504–3519, Barcelona, Spain (Online). International Committee on Computational Linguistics.

David Brambila. 1976. *Diccionario rarámuri-castellano (tarahumar)*. Obra Nacional de la buena Prensa.

Shweta Chauhan, Philemon Daniel, Archita Mishra, and Abhay Kumar. 2023. Adableu: A modified bleu score for morphologically rich languages. *IETE Journal of Research*, 69(8):5112–5123.

Luis Chiruzzo, Pedro Amarilla, Adolfo Ríos, and Gustavo Giménez Lugo. 2020. Development of a Guarani - Spanish parallel corpus. In *Proceedings of the Twelfth Language Resources and Evaluation Conference*, pages 2629–2633, Marseille, France. European Language Resources Association.

Luis Chiruzzo, Pavel Denisov, Alejandro Molina-Villegas, Silvia Fernandez-Sabido, Rolando Coto-Solano, Marvin Agüero-Torales, Aldo Alvarez, Samuel Canul-Yah, Lorena Hau-Ucán, Abteen Ebrahimi, Robert Pugh, Arturo Oncevay, Shruti Rijhwani, Katharina von der Wense, and Manuel Mager. 2024. Findings of the AmericasNLP 2024 shared task on the creation of educational materials for indigenous languages. In *Proceedings of the 4th Workshop on Natural Language Processing for Indigenous Languages of the Americas (AmericasNLP 2024)*, pages 224–235, Mexico City, Mexico. Association for Computational Linguistics.

Jorge Asillo Congora, Julio Santisteban, and Ricardo Lazo Vasquez. 2025. Ucsp submission to the americasnlp 2025 shared task. In *Proceedings of the 5th Workshop on Natural Language Processing for Indigenous Languages of the Americas (AmericasNLP 2025)*, Albuquerque, New Mexico. Association for Computational Linguistics.

Alexis Conneau, Ruty Rinott, Guillaume Lample, Adina Williams, Samuel Bowman, Holger Schwenk, and Veselin Stoyanov. 2018. Xnli: Evaluating cross-lingual sentence representations. In *Proceedings of the 2018 Conference on Empirical Methods in Natural Language Processing*, page 2475. Association for Computational Linguistics.

Ona De Gibert, Raúl Vázquez, Mikko Aulamo, Yves Scherrer, Sami Virpioja, and Jörg Tiedemann. 2023. Four approaches to low-resource multilingual nmt: The helsinki submission to the americasnlp 2023 shared task. In *Proceedings of the Workshop on Natural Language Processing for Indigenous Languages of the Americas (AmericasNLP)*, pages 177–191.

Abhimanyu Dubey, Abhinav Jauhri, Abhinav Pandey, Abhishek Kadian, Ahmad Al-Dahle, Aiesha Letman, Akhil Mathur, Alan Schelten, Amy Yang, Angela Fan, and 1 others. 2024. The llama 3 herd of models. *arXiv e-prints*, pages arXiv–2407.

Abteen Ebrahimi, Ona de Gibert, Raul Vazquez, Rolando Coto-Solano, Pavel Denisov, Robert Pugh, Manuel Mager, Arturo Oncevay, Luis Chiruzzo, Katharina von der Wense, and Shruti Rijhwani. 2024. Findings of the AmericasNLP 2024 shared task on machine translation into indigenous languages. In *Proceedings of the 4th Workshop on Natural Language Processing for Indigenous Languages of the Americas (AmericasNLP 2024)*, pages 236–246, Mexico City, Mexico. Association for Computational Linguistics.

Abteen Ebrahimi, Manuel Mager, Arturo Oncevay, Vishrav Chaudhary, Luis Chiruzzo, Angela Fan, John Ortega, Ricardo Ramos, Annette Rios Gonzales, Ivan Meza-Ruiz, and 1 others. 2022. Americasnli: Evaluating zero-shot natural language understanding of pretrained multilingual models in truly low-resource languages. In *Proceedings of the 60th Annual Meeting of the Association for Computational Linguistics (Volume 1: Long Papers)*, pages 6279–6299.

Abteen Ebrahimi, Manuel Mager, Shruti Rijhwani, Enora Rice, Arturo Oncevay, Claudia Baltazar, María Cortés, Cynthia Montaño, John E. Ortega, Rolando Coto-solano, Hilaria Cruz, Alexis Palmer, and Katharina Kann. 2023. Findings of the AmericasNLP 2023 shared task on machine translation into indigenous languages. In *Proceedings of the Workshop on Natural Language Processing for Indigenous Languages of the Americas (AmericasNLP)*, pages 206–219, Toronto, Canada. Association for Computational Linguistics.

Hermenegildo Espejo Apikai, Ketty Betsamar García Ruiz, and 1 others. 2021. Awajún chicham jintiatin etejamu. vocabulario pedagógico awajún.

Isaac Feldman and Rolando Coto-Solano. 2020. Neural machine translation models with back-translation for the extremely low-resource indigenous language Bribri. In *Proceedings of the 28th International Conference on Computational Linguistics*, pages 3965–3976, Barcelona, Spain (Online). International Committee on Computational Linguistics.

Fangxiaoyu Feng, Yinfei Yang, Daniel Cer, Naveen Arivazhagan, and Wei Wang. 2022. Language-agnostic

BERT sentence embedding. In *Proceedings of the 60th Annual Meeting of the Association for Computational Linguistics (Volume 1: Long Papers)*, pages 878–891, Dublin, Ireland. Association for Computational Linguistics.

Luciana Ferrer and Pablo Riera. Confidence intervals for evaluation in machine learning.

Ana-Paula Galarreta, Andrés Melgar, and Arturo Oncevay. 2017. Corpus creation and initial smt experiments between spanish and shipibo-konibo. In *Proceedings of the International Conference Recent Advances in Natural Language Processing, RANLP 2017*, pages 238–244.

Edward Gow-Smith and Danae Sánchez Villegas. 2023. Sheffield's submission to the AmericasNLP shared task on machine translation into indigenous languages. In *Proceedings of the Workshop on Natural Language Processing for Indigenous Languages of the Americas (AmericasNLP)*, pages 192–199, Toronto, Canada. Association for Computational Linguistics.

Yvette Graham, Timothy Baldwin, Alistair Moffat, and Justin Zobel. 2013. Continuous measurement scales in human evaluation of machine translation. In *Proceedings of the 7th Linguistic Annotation Workshop and Interoperability with Discourse*, pages 33–41, Sofia, Bulgaria. Association for Computational Linguistics.

Ximena Gutierrez-Vasques, Gerardo Sierra, and Isaac Hernandez Pompa. 2016. Axolotl: a web accessible parallel corpus for Spanish-Nahuatl. In *Proceedings of the Tenth International Conference on Language Resources and Evaluation (LREC'16)*, pages 4210–4214, Portorož, Slovenia. European Language Resources Association (ELRA).

Barry Haddow, Rachel Bawden, Antonio Valerio Miceli Barone, Jindřich Helcl, and Alexandra Birch. 2022. Survey of low-resource machine translation. *Computational Linguistics*, 48(3):673–732.

Hansi Hettiarachchi, Tharindu Ranasinghe, Paul Rayson, Ruslan Mitkov, Mohamed Gaber, Damith Premasiri, Fiona Anting Tan, and Lasitha Uyangodage, editors. 2025. *Proceedings of the First Workshop on Language Models for Low-Resource Languages*. Association for Computational Linguistics, Abu Dhabi, United Arab Emirates.

JANE H. Hill and Kenneth C. Hill. 1978. Honorific usage in modern nahuatl: The expression of social distance and respect in the nahuatl of the malinche volcano area. *Language*, 54:123.

Edward J Hu, yelong shen, Phillip Wallis, Zeyuan Allen-Zhu, Yuanzhi Li, Shean Wang, Lu Wang, and Weizhu Chen. 2022. LoRA: Low-rank adaptation of large language models. In *International Conference on Learning Representations*.

Diego Huarcaya Taquiri. 2020. Traducción automática neuronal para lengua nativa peruana. *Bachelor's thesis, Universidad Peruana Unión*.

Jonathan Hus, Antonios Anastasopoulos, and Nathaniel R. Krasner. 2025. Machine translation using grammar materials for llm post-correction. In *Proceedings of the 5th Workshop on Natural Language Processing for Indigenous Languages of the Americas (AmericasNLP 2025)*, Albuquerque, New Mexico. Association for Computational Linguistics.

Ben Hutchinson. 2024. Modeling the sacred: Considerations when using religious texts in natural language processing. In *Findings of the Association for Computational Linguistics: NAACL 2024*, pages 1029–1043, Mexico City, Mexico. Association for Computational Linguistics.

Oana Ignat, Zhijing Jin, Artem Abzaliev, Laura Biester, Santiago Castro, Naihao Deng, Xinyi Gao, Aylin Ece Gunal, Jacky He, Ashkan Kazemi, Muhammad Khalifa, Namho Koh, Andrew Lee, Siyang Liu, Do June Min, Shinka Mori, Joan C. Nwatu, Veronica Perez-Rosas, Siqi Shen, and 3 others. 2024. Has it all been solved? open NLP research questions not solved by large language models. In *Proceedings of the 2024 Joint International Conference on Computational Linguistics, Language Resources and Evaluation (LREC-COLING 2024)*, pages 8050–8094, Torino, Italia. ELRA and ICCL.

INALI. 2012. Catálogo de las lenguas indígenas nacionales en riesgo de desaparición. https://www.cdi.gob.mx/dmdocuments/lenguas_indigenas_nacionales_en_riesgo_de_desaparicion_inali.pdf/.

Katharina Kann and Hinrich Schütze. 2016. Single-model encoder-decoder with explicit morphological representation for reinflection. In *Proceedings of the 54th Annual Meeting of the Association for Computational Linguistics (Volume 2: Short Papers)*, pages 555–560, Berlin, Germany. Association for Computational Linguistics.

Tom Kocmi, Christian Federmann, Roman Grundkiewicz, Marcin Junczys-Dowmunt, Hitokazu Matsushita, and Arul Menezes. 2021. To ship or not to ship: An extensive evaluation of automatic metrics for machine translation. In *Proceedings of the Sixth Conference on Machine Translation*, pages 478–494, Online. Association for Computational Linguistics.

Philipp Koehn and Christof Monz. 2006. Manual and automatic evaluation of machine translation between European languages. In *Proceedings on the Workshop on Statistical Machine Translation*, pages 102–121, New York City. Association for Computational Linguistics.

Grzegorz Kondrak. 2005. N-gram similarity and distance. In *International symposium on string processing and information retrieval*, pages 115–126. Springer.

Vladimir I Levenshtein and 1 others. 1966. Binary codes capable of correcting deletions, insertions, and reversals. In *Soviet physics doklady*, volume 10, pages 707–710. Soviet Union.

Xi Victoria Lin, Todor Mihaylov, Mikel Artetxe, Tianlu Wang, Shuohui Chen, Daniel Simig, Myle Ott, Naman Goyal, Shruti Bhosale, Jingfei Du, and 1 others. 2021. Few-shot learning with multilingual language models. *arXiv preprint arXiv:2112.10668*.

Chi-kiu Lo. 2019. YiSi - a unified semantic MT quality evaluation and estimation metric for languages with different levels of available resources. In *Proceedings of the Fourth Conference on Machine Translation (Volume 2: Shared Task Papers, Day 1)*, pages 507–513, Florence, Italy. Association for Computational Linguistics.

Chi-kiu Lo. 2020. Extended study on using pretrained language models and YiSi-1 for machine translation evaluation. In *Proceedings of the Fifth Conference on Machine Translation*, pages 895–902, Online. Association for Computational Linguistics.

James Loriot, Erwin Lauriault, and Dwight Day. 1993. *Diccionario Shipibo-Castellano*. Ministerio de Educación del Perú, Perú.

Tom Lupicki, Lavanya Shankar, Kaavya Chaparala, and David Yarowsky. 2025. JHU's submission to the AmericasNLP 2025 Shared Task on the Creation of Educational Materials for Indigenous Languages. In *Proceedings of the 5th Workshop on Natural Language Processing for Indigenous Languages of the Americas (AmericasNLP 2025)*, Albuquerque, New Mexico. Association for Computational Linguistics.

Manuel Mager, Diónico Carrillo, and Ivan Meza. 2018. Probabilistic finite-state morphological segmenter for wixarika (huichol) language1. *Journal of Intelligent & Fuzzy Systems*, 34(5):3081–3087.

Manuel Mager, Özlem Çetinoğlu, and Katharina Kann. 2019. Subword-level language identification for intra-word code-switching. In *Proceedings of the 2019 Conference of the North American Chapter of the Association for Computational Linguistics: Human Language Technologies, Volume 1 (Long and Short Papers)*, pages 2005–2011, Minneapolis, Minnesota. Association for Computational Linguistics.

Manuel Mager, Abteen Ebrahimi, Shruti Rijhwani, Arturo Oncevay, Luis Chiruzzo, Robert Pugh, and Katharina von der Wense, editors. 2024. *Proceedings of the 4th Workshop on Natural Language Processing for Indigenous Languages of the Americas (AmericasNLP 2024)*. Association for Computational Linguistics, Mexico City, Mexico.

Manuel Mager, Elisabeth Mager, Katharina Kann, and Ngoc Thang Vu. 2023. Ethical considerations for machine translation of indigenous languages: Giving a voice to the speakers. In *Proceedings of the 61st Annual Meeting of the Association for Computational Linguistics (Volume 1: Long Papers)*, pages 4871–4897, Toronto, Canada. Association for Computational Linguistics.

Manuel Mager, Arturo Oncevay, Abteen Ebrahimi, John Ortega, Annette Rios, Angela Fan, Ximena Gutierrez-Vasques, Luis Chiruzzo, Gustavo Giménez-Lugo, Ricardo Ramos, Ivan Vladimir Meza Ruiz, Rolando Coto-Solano, Alexis Palmer, Elisabeth Mager-Hois, Vishrav Chaudhary, Graham Neubig, Ngoc Thang Vu, and Katharina Kann. 2021. Findings of the AmericasNLP 2021 shared task on open machine translation for indigenous languages of the Americas. In *Proceedings of the First Workshop on Natural Language Processing for Indigenous Languages of the Americas*, pages 202–217, Online. Association for Computational Linguistics.

Enrique Margery Peña. 2005. Diccionario fraseológico bribri-español/español-bribri. *, second edition. Editorial de la Universidad de Costa Rica.*

Nitika Mathur, Timothy Baldwin, and Trevor Cohn. 2020. Tangled up in BLEU: Reevaluating the evaluation of automatic machine translation evaluation metrics. In *Proceedings of the 58th Annual Meeting of the Association for Computational Linguistics*, pages 4984–4997, Online. Association for Computational Linguistics.

Elena Mihas. 2011. Añaani katonkosatzi parenini, el idioma del alto perené. *Milwaukee, WI: Clarks Graphics.*

Héctor Erasmo Gómez Montoya, Kervy Dante Rivas Rojas, and Arturo Oncevay. 2019. A continuous improvement framework of machine translation for Shipibo-konibo. In *Proceedings of the 2nd Workshop on Technologies for MT of Low Resource Languages*, pages 17–23, Dublin, Ireland. European Association for Machine Translation.

Oscar Moreno, Yanua Atamain, and Arturo Oncevay. 2024. Awajun-OP: Multi-domain dataset for Spanish–awajun machine translation. In *Proceedings of the 4th Workshop on Natural Language Processing for Indigenous Languages of the Americas (AmericasNLP 2024)*, pages 112–120, Mexico City, Mexico. Association for Computational Linguistics.

Carla Victoria Jara Murillo. 2018a. *Gramática de la lengua bribri*. éditeur non identifié.

Carla Victoria Jara Murillo. 2018b. *I ttè: historias bribrís*. ,second edition. Editorial de la Universidad de Costa Rica.

Carla Victoria Jara Murillo and Alí García Segura. 2013. *Se'ttö bribri ie: Hablemos en bribri*. Programa de Regionalización Interuniversitaria CONARE.

John E Ortega, Richard Alexander Castro-Mamani, and Jaime Rafael Montoya Samame. 2020. Overcoming resistance: The normalization of an Amazonian tribal language. In *Proceedings of the 3rd Workshop on Technologies for MT of Low Resource Languages*, pages 1–13, Suzhou, China. Association for Computational Linguistics.

Kishore Papineni, Salim Roukos, Todd Ward, and Wei-Jing Zhu. 2002. Bleu: a method for automatic evaluation of machine translation. In *Proceedings of the 40th Annual Meeting of the Association for Computational Linguistics*, pages 311–318, Philadelphia, Pennsylvania, USA. Association for Computational Linguistics.

Lawrence Philips. 1990. Hanging on the metaphone. *Computer Language*, 7(12):39–43.

Maja Popović. 2017. chrF++: words helping character n-grams. In *Proceedings of the Second Conference on Machine Translation*, pages 612–618, Copenhagen, Denmark. Association for Computational Linguistics.

Beatrix Potter. 1904. *Benjamin Bunny*. Frederick Warne Co., Inc., New York.

Juan Prieto, Cristian Martinez, Melissa Robles, Alberto Moreno, Sara Palacios, and Rubén Manrique. 2024. Translation systems for low-resource colombian indigenous languages, a first step towards cultural preservation. In *Proceedings of the 4th Workshop on Natural Language Processing for Indigenous Languages of the Americas (AmericasNLP 2024)*, pages 7–14, Mexico City, Mexico. Association for Computational Linguistics.

Prokopis Prokopidis, Vassilis Papavassiliou, and Stelios Piperidis. 2016. Parallel Global Voices: a collection of multilingual corpora with citizen media stories. In *Proceedings of the Tenth International Conference on Language Resources and Evaluation (LREC'16)*, pages 900–905, Portorož, Slovenia. European Language Resources Association (ELRA).

Robert Pugh, Marivel Huerta Mendez, Mitsuya Sasaki, and Francis Tyers. 2022. Universal Dependencies for western sierra Puebla Nahuatl. In *Proceedings of the Thirteenth Language Resources and Evaluation Conference*, pages 5011–5020, Marseille, France. European Language Resources Association.

Robert Pugh and Francis Tyers. 2021a. Investigating variation in written forms of Nahuatl using character-based language models. In *Proceedings of the First Workshop on Natural Language Processing for Indigenous Languages of the Americas*, pages 21–27, Online. Association for Computational Linguistics.

Robert Pugh and Francis Tyers. 2021b. Towards an open source finite-state morphological analyzer for zacatlán-ahuacatlán-tepetzintla Nahuatl. In *Proceedings of the 4th Workshop on the Use of Computational Methods in the Study of Endangered Languages Volume 1 (Papers)*, pages 80–85, Online. Association for Computational Linguistics.

Nathaniel R. Krasner, Justin Vasselli, Belu Ticona, Antonios Anastasopoulos, and Chi-kiu Lo. 2025. Machine translation metrics for indigenous languages using fine-tuned semantic embeddings. In *Proceedings of the 5th Workshop on Natural Language Processing for Indigenous Languages of the Americas (AmericasNLP 2025)*, Albuquerque, New Mexico. Association for Computational Linguistics.

Rahul Raja and Arpita Vats. 2025. Fuse : A ridge and random forest-based metric for evaluating mt in indigenous languages. In *Proceedings of the 5th Workshop on Natural Language Processing for Indigenous Languages of the Americas (AmericasNLP 2025)*, Albuquerque, New Mexico. Association for Computational Linguistics.

Ricardo Rei, Craig Stewart, Ana C Farinha, and Alon Lavie. 2020. COMET: A neural framework for MT evaluation. In *Proceedings of the 2020 Conference on Empirical Methods in Natural Language Processing (EMNLP)*, pages 2685–2702, Online. Association for Computational Linguistics.

Rubén Romano and Sebastián Richer. 2008. Ñaantsipeta asháninkaki birakochaki. `http://www.lengamer.org/publicaciones/diccionarios/`.

Robert C. Russell. 1918. Soundex system of phonetic indexing.

Mitsuya Sasaki. 2014. A dialectological sketch of Ixquihuacan Nahuatl. , 35(TULIP):139–170.

Petra Schroeder. 2014. *Gramática del Náhuatl de San Miguel Tenango, Zacatlán, Puebla*. Summer Institute of Linguistics. [Draft publication].

Petra Schroeder. 2015. *Phonology of Nahuatl de San Miguel Tenango, Zacatlán, Puebla*. Summer Institute of Linguistics. [Draft publication].

Petra Schroeder and David H. Tuggy. 2010. The consonantal prefixes of San Miguel Tenango Nahuatl, Zacatlán. *Etnografía del estado de Puebla, zona norte*, pages 112–117.

Jorg Tiedemann. 2012. Parallel Data, Tools and Interfaces in OPUS.

Adolfo Constenla Umaña, Feliciano Elizondo Figueroa, and Francisco Pereira Mora. 2004. *Curso básico de bribri*. Editorial de la Universidad de Costa Rica.

Justin Vasselli, Arturo Martínez Peguero, Junehwan Sung, and Taro Watanabe. 2024. Applying linguistic expertise to LLMs for educational material development in indigenous languages. In *Proceedings of the 4th Workshop on Natural Language Processing for Indigenous Languages of the Americas (AmericasNLP 2024)*, pages 201–208, Mexico City, Mexico. Association for Computational Linguistics.

Justin Vasselli, Haruki Sakajo, Arturo Martínez Peguero, Frederikus Hudi, and Taro Watanabe. 2025. Leveraging Dictionaries and Grammar Rules for the Creation of Educational Materials for Indigenous Languages. In *Proceedings of the 5th Workshop on Natural Language Processing for Indigenous Languages of the Americas (AmericasNLP 2025)*, Albuquerque, New Mexico. Association for Computational Linguistics.

Ashish Vaswani, Noam Shazeer, Niki Parmar, Jakob Uszkoreit, Llion Jones, Aidan N Gomez, Łukasz Kaiser, and Illia Polosukhin. 2017. Attention is all you need. *Advances in neural information processing systems*, 30.

Raúl Vázquez, Yves Scherrer, Sami Virpioja, and Jörg Tiedemann. 2021. The Helsinki submission to the AmericasNLP shared task. In *Proceedings of the First Workshop on Natural Language Processing for Indigenous Languages of the Americas*, pages 255–264, Online. Association for Computational Linguistics.

Jules Verne. 1874. *A Journey to the Centre of the Earth.* Scribner, Armstrong & Co., New York.

Ruvan Weerasinghe, Isuri Anuradha, and Deshan Sumanathilaka, editors. 2025. *Proceedings of the First Workshop on Natural Language Processing for Indo-Aryan and Dravidian Languages.* Association for Computational Linguistics, Abu Dhabi.

Linting Xue, Noah Constant, Adam Roberts, Mihir Kale, Rami Al-Rfou, Aditya Siddhant, Aditya Barua, and Colin Raffel. 2021. mt5: A massively multilingual pre-trained text-to-text transformer. In *Proceedings of the 2021 Conference of the North American Chapter of the Association for Computational Linguistics: Human Language Technologies*, pages 483–498.

Mahshar Yahan and Mohammad Amanul Islam. 2025. Leveraging large language models for spanish-indigenous language machine translation at americas-nlp 2025. In *Proceedings of the 5th Workshop on Natural Language Processing for Indigenous Languages of the Americas (AmericasNLP 2025)*, Albuquerque, New Mexico. Association for Computational Linguistics.

Richard Zemel and Toniann Pitassi. 2000. A gradient-based boosting algorithm for regression problems. *Advances in neural information processing systems*, 13.

A Dataset Statistics for ST1

Table 7 shows the number of sentences for each language in the dataset.

LANGUAGE	TRAIN SOURCE	TRAIN
Chatino (ctp)	(Ebrahimi et al., 2023)	357
Asháninka (cni)	(Ortega et al., 2020; Romano and Richer, 2008; Mihas, 2011)	3,883
Otomí (oto)	(Mager et al., 2021)	4,889
Aymara (aym)	(Prokopidis et al., 2016; Tiedemann, 2012)	6,531
Bribri (bzd)	(Feldman and Coto-Solano, 2020; Margery Peña, 2005; Murillo, 2018a; Umaña et al., 2004; Murillo and Segura, 2013; Murillo, 2018b)	7,508
Wixarika (hch)	(Mager et al., 2018)	8,966
Shipibo-Konibo (shp)	(Montoya et al., 2019; Galarreta et al., 2017; Loriot et al., 1993)	14,592
Rarámuri (tar)	(Brambila, 1976)	14,720
Nahuatl (nah)	(Gutierrez-Vasques et al., 2016)	16,145
Awajun (agr)	(Moreno et al., 2024)	21,964
Guarani (grn)	(Chiruzzo et al., 2020)	26,032
Wayuunaiki (guc)	(Prieto et al., 2024)	59,715
Quechua (quy)	(Agić and Vulić, 2019; Huarcaya Taquiri, 2020)	125,008

Table 7: Dataset statistics for ST1, together with the sources for the tr Languages are listed in increasing order of available training data. Americ indigenous languages from a set of different sources (please see the corre

B ST1 Ranking

Table 8 shows the main ranking of all submitted systems for ST1.

RANK	TEAM	VER.	COUNT	TOT. BLEU	TOT. CHRF	TOT. CHRF++
					TRACK 1: SPA-XXX	
1	GMU	2	13	43.72	324.12	285.37
2	Syntax Squad	1	11	36.24	265.50	233.07
3	Syntax Squad	2	1	2.02	30.13	26.31
4	UCSP	1	1	0.07	21.73	16.75
-	GMU	1	13	31.83	273.23	244.56
					TRACK 2: XXX-SPA	
1	GMU	2	13	93.44	368.14	346.06
2	Syntax Squad	1	11	75.31	279.68	261.19
3	UCSP	1	1	1.52	20.70	17.87
-	GMU	1	13	99.19	363.52	343.34

Table 8: Main ranking of all submitted systems for ST1. VER denotes the t denotes the number of languages a particular system was submitted for, w total sum of the metric score across submissions. The final three column languages of the shared task, with CHRF++ being used to calculate the c

C ST1 Full Results

Table C shows the full results of ST1.

LANG.	TEAM	VER.	BLEU	CHRF	CHRF++
TRACK 1: SPA-XXX					
agr-spa	GMU	0	16,81	38,73	36,59
agr-spa	GMU	1	15,17	38,73	36,52
agr-spa	Syntax Squad	0	13,21	36,11	33,70
aym-spa	GMU	0	6,51	27,50	26,09
aym-spa	Syntax Squad	0	5,89	27,53	25,78
aym-spa	GMU	1	5,17	26,49	25,23
bzd-spa	GMU	0	6,98	29,14	27,86
bzd-spa	GMU	1	6,11	28,77	27,41
bzd-spa	Syntax Squad	0	5,87	27,53	26,22
cni-spa	GMU	0	5,32	23,72	22,44
cni-spa	GMU	1	4,00	22,94	21,57
cni-spa	Syntax Squad	0	3,06	21,34	20,13
ctp-spa	GMU	1	11,74	28,04	26,16
ctp-spa	GMU	0	3,76	15,60	14,47
grn-spa	GMU	0	13,81	34,93	33,84
grn-spa	GMU	1	11,23	33,57	32,31
grn-spa	Syntax Squad	0	15,14	26,15	24,70
guc-spa	GMU	1	4,20	26,00	23,93
guc-spa	GMU	0	2,92	25,06	23,10
guc-spa	Syntax Squad	0	3,14	16,19	14,40
hch-spa	GMU	0	5,46	25,91	24,37
hch-spa	GMU	1	4,69	25,53	24,04
hch-spa	Syntax Squad	0	3,98	23,69	22,02
nah-spa	GMU	0	7,22	27,14	25,58
nah-spa	GMU	1	5,08	26,18	24,31
nah-spa	Syntax Squad	0	4,00	15,40	13,88
oto-spa	GMU	0	2,25	19,69	18,24
oto-spa	Syntax Squad	0	1,50	19,91	17,80
oto-spa	GMU	1	1,36	17,76	15,99
quy-spa	GMU	0	12,27	34,64	33,02
quy-spa	GMU	1	10,38	33,50	31,77
quy-spa	Syntax Squad	0	10,60	33,26	31,71
quy-spa	UCSP	0	1,52	20,70	17,87
shp-spa	GMU	0	13,83	39,93	38,01
shp-spa	GMU	1	12,55	39,40	37,43
shp-spa	Syntax Squad	0	8,94	32,58	30,83
tar-spa	GMU	0	2,07	21,53	19,72
tar-spa	GMU	1	1,75	21,23	19,39

LANG.	TEAM	VER.	BLEU	CHRF	CHRF++
		TRACK 2: XXX-SPA			
spa-agr	Syntax Squad	0	7,82	40,10	35,16
spa-agr	GMU	1	8,64	39,75	35,09
spa-agr	GMU	0	1,30	19,16	16,67
spa-aym	Syntax Squad	0	1,96	31,61	27,72
spa-aym	Syntax Squad	1	2,02	30,13	26,31
spa-aym	GMU	1	1,14	26,26	22,91
spa-aym	GMU	0	0,88	23,12	20,45
spa-bzd	Syntax Squad	0	4,55	21,68	22,77
spa-bzd	GMU	1	4,41	21,56	22,51
spa-bzd	GMU	0	3,85	19,42	20,61
spa-cni	Syntax Squad	0	2,43	26,96	23,17
spa-cni	GMU	1	2,47	25,60	22,22
spa-cni	GMU	0	3,63	24,62	21,77
spa-ctp	GMU	0	1,64	15,04	13,33
spa-ctp	GMU	1	1,27	15,31	12,25
spa-grn	GMU	0	5,47	32,50	29,95
spa-grn	GMU	1	4,04	27,23	25,00
spa-grn	Syntax Squad	0	3,46	17,84	16,21
spa-guc	GMU	1	1,48	27,42	22,93
spa-guc	Syntax Squad	0	0,11	15,86	12,83
spa-guc	GMU	0	0,20	10,94	9,12
spa-hch	Syntax Squad	0	11,07	30,47	26,77
spa-hch	GMU	1	10,04	29,59	26,14
spa-hch	GMU	0	5,98	27,00	23,59
spa-nah	GMU	1	2,02	23,82	20,33
spa-nah	GMU	0	0,64	18,76	15,98
spa-nah	Syntax Squad	0	0,65	15,73	12,64
spa-oto	Syntax Squad	0	0,76	14,16	12,02
spa-oto	GMU	1	1,33	13,23	11,31
spa-oto	GMU	0	0,98	11,55	10,03
spa-quy	GMU	1	3,70	38,02	32,70
spa-quy	GMU	0	3,80	36,30	31,68
spa-quy	Syntax Squad	0	3,07	36,14	31,01
spa-quy	UCSP	0	0,07	21,73	16,75
spa-shp	GMU	1	2,79	21,99	19,46
spa-shp	GMU	0	2,68	19,39	17,49
spa-shp	Syntax Squad	0	0,37	14,94	12,76
spa-tar	GMU	0	0,77	15,45	13,89
spa-tar	GMU	1	0,39	14,35	12,53

Table 9: Full results of ST1.

D ST3 Results

Table 10 shows the results for ST3 broken down between semantics and fluency scores.

Method	Guarani		Bribri		Nahuatl		Average	
	Semantics	Fluency	Semantics	Fluency	Semantics	Fluency	Semantics	Fluency
ChrF++	0.63	0.5323	0.4078	0.3018	0.5681	0.4929	0.5353	0.4424
BLEU	0.4207	0.3314	0.3515	0.2908	0.4257	0.351	0.3993	0.3244
Tekio_1	**0.6899**	0.6474	0.6369	0.5236	0.6069	0.5618	**0.6446**	0.5776
Tekio_2	**0.6899**	0.6474	**0.6404**	0.5307	0.5789	0.5381	0.6364	0.5721
Tekio_3	0.603	<u>0.7411</u>	0.6002	0.5657	0.49	0.5203	0.5644	0.609
Tekio_4	0.6054	**0.7433**	0.6036	0.5634	0.4972	0.5248	0.5687	<u>0.6105</u>
RaaVa_1	0.6367	0.5227	0.4644	0.3187	0.5818	0.5	0.561	0.4471
RaaVa_2	0.6518	0.6073	0.5852	0.4667	0.5896	0.5423	0.6089	0.5388
RaaVa_3	0.6793	0.6284	0.5689	0.5355	**0.625**	0.5722	0.6244	0.5787
RaaVa_4	0.6793	0.6284	0.5689	0.5355	**0.625**	0.5722	0.6244	0.5787
RaaVa_5	<u>0.6816</u>	0.6584	0.6314	**0.5862**	0.6165	**0.5991**	<u>0.6432</u>	**0.6146**
RaaVa_6	0.6661	0.628	<u>0.6372</u>	<u>0.5768</u>	<u>0.621</u>	<u>0.5927</u>	0.6414	0.5992
LexiLogic	0.6512	0.5608	0.4233	0.274	0.5645	0.488	0.5463	0.4409

Table 10: Pearson correlation scores of each submitted system with adequacy (semantics) and fluency of the annotated instances in the test dataset for ST3. The best score(s) for each column is bolded, while the second best score is underlined.

Author Index

Association for Computational Linguistics
209 N. Eighth Street
Stroudsburg, Pennsylvania 18360

ISBN 979-8-3313-1911-3

CURRAN ASSOCIATES INC.
proceedings.com